MARY MAGDALENE: THE ILLUMINATOR

William Henry

ADVENTURES UNLIMITED PRESS

MARY MAGDALENE: THE ILLUMINATOR

The Woman Who Enlightened Christ

William Henry

Mary Magdalene: The Illuminator

Published by
Adventures Unlimited Press
Kempton, Illinois 60946 USA

www.adventuresunlimitedpress.com

ISBN 1-931882-63-0

Printed in the United States of America

Cover art by Dana Augustine

10 9 8 7 6 5 4 3 2

MARY MAGDALENE: THE ILLUMINATOR

The Woman Who Enlightened Christ

Dedicated to the 3 wise ones
and to the Bird of Light that delivered them.

Visit William Henry at his web site at:

www.Williamhenry.net

CONTENTS

And as we wind on down the road,
Our shadows taller than our souls
There walks a lady we all know
Who shines white light and wants to show
How everything still turns to gold
And if you listen very hard
The tune will come to you at last
When All are One and One is All
To be a rock and not to roll

Led Zeppelin, "Stairway to Heaven"

THE ILLUMINATOR

I.
THE GOLDEN LEGEND

This book is primarily about the "supreme initiate" of Jesus, Mary Magdalene: one of the most mysterious of all literary figures. Said to be a prophetess who 'knew the All', a priestess of Isis and Ishtar, a "holy harlot," who seduced men from the Eastern and Western world (including a messiah), a shining example of conversion from "sin", a mother of future kings, and a perfumer, she's as alluring as the "mare among stallions" the Egyptians' enemies set loose in war to drive the pharaoh's stallions wild. The source of her power to captivate is her refusal to be put in a box: whether it be an alabaster box, a prostitute box, a sinner box, a Christian box, a box of Gospels, or a goddess box.

So, in this book we will search for Mary Magdalene (MAG-duh-luhn, MAG-duh-leen) outside the box.

Even more, this book is a search for the lost esoteric teaching *of* Jesus (as opposed to the exoteric story *about* him) ***and*** Mary Magdalene (referred to, for convenience, as MM), which she taught and for which the popular thirteenth century French chronicler Jacobus says she earned the distinction *Illuminata* and *Illuminatrix* – the Illumined and Illuminator. *Webster's* says *Illuminati* literally meant 'enlightened ones' in Latin. It comes from *illuminare*, to light up. It means 'persons who had received baptism'. Hence, they were 'lit up'.

Sometime around 1267 Jacobus de Voragine, the Archbishop of Genoa (Northern Italy), known as the 'father of the poor', compiled a valuable source book on the lives of the Christian saints entitled the *Golden Legend.* It is said that no book other than the Bible was so widely read during the late Middle Ages. This encyclopedia of wonders, mysteries and intrigue was one of the first books published when the new literary language, English, appeared in the late 15th century. It was written for the common people and widely embraced by them. Jacobus' work, which he titled *Legend of the Saints,* was so influential that after his death he was venerated as a saint, and invoked as 'the peacemaker'. The attacks on the work by the Reformers sent the book into oblivion until it was revived in 1892.

The curious thing about Jacobus' legends is that the original authors remain 'hidden'. One commentator writing in the introduction to *The Golden Legend* notes that this 'author' is the masses, the people themselves. "The true matter of the legend is fashioned by the mind and soul of the people, and added to, or even at times substituted for, what is authentically known about the saints." These substitutions spring from the hearts and minds of the people. They are made to suit the ideals of the people and to fill the needs of the current era psyche.

A hallmark of Jacobus' work is his radical etymologies and use of apocryphal sources to reveal a parallel tradition to that of 'official' Christianity.

An example of his method is the name Mary Magdalene. Jacobus says Mary is interpreted *anmurum mare*, bitter sea, or light-giver, or enlightened. Magdalen is the same as *manens rea* and means armed, unconquered and magnificent. This postulates a far different MM from the Church's image of Mary as a repentant prostitute.

THE TEMPLAR

The enormous popularity of Jacobus' work – which no doubt raised a few eyebrows when it revealed that Mary Magdalene was actually a 'magnificent enlightened one' -- corresponded with the glory days of the Knights Templar, also known as 'The Poor Knights of Christ and the Temple of Solomon'. In the early 1100's this mystic military Order claimed ownership of a mysterious ancient secret they discovered at the site of Solomon's Temple (*Sol's Temple* or *Soul's Temple*) in Jerusalem. The Templars based themselves at the Dome of the Rock, an Islamic shrine atop Mount Moriah which they renamed the Temple of the Lord.

The list of what the Templars potentially discovered – the "bones" the inquisitive Templars dug up -- during their cryptic excavations within the Temple is impressive: The Ark of the Covenant, the Holy Grail, the secrets of sacred geometry, the ancient super science of the Anunnaki gods of Sumeria, the secrets of building vortexes.

Some claim the core of the Templar discovery was a secret about or even belonging to Mary Magdalene. A mysterious human skull called a 'dead head' (that was capable of turning a wasteland into a garden) symbolized this epic lost secret of the Templars. As we will see, MM is frequently painted holding a human skull.

All the occult mysteries speak of a key that is required to unlock mystical secrets of enlightenment. Specifically, the lost secret of the Templars, this study illuminates, is about building a better human through the release of secretions from the astounding manufacturing plant of spiritual oils, the human brain. This oil or *essence* was the key secret of Mary Magdalene and the *Essenes* recovered by the Templars, from between the temples. The skull is a protective box for the brain, eyes and hearing organs. It is the Cup of Life, the Grail, that catches these secretions from the brain. Without "the key" vibrating in our brains and radiating throughout our bodies no one can gain the higher knowledge of the gods.

Ultimately, the secret we will pursue in these pages, concerns the human body. The bones of the human body are the flexible frame work of the soul's temple (Solomon's Temple). Bone is the foundation of the body. In its archives are found the secret of the ages. They represent the foundation stones upon which sits the Temple of the Brain.

The Templar's discovery and exploitation of the temple's secrets led to the Order's rapid ascent as a political and financial power. It has been claimed that the Templars' ultimate objective was to restore true Gnostic monotheism to the world, uniting Christianity, Judaism and Islam in a New Kingdom of Heaven on Earth. The 'new' humans that inhabited this New Jerusalem (or New Atlantis) would know and embody the secret of the Kingdom of Heaven within the brain and its capability of producing manna, dew, the food of the gods, the elixir of life, the sacred Soma, the tonic of immortality, for these terms all refer to the cosmic *esse* or *brain substance*.

One fruit of the Templar's discovery is the cathedrals of France, the womb-like instruments designed to tune the body-brain-mind-soul to the Light. Between 1130 and 1200 57 of these 'Templar keys' were started in France, which incorporated a fundamentally new sacred architecture, known as 'Gothic'. The first big 'vessel of light' was St. Denis, in Paris. Abbot Suger, a close friend of Templar founder Bernard de Clairvaux supervised the construction. It has been proposed that he was given access to parts of the secrets retrieved by the Templars. We will examine powerful evidence of this later.

Of course, the possibility of such an enlightened civilization threatened the Catholic Church. Even more, they were a threat to King Philip the Fair of France, whose reign desperately needed the vast Templar wealth, and who feared their magical powers. This prompted the wily king and his cunning counselors to demand that the feeble French Pope Clement V suppress the Templars. On that unlucky Friday, the 13th of October, 1307 King Philip declared Inquisition. He had all the Templars arrested on the grounds of heresy. The Templars were tortured. Some gave astounding confessions, including spitting on the cross and worshipping the Head of God.

THE ATON

The forty or so years between Jacobus' publishing of the *Golden Legend* and the demise of the Templars saw the emergence of a new world order and the appearance of a new Magdalene. As the 'illuminata', the enlightened, Jacobus upholds, the Magdalene was illumined with the light of perfect knowledge in her mind and illumined with the light of glory in her body. In this case *glory* describes the splendor and bliss of heaven. *Glorify* means apotheosize, to raise-up, to make one a god. It also literally means to illuminate = to give light = *glow ray(s)*.

By 'light', I believe, is meant something more like the meaning of the term when used by the Egyptian mystic Akhenaton, that is, glowing rays of *love* and *spiritual consciousness* from ATON = the Lord. I'll refer to it as 'Love-Light'.

Akhenaton, Nefertiti and family receive the rays of the ATON. The hands from the ATON offer the Key of Life.

Akhenaton inhales the Key of Life from ATON and then breathes it into his daughter's face.

Akhenaton's emphasis on light is one 'fingerprint' that has led researchers such as Robert Feather, author of *The Secret Initiation of Jesus at Qumran*, to investigate the connection between the teachings of Jesus and the Qumran-Essenes and the religion of the Disk. In fact, a generation of scholars of the Essenes of Qumran and their writings, the Dead Sea Scrolls and Nag Hammadi Scrolls, believe that the Essenes discovered the "torch of illumination" that the followers of Akhenaton hid after his reign.

Akhenaton and his bride, Nefertiti, had a profound influence on the First Christians, including bequeathing to them a spiritual technology for embodying the light. Though they left no written teaching the inscriptions that tell of it say Akhenaton placed the Love-Light in the hearts of his subjects. Depictions show him inhaling the Key of Life from the ATON and then breathing this consciousness into his daughter.

Jesus (called ADON or ADONOI = Lord) also transmitted the Holy Spirit to the disciples by breathing upon them. As Jesus' chief initiate it is probable that MM received the Holy Spirit and advanced spiritual consciousness in this manner. Importantly, Nefertiti is portrayed receiving the rays of love in an alabaster jar. Mary Magdalene was later referred to as "the woman with the alabaster jar" that contained a precious oil or ointment. It is believed the alabaster ('Egyptian crystal') box of Mary Magdalene was made from alabaster mined at the lost city of *Alabastron*, noted by classical authors. This was Akhetaten (The Horizon of Aten) built by Akhenaton. One of our primary quests in this book will be to search for the secrets of MM's anointing oil and how it may have caused her to glow-rays of Love-Light.

COSMIC RAYS

In the several minutes it took to read this far several hundred cosmic rays will have passed through your head and penetrated into your body. The passage of cosmic rays through your body can leave various fluids within your body momentarily ionized. Nobel prize winner H J Muller found that mutations and changes in human genes can be caused by ionizing radiation such as cosmic rays. Therefore it is thought that cosmic rays may be capable of changing your DNA make-up by hitting individual cells, and may even have human evolution implications. However, it should be stressed that this is a very rare occurrence as cosmic rays of an energy high enough to cause such changes are rare at ground level. Still, these "blue apples" from heaven (the alchemical symbol for the ultimate, the impossible) are to be found. I will show that Jesus and MM were deeply interested in this topic.

Science is rapidly approaching a new understanding of cosmic rays, which heretofore have been a puzzle. It has long been hypothesized that they accelerate human evolution. This raises a bit of a paradox. At the apex of human evolution is our colonization of the moon and beyond. One barrier to this colonization is the harmful cosmic rays. The astronaut has a couple of options available to him to reduce the radiation, which include wearing a protective spacesuit as well as shielding the spaceship. Lead would be the ideal material for this job, however it is very heavy and would not be suitable for a spaceship. A substitute for lead therefore has to be found.

In the theosophical tradition they speak of the seven cosmic rays. As each ray is mastered the initiate becomes clothed in the energy of the ray until finally they are an illumined one. The mastery of the seven rays is described in Gnostic texts as putting on a spiritual garment, a *robe of glory*. This garment, veil, sheath or covering is necessary equipment for the soul as it journeys through the halls (holes) of the mystic mansions of creation, a journey MM is credited with taking in the *Gospel of Mary*. NASA, and other space agencies, would be well served were they to study this Gnostic work, as well as the *Hymn of the Pearl*, which describe this garment of light.

The secretion of the oil of *Krist* or *Chrestos* in the skull, called Gulgotha, the place of crucifixion, in the bible, and the igniting of our real spiritual light which produces the garment of light, I hypothesize, is the secret possessed by Mary Magdalene for which she was given the title the Illuminator.

This is quite an amazing study. An almond-shaped area of the brain, the amydala (uh-mig-dah-la) is the brain's fear center (we share it with fishes). It is the part of the brain that decodes emotions. Stimulation of the amygdala – which sounds like Magdala or Magdalene -- produces lust and memories of sexual experiences. By inhaling chemicals or hearing certain sounds we can stimulate the neurons of the amygdala to open ourselves to channels of higher level experiences.

THE WATERS OF LIFE

Jacobus says MM was called "illuminatrix" because she "drank avidly" of the (love) light which afterward she poured out (glowed, rayed) in abundance, and through "inward contemplation" (or manipulation of the hidden power of the human brain) she received the light with which she later brought *gnosis* or enlightened others.

As we study this story through the lens of mystic anatomy and in the light of neuroscience we will see that what Jacobus is describing is the rising of a wondrous oil (called *Chrestos* by the Essenes) in the sacral ("sacred") or lower part of the spinal cord and its passage into the pineal gland (the "lamp" or "candle") referred to as the "third eye" in the center of the human brain. When this lamp is lit illumination results. This oil becomes more than a fuel. It oils the body's spiritual machinery. It purifies the body, and may give it a beautiful opalescent color characteristic of the Shining Ones, the illumined ones.

Scanning electron microscopy has revealed that the human pineal is covered by unusual faceted, geometric crystalline structures called calcite microclusters and "Brain sand" that effectively make it an antenna sensitive to electromagnetic stimulation which, I propose, the ancients referred to as "waters of life". The cell phone industry is studying these crystalline structures on the pineal and is describing the gland as a "wireless transmitter" capable of receiving even faint messages through resonance. They think the pineal gland is a natural wireless transmitter.

URSA MAJOR: THE CELESTIAL SPRING

So, who's calling us? From what distant shore does this transmission arise? Ancient legends of numerous cultures and modern astrophysics are crystal clear. The constellation of seven stars known as the Big Dipper is one source of higher energy charged particles known as cosmic rays that MM may have captured and rode, like a beam of light.

In January, 2005 *New Scientist* magazine reported that a celestial "spring" of mysterious particles that slam into Earth from all directions may have been discovered by a US physicist. Glennys Farrar, a physicist at New York University in New York City used a new analysis technique to identify five Ultra High Energy Cosmic Rays appearing to originate from the same area of space. They came from a 'hole' about as large as a full Moon seen from Earth and from the direction of Ursa Major.

As *New Scientist* reported, when Farrar and colleagues searched celestial databases to find what objects lay along that line of sight, she found essentially nothing but empty space for quite some distance. But then, at 550 million light years from Earth, she discovered two crowded galaxy clusters - containing about 50 galaxies - crashing into each other. Farrar concluded that the five cosmic rays were accelerated to high energies by the galactic collisions themselves or by some other phenomena within the galaxies. She cites several possibilities for the underlying source of the cosmic rays. It could be a long-lived process - such as a super-massive black hole slurping up surrounding matter. Another possibility is magnetic shocks produced by the colliding galaxy clusters. A third source is a sudden, cataclysmic event called 'starburst', when an explosion of matter and energy at the center of a galaxy gives off a gamma-ray burst.

The Big Dipper is also known as the Shepherd, Meru, the Casket of Osiris, the Plough, and the Great Bear. The word *bear* has additional meaning when interpreted as a verb. *To bear* means to bring forth, support, sustain and affirms the idea of a sustaining vibration ringing from the Great Bear. It puts us in a better position to understand what was really meant when Jesus appears in the book of Revelation holding seven stars in his hand. I propose these seven stars are cosmic rays from the Big Dipper. They interface with the seven chakras or energy centers of the body.

Gregg Rigby, author of *On Earth As It Is In Heaven*, has discovered that a ground pattern, which is a duplication of the seven stars of Ursa Major, exists in Northern France. The ancient peoples were aware that the earth acts a mirror to the energies of the cosmos. Ursa Major has been associated with wisdom and those who come to teach it. The seven points that make up the pattern are marked by Gothic cathedrals, suggesting that the Templars understood "the mystery of the seven stars" and marked the locations where their energy was concentrated.

As the cosmic vibrations or Waters of Life from Ursa Major, also known as the Dove, pour over the Earth this is the descent of the Holy Spirit, symbolized in Christian art by a dove. As the data provided by Gnostic accounts reveals, Jesus and Mary Magdalene knew the secret of the 'en-Christed' pineal and its ability to refine the oil and release *secretions* that contain the *secrets* of life. *Christos!* It is this oil that causes the flash of light, the raising of illumination of consciousness – or – glow-ray-fi-cation - of the individual.

The essential human dilemma, however, is that our (pineal) candles are not lit. None of our elevators goes to the top. This is because our pineal glands are encrusted or calcified. De-calcifying the pineal is the same as enjoying it, en-Christing it.

THE DESPOSYNI

The transformation caused by en-Christing oneself has genetic, biological and chromosomal consequences. It also has ethnic attributes. A new strain of humans may have arisen in the blink of an eye as a result of Jesus and Mary Magdalene's use of such a transmutational Force. The account in the book of Genesis of the 'Sons of God and Daughters of Men' is another example of the genetic infusion I am describing. This mating of the worlds also represented an infusion of fields of consciousness, one human, one nonhuman, 'extra' or 'ultraterrestrial'. There are many documented cases of electromagnetic effects in conjunction with paranormal phenomena.

This implantation or blossoming of genes with cosmic rays and interlacing of human and nonhuman fields of consciousness adds a new dimension to the hunting of the *Desposyni*, a Greek word dusted off and brought to light in the early 1960s by Father Malachi Martin that literally meant "belonging to the Lord." It was a sacred name reserved only for Jesus' blood relatives, especially James the Just, as the legitimate apostolic successors of Jesus, rather than Peter. Some claim the Desposyni also included the blood relatives of Jesus and Mary Magdalene. After the Crucifixion, the Desposyni were murdered by the Romans and despised by the Church. Many fled to France with Mary Magdalene.

The family of Jesus and Mary Magdalene was persecuted for many reasons, but none would be more epic than if it was because they were a higher, hybrid form of 'enchristed' human who threatened the Church's authority. Alchemy historian Jay Weidner has called this higher form of human *Homo Luminous*, the illumined human. Set to unleash the secrets of the ages, and possibly create a planet full of spiritually actualized Christ-like beings, Jesus was executed as a revolutionary by the Roman world order.

What happened to these lost teachings? It is claimed the Templars benefited from documents passed down from the Desposyni in their excavations at Solomon's Temple.

This book upholds Mary Magdalene as the supreme initiate of Jesus, and the 'mother' of the Desposyni, who was conversant in the secrets of the Kingdom of Light and the Secret of the Temple (the brain, the dome). She was a light bearer, most certainly. In addition, she was conversant in the secrets of the Cross, also called the Stairway to Heaven and the key to the means by which it was scaled, *bliss*, the state of mind created by Christos and the key required to enter the Kingdom.

The noun bliss has only one meaning: a state of extreme happiness. It is freedom from attachment, freedom from unconditioned responses. It is freedom from fear. It is pure love. It was this knowledge that transformed Jesus from a wise man into his godlike status. Its synonyms are beatitude, blessedness, cheer, and joy. These come very close.

Bliss is sometimes referred to as 'the seventh heaven'. This is straight out of cabalistic doctrine. Seven corresponds to the seven devils of which Mary Magdalene was cured, the seven days of creation, the seven rungs of perfection, seven chakras, seven celestial stairs, the seven heads of the wise *naga* serpent of the underworld, the seven branches of the shaman's cosmic and sacrificial tree.

All the different aspects of seven symbolism returns us to the single problem focused on by Jesus and Mary Magdalene: the secret of bliss, ecstasy or *merry ness*. This pure unadulterated faith and practice *of* Jesus ***and*** MM is what we seek.

THE PURE ONES

In the Nazarene tradition, the title given to those who achieved this exalted and blissful state was "the *Poor Ones*" (Galatians 2:10, James 2:3-5) or *ebyon* in Hebrew. The Ebyonites or Ebionites are considered heretics. They recognized Jesus as Messiah, but not as God. Importantly, the Ebionites revered the Desposyni.

In *Journey of the Magi* Paul William Roberts notes that the word translated as 'poor' - *drigu* - is the origin of the Persian 'Darvish' or 'Dervish' - a name still used for certain (whirling) sects of Muslim Sufi mystics - and it had a specific and special sense, meaning a pure, devout, and humble person, a true follower of Zoroastrian doctrine: a believer. A dervish was also known as 'one at the door to enlightenment'. (For more on the dervishes please see my book *Egypt: The Greatest Show On Earth*).

The *Poor* originally was applied to Christians because they came from lower social groups and tended to be poor (Gal. 2:10, Acts 11:28-30, 24:17, Rom. 15:25-31, 1 Cor. 1:26-29, 16:1-2, 2 Cor. 8-9). This term refers not only to their humble ways, but also to their "low" or "poor" opinion of Jesus, so it is said, and to their demotion of him from Son of God to ordinary man who became the Cosmic Christ through an anointing oil or perfume provided by Mary Magdalene. Remember, Jesus said: "*Blessed are the poor, for the kingdom of Heaven is theirs.*"[Mat. 5:3] In light of this, it is reasonable to propose that *poor* is a play on *pure*. It refers to a blissful state of mind, a way of being created by Christos. The Poor were also known as "the Children of the Light." Let us remember that the Templars called themselves Poor Knights and Jacobus was known as a 'poor man', as well as the Peacemaker. In a moment, we will meet another group of 'poor' people who mightily influenced the re-imaging of Mary Magdalene.

Obviously, Jacobus' tale of the illumined Magdalene, whose story prompts us to look inward to the functioning of our mystic anatomy, is far different from the image of a fallen and redeemed 'Madge' from Magdala presented by the Church. As powerful and inspirational as this image is -- if a person as low as she can be redeemed, anyone can -- it is a false image. As we will see, it arose from a wild misinterpretation in the sixth century.

When Jacobus dove into the story of the Magdalene seven centuries later he emerged with a shining new Magdalene. His 'enlightening' of Mary Magdalene is radical, controversial and contrary to the Christian folk images of her. However, we will be exploring biblical and other literary evidence that supports the re-enlightening of the woman the Gospels call the Apostle of the Apostles. She was a hard core esoteric researcher and practitioner.

For the record, this sort of re-imaging, rediscovery or accentuation of the positive attributes of historic figures happens. Jesus, himself, has gone through several historical re-visions or makeovers.

The 'historical preservation' activities at Mount Vernon, the home of George Washington are a prime current-era example of the way in which, by simply shifting the light, new facets or new dimensions of a figure's personality are revealed. Through computer imaging and forensics scientists have determined that Washington was once a buff stud. Before Washington was middle-aged and the father of America, he was a tall, strapping 19-year-old surveyor who still had all his teeth. At Mount Vernon Estate and Gardens a new, life-size image of Washington with auburn hair and gray-blue eyes has appeared. The folks at Mount Vernon are hoping the new George will help Americans see him as he was before he was famous, before Gilbert Stuart painted him in the portrait that appeared on the dollar bill, back when he was an "adventurous, athletic, risk-taking, courageous kind of action hero," Jim Rees, the estate's executive director, told the *Washington Post*. Reading between the lines, we are witnessing the remaking Washington for marketing purposes. Fortunately, they're rebuilding his distillery too.

The focus at Mount Vernon is on the physical image and persuading teens to look up to Washington.

If you want to look up to Washington forget about his teen years. Try visiting the U.S. Capitol. There one can see the father of the country deified. In 1865 Constantino Brumidi painted "The Apotheosis of George Washington" in the eye of the Rotunda of the U.S. Capitol. It shows Washington raised from a man into a god-man. He was deified and now is in the company of Zeus, Athena, Osiris and other great civilizers. The transformation of Washington into *divus* Washington and his ascension to the stars is an important example of how the story of 'messianic' figures is conveyed orally and visually. But that story is for another book. Our interest is in the apotheosis of Mary Magdalene.

My proposal is that Jacobus was responsible for turning the crystal and revealing a hidden facet to Mary Magdalene -- the Illuminator. This is an apotheosized Magdalene we can look up to. While other authors dropped 'the Illuminator bomb' in their books, none have attempted to present evidence for why Mary Magdalene earned this distinction. This is the aim of this book.

In the 'Good Book' Mary Magdalene first appears in the Gospel of Luke[8:2-3] as one of several apparently wealthy women Jesus cures of possession, who join him and the Apostles and provided for them.

Says Luke: "The Twelve accompanied Him, and also some women who had been cured of evil spirits and maladies: Mary called the Magdalene, from whom seven devils had gone out, Joanna, the wife of Herod's steward Chuza, Susanna, and many others who were assisting them out of their means". [Lk 8:1-3]

Mary Magdalene is next found embalming Jesus with oil. Next, standing at the foot of the cross (Mark 15:40; Matthew 27:56; John 19:25; Luke 23:49). She assisted in the entombment of Jesus, and she was the first recorded witness of the Resurrection.

The oil.

The cross.

The tomb.

The gate.

These are among the greatest mysteries ever. At the center of all of them is MM, the Illuminator.

To aid us in our quest to illuminate the mysteries of the oil, cross, tomb and gate we will be using symbols of a mystic religion that circulated in France shortly after the time of Jacobus. The Cathars of Southern France, who called themselves 'the Pure Ones' and whose lineage is traced to the Essenes and the Gnostics, constructed a symbol system that symbolist Harold Bayley says became the repository for their secret tradition or gospel of Jesus. These symbols are among the most remarkable to be found anywhere. They were created by a group who claimed to be descendents of the Desposyni who fled into the Alpine valleys to escape the persecutions of Nero and Diocletian. Their aim was to destroy the Catholic Church and teach their purer gospel.

These mystics called themselves the Albigenses. They were known as the "Good people," *Bon* (French for 'good'). Their Italian name "Cathari" is from a Greek root signifying "the Pure Ones". The *Bon* are obviously the *Ebyon* (e-bon-ites or ebionites), the poor ones.

The Cathars enjoyed immense popularity during the 12-13th centuries, coincident with the rise of the Templars and the ascension of Mary Magdalene in literary and mystic circles. This was probably not a coincidence.

The Pure Ones claimed to possess a direct revelation from Jesus. They believed that he was an angel who had come to awaken the souls asleep in matter. They considered all humans to be angels in a "dormant" divine state, angels imprisoned with a physical being. Human beings are descendents of fallen angels and are thus angels themselves, either by heredity or by the transmigration of souls. There exists only one sin: a rupture with God. Thus the human being– lives on this earth to pay penitence, to expiate its rupture from God, and to win back its angelic status.

These Good Christians called their church AMOR ('love'). These innocents were slaughtered en masse by what we today would call a terrorist organization -- the Church of ROMA, the Catholic Church -- in the first European genocide in order to prevent their competing religious beliefs – the revived religion *of* Jesus -- from spreading.

The keynote of the Cathar character was industry, and it is said that the axiom "Work is Prayer" had its origin among them. It is noteworthy that their primary industry was paper manufacturing.

The Cathars created a language of symbols and emblems that, beginning in 1280, were used as trademarks, decorative devices and watermarks to covertly convey the teachings of their religion after the genocide. Fashioning these symbols out of wire, they pressed them between pages of paper leaving them embedded for posterity. When the paper was *held to the light*, voila, the symbol appeared between the pages.

In the early 20th century Harold Bayley collected many of these symbols. He proposed that these emblems are actually thought-fossils or thought-crystals in which lie enshrined the original mystic religion of Christianity.

One of the first emblems Bayley presents in his book *The Lost Language of the Symbolism* is a pair of holy spectacles shown on the next page. These spectacles, says Bayley, possessed a fairy-like faculty to reveal surprising wonders. Among other purposes this symbol enabled the Cathars to recognize one another.

The emblem shown below combines the heart, the three rays and the word ‘le bon’, the Good. The three rays appear repeatedly in mystic teachings. They symbolize the three lights of enlightenment. Interestingly, Akhenaton’s daughter points to a 3-rayed symbol that could be a match for the three rays.

The Cathars were the Bon or Good People.

The Bible states that God is Light and also that God is Love. John tells us that when the Love-Light is developed from within us, when we can see, we shall love our fellow travelers as God has loved us. It is then that we shall know the first and last wonders of the Kingdom of Heaven on Earth: we are all One.

2.
THE TOWER OF LIGHT

The bible provides no personal details of Mary Magdalene's age, appearance, status or family. According to Jacobus' legendary account, she was of noble ("blue blood") lineage. Her father was called Syrus, and her mother Eucharia. Together with her 'brother' Lazarus and her 'sister' Martha, she was the possessor of the fortified town of Magdala, often identified as a hamlet 120 miles north of Jerusalem on the Sea of Galilee. Magdala was a wealthy town known for its opulence. The Romans destroyed it because of the moral depravity of its inhabitants. As Rome was a state organized around inflicting terror this 'moral depravity' must have really been something if it even offended Rome.

Like other women of high birth, including Isis in Egypt, Mari-Inanna and Ishtar of Mesopotamia, and Asherah in Canaan, Mary Magdalene was associated with a pillar or tower. Her name 'Magdalene', it is widely claimed, means 'Watch tower' or simply 'Tower' and refers to the 'tower' at Magdala.

Magdala is one of those multi-faceted jewels or kaleidoscopic literary catchwords (like 'rosebud' and 'illuminati') whose meaning depends entirely upon the perspective of the viewer. The sound alike name *Magada* is suggested as an alternate. The common root is *mag* (to *move* in Sanskrit), which gives us so many words indicating authority, wisdom and superiority: Magnum ('great'), magnificent, magnanimous, magic, mogul, majesty, majestic. The Magi, the occult masters of Iran, were widely known for their Christ-seeking skills.

Interestingly, it is thought that *May* is derived from *mag*. It was around the phallic May-pole (*majka* or *maj*), a vertical post or tower that symbolically connects heaven and earth, that the ancients danced the ringdance to celebrate Beltane, when, in a mist, the ancient Shining Ones came through the air to teach skill, knowledge and perfect wisdom in the form of Four Grail Treasures. This dance is still performed today. I will use • to symbolize the tower from the top down perspective and ⊙ as a symbol for the tower with a ring around it. Importantly, this symbol is also the Egyptian glyph for 'sun' and 'light'.

The suffix *dala* of Mag-dala offers some interesting and helpful associations of its own, appearing in the curiously resonant *amgydala*, and also in *mandala* (Sanskrit for circular or round, ○), ritualistic geometric designs or energy patterns symbolic of the universe, used in Hinduism and Buddhism as an aid to meditation. Another *dala* word is *Dalai* Lama, the title of the spiritual and political leader of Tibet who is believed to be the incarnation of Avalokiteshvara, the Buddha of Compassion, whose soul jumps like a fish into the body of an infant upon the Dalai Lama's death.

FISH TOWER

In *The Magdalene Legacy* Laurence Gardner observes that biblical locations are often cited with different names. In Matthew, Mark and John, for instance, the Crucifixion site, located near the Temple of Solomon, is named as Golgotha, while in Luke it is given as Calvary. Both names (Hebrew, *Gulgoleth*: Aramaic, *Gulgota*; Latin, *Calvaria*) derive from words that mean 'skull', and the meaning of the place name, as given in all the four Gospels is the same, 'the place of the skull'. The place name comes from *Gilgal*, the biblical location where Elijah ascended into a whirlwind or Merkaba.

Magdala, notes Gardner, was a fishing town on the Sea of Galilee. The Jewish *Talmud* (or *Dala-mud*, when the 't' is exchanged for the 'd' as is allowed) identifies it as Magdal Nunaiya, meaning 'Fish Tower' in Aramaic. "Tower of the Fisherman" is another suggested meaning.

Other times Magdala's full name is cited as *Magdala Tarichae*a. It is likely this is the name by which this town was known in Mary Magdalene's time. Tarichaea means salted fish, so Magdala's full name might be 'the tower of salted fish'. If the name of the town was 'Tower of Salted Fish', it's no surprise that its main business was fishing.

It would be most interesting if Fish Tower, or especially, Tower of the Fisherman, were the intended meaning and acceptable alternative name of Mag Dalen in the Gospels. The fish is one of the primary symbols of the Christian movement. It is usually thought to derive from the Greek for fish (*ichtys*), an acrostic of 'Jesus Christ, Son of God, Savior'. Shown here are examples of fish glyphs, dolphins actually, from the Good people of France. Among the Greeks, Bayley notes in *The Lost Language*, the Dolphin was venerated as the Savior. Here, the dolphin and the fleur de lis, the 'flower of light', are combined.

The dolphin and the flower of light are combined in this symbol of the Good people.

The three-rayed or three-petaled fleur-de-lis is a deeply mystical symbol. Its origins with French monarchs stems from the baptismal lily used in the crowning of King Clovis I, the founder of the Merovingian dynasty. According to Lynn Picknett and Clive Prince, the authors of *The Templar Revelation*, " ...the Merovingian kings, from their founder Merovee to Clovis (who converted to Christianity in 496) were 'pagan kings of the cult of Diana". The Bear was an animal of the Goddess Diana.

To further enhance its mystique, a legend eventually sprang up that ***a vial of OIL descended from HEAVEN*** to anoint and sanctify Clovis as King. The thus "anointed" Kings of France later maintained that their authority was directly from God (via an oil) … without the mediation of either the Emperor or the Pope.

The fleur-de-lis symbolizes the sacred (heavenly) origin of the Merovingian dynasty and then became a symbol of the entire Christian French Kingdom. Modern, controversial, theories about the Holy Grail see in the fleur-de-lis a symbol of the mythical holy origin of the French nation in the union of legendary King Merovee with Jesus and Mary Magdalene's descendants (more momentarily).

Fish formed like a column or tower or Fish tower.

Shown here is a fish glyph of the Good People Bayley describes as a "nondescript kind of ***fish formed like a column or tower***, *passing, Maypole-like, through the ring or O of I O.*" That's a fish, a tower, and a ring.

This fish glyph and Bayley's intriguing description ring of the meaning of Magdala, the Fish Tower. It symbolizes the unity of male (I) and female (O). Hence, it is symbolically linked to the May or Mag Pole ☉.

The emphasis on the fish passing through the ring in the fish tower provides another fascinating link to Magdala. As noted, Terichea is another name for Magdala. This place name, Terichea, rings of *trachea*, the tube that carries air from the mouth to the lungs also called a windpipe. Trachea is always associated with a tube. A tube is a canal. A canal usually contains water or fluid. This word and symbol poetry of the fish and the ring suggests a connection between Tarichea (Magdala) and a tube through which 'fish' run in water.

Christian paintings in the catacombs often testify to the connection of fish with baptismal or *living water*. In its mystical Jewish derivation *the living water* is the cosmic waters coming directly from the heavens (especially the seven stars of the Dove) which was thought to contain living creatures, or fish. Here, the pun involving the ring is illuminated. A 'ring' is a circular object, but it is also a sound created by a bell, a vibration.

The heavenly fish who lived in the living waters were called 'mer man'.

The most well known ruler of the waters is Neptune, the "the artful creator" who carried the three-pronged trident ♆. In Atlantis he was Poseidon. In Sumeria he was the mer-man, Enki, the Lord of Wisdom and Lord of the Waters. In Babylon he was Oannes. The Dogon tribe of Mali called him Nommo and said he came from Sirius.

A mer-man.

This scene portrays as fish-garbed apkullu *priest sprinkling a holy liquid from a bucket in front of a deity. The meaning of the cross symbol is uncertain. It is likely that the god the liquid is offered to is Enki, the Lord of Wisdom and Waters.*

This cylinder seal portrays a sacred tree or tower operated by two winged genii holding buckets of holy liquid. To the right a fish-man also holds a bucket and a cone. Mesopotamia. 800-600 B.C.

Priests in fish suits tend a radiant pillar (I) surmounted by a winged ring ridden by Enki or E.A., the god of wisdom. Is this the Fish Tower ?

We find the identical theme, two fish grasping a line of hope or salvation, in the Early Christian symbol of the *anchor* and axis or *pillar* from the catacomb of Domitilla, Rome's oldest and largest Christian cemetery. The anchor transforms into a 'cross' with a female circle or disk.

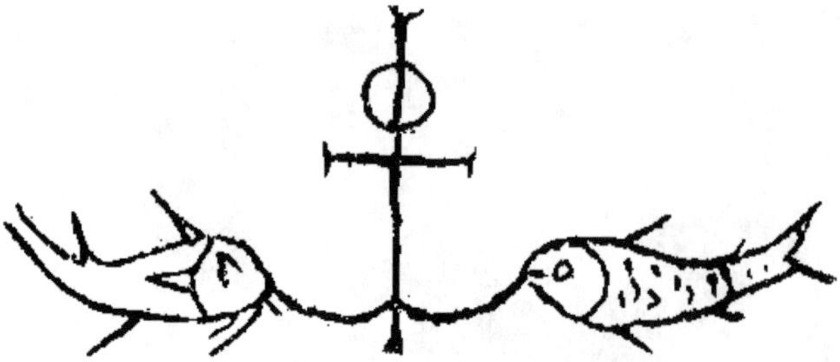

Christian graffiti from the catacomb at Domitilla, Rome. Mythologist Barbara Walker notes that the anchor cross was a variant of the Egyptian ahkh or key of life ☥ *that represented the union of Isis and Osiris. Egyptian deities carried it as a symbol of the water and the gift of eternal life.*

The match between these two emblems -- both portray two fish beside a pillar (or tower?) topped by a ring or a disk -- is obvious and leads to powerful and interesting questions. Is this pillar or tower the so-called Fish Tower of Magdala AND the 'tree' or 'cross' MM stood beside? What is the connection between the ring on the Christian symbol and the ring, winged disk or wheel of Enki? Finally, what is the holy liquid the buckets contain? Is it the cosmic living waters?

Importantly, the book of Zecharia (14:8-9) prophesied that the Messiah (the source of the living waters) would cause the cosmic or living waters to flow from Jerusalem.

John was shown "a pure river of water of life, clear as a crystal," proceeding out from the throne of God in the heavenly Jerusalem in Revelation 22:1.This association will prove immensely useful momentarily when we discuss Mary Magdalene's French nome de plume, "Lady of the Waters".

THE SHEPHERD OF HERMAS

A beautiful allusion to the living waters and a tower is found in the *Shepherd of Hermas*, a first or second century AD work revered as a companion text to the Scriptures, but later abruptly excluded. Composed in Rome *c.* AD 139–155 it is a three-part collection of revelations given to Hermas, a devout Christian, by an angel (Shepherd). It made a highly significant impact on Early Christians who sandwiched it between the Acts of the Apostles and the Acts of Paul in the New Testament. In the book the Holy Spirit shows Hermas a great ***tower*** with bright square stones that was built by six angels upon the ***water***. The angel explains to Hermas that the tower built on water of glistening stones is the Church.

To fully comprehend the mystical knowledge presented in this 'forgotten' gospel, it is key to note that the name '*Hermas*' alludes to *Hermes Trismegistos*, the 'thrice great' philosopher, priest and king most famous for his law: As above. So below. The Greek god of alchemy, Hermes (the Enlightened One) was the son of the virgin mother, *Maya* (just like Buddha), another form of *Mary*. One of the most important Hermetic scriptures is called 'Poimandres' (*Shepherd of Men*). Like Jesus, Hermes (called Thoth in

Egypt) was also known as the 'Logos', the Word, which is the *Nous* or *Divine Mind.* In Rome, this god was called *Mercury*, from the Latin word *merx*, meaning *goods* or *merch*andise. I'll take the pun and suggest he was the god of the *mer(x)=Goods* people = *god's* people. These are the *mer men* and *mer maids.*

Hermes-Thoth's "magic wand," the caduceus with two serpents that wind around the rods, is the symbol for alchemy. Also called the Staff of Hermes, today it is the logo for the American and British medical associations. Z. Sitchin has traced it as far back as 2300 B.C. to the Sumerian "Lord of the Water," Enki. Indeed, water is the staff of life's hidden power.

In his painting by Giovanni Bellini (1460-65) on the next page Jesus stands in front of a relief of two standing figures in front of a candelabrum, or perhaps an incense burner, before which is a seated figure holding a caduceus, who may be Hermes or Thoth. On one level of interpretation the juxtaposition of Jesus with Thoth/Hermes is intended to convey the meaning that he had eclipsed the pagan cults of antiquity and instituted a new order. On another level, it suggests that Jesus was a master of alchemy and embodied its teachings.

As I ponder Bellini's painting I wonder if it is possible that the two figures who are receiving the caduceus wand (and likely its secrets) could be John the Baptist and Jesus.

Following the Bellini painting is a relief from the Temple of Abydos portraying Thoth raising Seti dressed as Osiris from the dead with the key of life. The identical scene can be seen in the 4th century image of Jesus raising Lazarus from the dead.

The Blood of the Redeemer, Giovanni Bellini. London, National Gallery.

Detail of The Blood of the Redeemer *showing a figure with a caduceus. Is this figure passing or transmitting the secrets of this wand to Jesus?*

Top. Thoth raises Seti as Osiris with the key of life.

Jesus raises Lazarus with a wand or (b)aton while MM anoints his feet. Is his wand or rod actually a ray of Aton? Vatican Museum.

Hermes also had a stone or pillar (tower), called the pillar of Hermes known as "The Emerald Tablet." A legend about this tablet says that Alexander the Great discovered it in the tomb of Hermes, which had been hidden by the priests in the deepest depths of the Great Pyramid. Hermes did the writing himself on a large plate of emerald, by means of a pointed diamond. Nothing surpassed the alchemical wisdom engraved on this Stone or Tower of Hermes. It contains the key that unlocks the mysteries of 'Egypt' (= the heavenly realms) or the secret wisdom of the ages = the means by which light the candle atop our inner Tower and to Cross the Waters of Life. The alchemical teaching of the Emerald Tablet explains why Wolfram pictured the Holy Grail as an engraved emerald tablet.

THE EGYPTIAN MEANING OF TOWER

In Egyptian literature and symbolism the tower delivers a specific message that must be tabulated in any search for the meaning of Magdala. In Egyptian hieroglyphic symbolism the tower is a determinative sign denoting height or the act of rising above the common level in life or society. A tower is featured in the hieroglyph for Heliopolis, , the great light 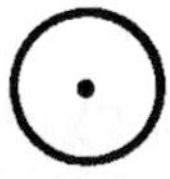 or wisdom center of ancient Egypt, which some believe is the location of the pillar of Hermes. The obelisk or pillar at Heliopolis marked the return of the Sun or Son of God.

The pharaoh Thutmosis III originally erected the

obelisks of Heliopolis around 1490-1436 BC. His ruler ship would witness the founding one of the most mysterious dynasties in all Egyptian history, a dynasty that included such illustrious names as Akhenaton and Tutankhamun. According to Gardner and others, it was also Tuthmosis III who established a mystery school of the original Rosicrucians, the *Therapeutate* – meaning 'physicians of the soul'. The Essenes later adopted this name.

Heliopolis was originally named *An* or *Annu*. This may also have been the word for the pillar or tower. It is revealing that in Aramaic *nun* means fish. Jesus is a generic from of Joshua, the name of the son of Nun who spied upon the sons of the Giants in Numbers 13. *A nun* is a female servant of Christ who has taken the three vows of poverty, chastity and obedience. *Nun* comes from the Old French *nonne*, which is traced to *Oannes*, the Babylonian name for Enki, the Lord of Waters, shown a moment ago as a Merman, half man and half fish. *Mer* is an Egyptian term for both "waters" and "mother love." One of Egypt's oldest names was *Ta Mera*, 'land of waters' or 'land of love'.

It is fascinating enough that the seed sound *nu* has for so long been associated with the concepts of the water, tower and the fish and that these concepts merge in the word Magdala, meaning the Fish Tower, and in the name Mary Magdalene. However, these connections are made even more intriguing by the fact that nun, when spelled 'none', is a quantity, zero, O. None comes from *non* or *n'an*, *ne*, not, and *an*, one, and means not any. To have none is to have zero, a quantity represented by the symbol O, which is a ring.

Continuing, *Annu/Heliopolis* was the city of the Sun and the home of the ben-nu. According to a famous legend recorded by the Greek historian Herodotus, the ancient Egyptians believed that every 500 years a wondrous bird, called the 'bennu' (*phoenix* in Greek), would travel to Egypt from Arabia carrying with it the wrapped, embalmed body of its parent. It would deliver this 'egg' at Heliopolis, where it would be put into a furnace and buried at the Temple of the Phoenix. Then, out of the ashes, another phoenix would be born.

The temple of Ra (Ray) at Heliopolis is said to have been a special depository for royal records, and Herodotus states that the priests of Heliopolis were the best-informed in matters of history of all the Egyptians. Plato, Solon, Pythagoras, and other Greek philosophers until the time of Strabo (1st century BC) are claimed to have frequented the schools of philosophy and astronomy. During the Amarna Period, king Akhenaton built here a temple and introduced monotheistic worship of Aton, the deified galactic disc.

A legend of antiquity says that during the Flight to Egypt, when Mary, Joseph and the baby Jesus fled from 'Bethelehem' ('House of Bread') to escape the certain death at the hands of Herod, they rested in Heliopolis where the Egyptian priest Manetho (c. 280 BC) says Moses was initiated. The royal family remained in exile in Egypt for several years. All the while the young Jesus would likely have been preparing for his later life mission.

The Hebrews called Heliopolis 'On', An, or *Aven*, or 'House of the Sun' or 'House of ☉ (Sun, light, gold).

There is a famous well or fountain at Heliopolis, in which, according to Egyptian tradition, the Sun God Ra bathed his face when he rose upon the Earth for the first time. This well still exists at *Matariyah.* It is stated in the apocryphal tradition that the Virgin Mary rested by this well, and drew from it the water with which she washed the clothes of Jesus, and that wherever the water fell *basalm-bearing* plants sprang up; ***drops of the oil*** made from them were always mixed with the water used in baptizing Christians.

This legend makes clear that from an early age Jesus was baptized with an oil, possibly of cosmic origins. I say this for when Hermes' As above. So below law is invoked, this tale hints that Mary knew of a way to channel the *cosmic* or *living waters* from a heavenly well through specific plants to create an aromatic purifying balm, balsam or oil. In his adult years Jesus is, once again, anointed with oil. Mary Magdalene is mentioned in Luke 8:3 as one of the three wealthy women who "ministered to Christ of their substance".

This 'ministering substance', what is it?

This holy liquid or substance is an *oil* or *balsam,* quite likely a fragrant *ointment.* What function did it serve? Ointments are usually used in medications or perfumes. Interestingly, it seems MM's oil served this healing function as it made the adult Jesus holy or whole (360). It rang or vibrated in resonance with the holy waters ≋.

In addition, I find it highly intriguing that Jesus *'saved'* humanity soon after MM anointed him with this oil. It makes me wonder if MM's *salve* had something to do with *how* Jesus *saved.* After all, his anointing ultimately brought about *salvation* (sal-va-*shen*), which I will term our release from confinement on Earth and our return to the Light. We are being led to the possibility that MM's oil was a salve that saves. It was a salvation salve that brought freedom to spiritual slaves.

SPIT AND THE TOWER OF SILOAM

A salve that saves? A salvation salve? To get to the inner meaning of the Christian tradition, which describes a 'substance' mixed with the water (probably the holy *living waters = cosmic rays* ♆ , ≋) and used in Early Christian baptisms, we must remember how Jesus healed.

In particular, let us remember that *saliva*, a watery mixture of secretions that formed a frothy substance, is mentioned in the bible as one of the methods by which Jesus altered disease. Three times Jesus used spit to heal people. Did you ever wonder why?

In Mark 7:32-35, a deaf man with a speech impediment was brought to Jesus. Jesus put his finger in the man's ears and, spitting, touched his tongue, then looked up to Heaven and groaned, and said to him, "Ephatha!" (that is, "Be opened!") And immediately the man's ears were opened, his speech impediment was removed, and he spoke plainly. In Mark 8:22-25, in Bethsaida, a blind man was brought to Jesus. Jesus took the blind man outside the village. Putting spittle on his eyes, He laid hands on him and asked, "Do you see anything?" Looking up the man replied, "I see people looking like trees and walking." (Huh?) Then Jesus laid his hands on his eyes a second time and the man saw clearly, his sight was restored and he could see everything distinctly. Hmmm.

In John 9:1-7, Jesus meets up with a blind man who was blind from birth. Jesus spat on the ground and made clay with the saliva, and smeared the clay on the man's eyes, and said to him, "Go wash in the ***Pool of Siloam***" (in Jerusalem). So he went and washed, and came back able to see. In his book *The Wars of the Jews*, Flavius Josephus, a Jewish priest, tells us the location of Siloam had "that fountain of sweet and abundant water". It stands on the west slope of the Mount of Olives, the site of so many important biblical events including Jesus' Ascension. At its foot is the Garden of Gethsemane, where Jesus' tomb was located and where MM discovered the risen Jesus.

The Pool of Siloam (same as *Shiloah*) was built near the ancient community that was built around the "serpent-stone", called Zoheleth. I was excited to learn it is the site of the legendary ***Tower of Siloam***, whose collapse is discussed by Jesus in the *Gospel of John*[9:7] during a discourse on the problem of evil and how disaster can strike both the just and the unjust with equal ferocity. This is the only time this Tower (*Pole* or *Pool*) is mentioned. It must be significant even though the loss of life was not enormous. Eighteen people were killed. Therefore, it seems to me that another symbolic meaning to this Tower is inferred. Interestingly, the story of the collapse of this Tower rang in churches across America after the collapse of the Twin Towers on 9-11.

Wells are feminine, and it is likely the feminine principle was the object of adoration at Siloam. It is highly significant that the Tower of Siloam was located at the serpent-stone. The Celts of Ireland and the Hopi of Arizona are two examples of cultures that associate the serpent with healing springs or holy wells. The Hopi refer to round towers as "snake houses". Over 65 round towers, many rising over 100 feet high, spring from the countryside of Ireland. In *Sacred Geometry*, Nigel Pennick explains the symbolism of the circular form: "Like the Pagan temples, the round churches were microcosms of the world. In the late Middle Ages, they became the prerogative of an enigmatic and heretical sect, the Knights Templar. The round form of the church became especially connected with the order..."

In *Jesus, Last of the Pharaohs*, Ralph Ellis avers that round towers were modeled after the Egyptian Benben tower located in the Phoenix Temple at Heliopolis. He also links the round tower with the Pillar of Osiris. We will explore the Benben tower and the Pillar of Osiris momentarily.

I believe the symbolic core of this tower story is suggested by the definition of *Siloam*: "sent" or "sending." Sent means 'to cause to be conveyed by an intermediary to a destination'. It means 'to move'. This is useful to us as *mag* is the Sumerian word for move. Was the Tower of Siloam a tower/magdala *center*, ⊙, for 'sending' or 'moving' or 'conveying'?

Synonyms for send include forward, route, and ship. It is also a broadcast term meaning to emit or transmit. *Send forth* means to discharge material, as vapor or fumes: emit, give, give forth. It also means to demand to appear, come, or assemble: call.

The accumulation of these meanings sends me thinking. I wonder if this ambiguous Tower of Siloam and the *Pool* (Pole) was a place where 18 people were physically delivered elsewhere, as for instance, through some sort of porthole, ☉. Of course, this sounds simply too good to be true.

Alternatively, I wonder, could Siloam have been a place where a transmitting tower was located that emitted a vapor from underground that sent a scent that sent one elsewhere, spiritually speaking? Oracle centers, such as the goddess' at Delphi, emitted a supernatural vapor after all. According to the principles of feng shui, the round pagoda towers of Buddhism traps negative *ch'i*, or dragon energy located in the earth. Those of India, called *stupas* (Sanskrit, = mound) are chiefly pyramidal (*conical*) structures of masonry, tapering to an apex and elaborately adorned with carving and sculpture. Christian *steeples* spiraling chi through its spire (pole) perform the same function as the *stupa* (=*steeple*).

Might Silo-am have been a covered pit -- an underground *silo* -- or an above ground storage tower for storing sacred energy? Did Jesus know this? Is this why Jesus packed the man's eyes with mud made from his spit and sent him to the Tower of Siloam?

The interchange of Pole (Pool) and Tower brings up an important question. What, exactly, was pooled in the pool Jesus ordered the blind the man to bathe in? Could it have been a holy liquid like that harvested from the tower in the Babylonian depiction?

The Hindu *Vedas* proclaim that "all healing power is in the waters" (= ♆ and ≋). The well of water at Siloam obviously made the blind man well. Well, what do you know? We found one poetic meaning of *well.*

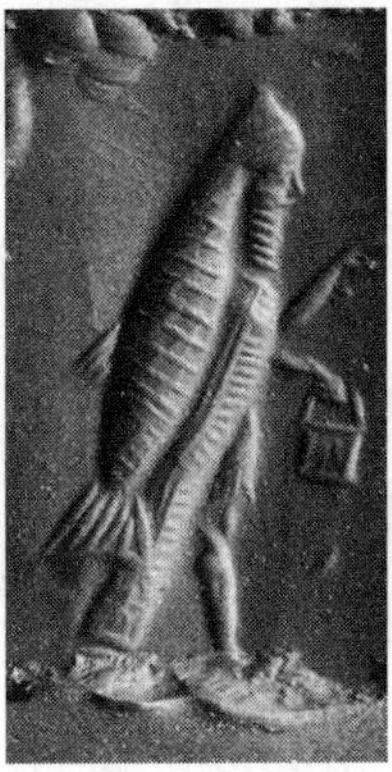

What is in the fish man's pail?

It is well worth noting that in Ireland there is a reference in the *Well of Kilmore* to *mystical fishes*. An old Druid writer sayd, "They do call the said fishes *Easa Seant*, that is to say, holie fishes." *Easa* contains the name E.A., the holy fish god.

For those who are willing, a magnificent pun wells up or arises from *Easa Seant* (holy fishes). It is phonetically the same as *Issa Sent*. *Saint* Issa is the Buddhist name for Jesus. Therefore *Ea-sa Sent* and *Issa Sent* are both names for the saintly mystical fish.

Jesus carries a lamb and a cauldron or pail.

A pool is usually associated with standing water (rain water) or other liquid. Here, we are talking about a mystical story. In this context suppose the holy water of the Tower at Salaom was a cosmic healing energy or vibration – standing waves -- that 'pooled', congealed or focused ⊙ around the tower. Now, suppose this tower broadcast this healing frequency, which triggered the release of a milky fluid (the cerebral spinal fluid) from within the brain that filled the network of hollow spaces (empty pools), called ventricles, inside the brain.

A hypothesis: Visitors to this Tower of Siloam 'saw the light'. The removal of the impenetrable *veil*, which shrouded the mysteries, was removed at this *well.* They were, well, cured of 'blindness'. They were illumined.

I'll bet that when the blind bathed in the Pool or Tower of Siloam it made the hair stand up on their arms. Their pineal glands were also activated, the third eye opened. Both the retina and the pineal gland are equipped with photoreceptor cells and may be considered photosensitive organs. This energy may have entered the pathways to the brain through the retina (which I have proposed is Jacob's Ladder) and it charged or 'lit' the wick of the pineal gland resulting in activation of latent psychic and spiritual processes. Mind can do every thing including so-called miracles. Stimulated properly the pineal gland can revitalize body, it can heal diseases and it can manipulate laws of physics.

Ultimately, Jesus' *salve* or *salivation* brought about *salvation*, *a-tone-ment*, *at-one-ment* or *atonement.* As the word *ment* is derived from the Latin *mentis* meaning *mind*, right here we have the complete explanation of purpose of this substance. It manifests *one mind*, the Christ Mind and In Sight. The Christ Mind creates a state of mind, oneness, with all creation. We become mystical fish bathing in the pool of living waters. Well, that's my take anyway.

3.
THE BIRD OF LIGHT AND THE ROUND TOWER

With our understanding that the cosmic or living waters are subtle vibrations from cosmic rays, it is instructive to note that the Egyptians portrayed the phoenix as the heron, the bird of light.

According to Egyptian legend, at the dawn of each new age the heron would alight from the "Isle of Fire" and land on top of a tall pillar, at Heliopolis. From its outstretched arms it would radiate light. It would then deliver a teaching, symbolized by the key of life, , that would transform humans into herons. This did not mean they transformed into birds. Rather, it meant they became phoenix, the people of the light. In Egyptian baptismal scenes the key of life was portrayed falling like 'water'. Later, it became the symbol for Ve***nu***s.

The hieroglyph of the heron, , called *shen*, is easily seen as the inspiration for the Christian fish symbol  of *sal-va-shen* (salvation). This answers to the strange mystic Jewish '*slave nation's*' association of the living waters (or cosmic rays) with the fish. (Interestingly, the English word pool comes from the French *poule*, hen. Jesus is the father hen who gathers his chicks.)

Is the heron atop the Magdala Tower *? Note the 3 rays the pole is emitting on the right.*

Intriguingly, the Egyptian hieroglyph for the *shepherd* shows a figure holding a pole with the heron glyph attached . The Bear people were called Shepherds. To me, this figure also resembles a 'fisher man' with a fishing rod or pole on its shoulder. Figuratively speaking, this figure has fished the mystical key of life out of the cosmic ocean. As the Good Shepherd Jesus embodied these characteristics and then taught others how to become mystical fish too.

In *The Healing Sun Code*, I concluded that the phoenix/heron legend probably originated with the appearance of a light from the heronry, the center of our galaxy, the Core the Mayans called 'the place of herons'.

The Druids called this center *Tula*, a Sanskrit word that means 'balance'. *Tula*, *Toowa*, *Tua*, *Tala*, *Tara*, *Towa, Torah*, *Tor*, and *Tower* are resonant terms. While modern science considers the galactic center a star nursery, ancient tradition reveals it is a *soul* nursery. This mother of cosmic energy is the likely intermediary of the life-giving "Living Waters" spring of Ursa Major. It appears the Egyptians discovered the key to utilize the Light of the Mother to *cure* the human condition. So did Jesus. They considered it the prima material, the original mother matter of the universe. This Love-Light apparently provided nourishment, a speculation deduced by the fact that the key of life symbol that represented this nourishment was often accompanied by a conical shaped hieroglyph meaning 'bread', 'manna'.

The Egyptian key of life and bread symbol.

The legend of the phoenix was connected with the ultra-mysterious *benben* stone, a conical-shaped stone containing cosmic rays the ancient Egyptians regarded as a cosmic emissary, the embodiment of the Divine Word. *The benben, like the tower is a symbol of ascent or a-shen-shen.* This was secreted away at Heliopolis before it disappeared around the time that the pyramids were built.

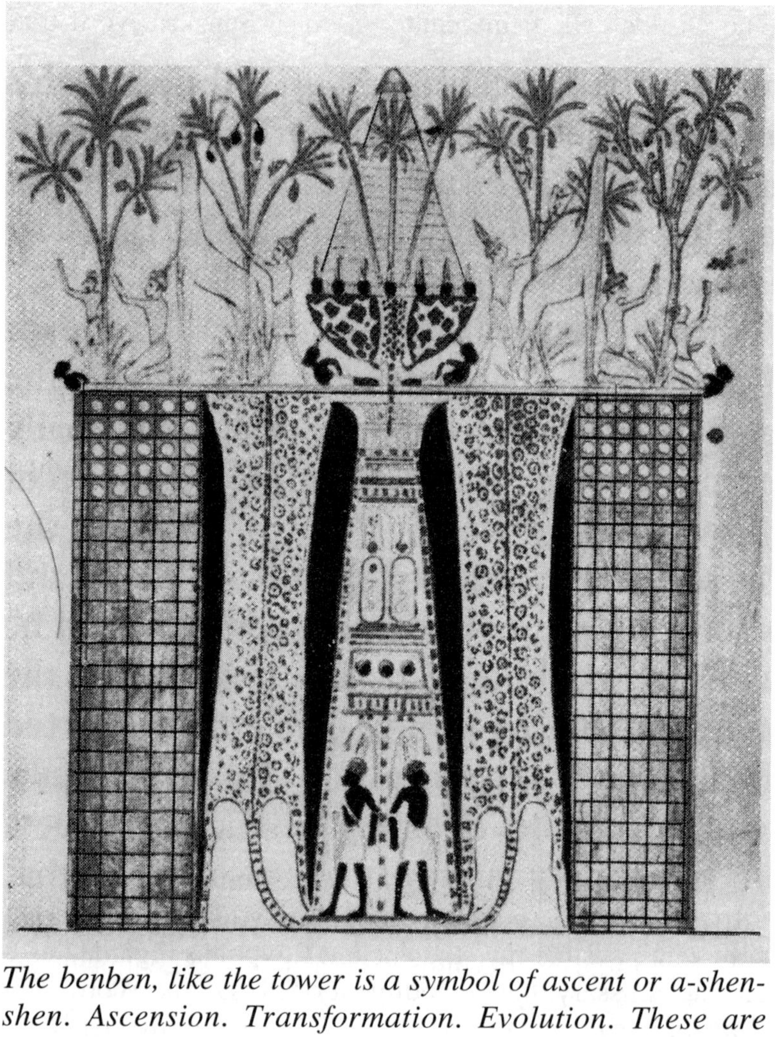

The benben, like the tower is a symbol of ascent or a-shen-shen. Ascension. Transformation. Evolution. These are alchemical concepts.

On the previous page we see a *drawing of a* ***tower***  that appears to illustrate the hieroglyph of Heliopolis. A *ben ben,* the *conical stone* or *egg* of the phoenix or heron tops this tower. This masterpiece tower was etched onto a gold plate made by Nubian goldsmiths and given to King Tutankhamun, who is the son or nephew of Akhenaton and Nefertiti.

I am intrigued by the repetition of the syllable *bon* (good=god) or *ben.* A cone matching the ben ben also appears in the East on the top of a sacred tower called *Meru* featured on the next few pages. Meru is the name of the celestial mountain, fountain, pillar or cosmic axis where the gods and the highest celestial beings dwell. This sounds like the galactic center. Like the ben ben atop the tower of Heliopolis, a 'ring' atop a 'cone'  ,  symbolized Meru. It is circular, and formed like a cone.

As we will explore momentarily, the Tower of Babel, the Gate of Heaven, was built by Nimrod in ancient Su-*Mer* or Su-Meru to replace the broken cosmic *axis* Meru and by its *access* to *ascend,* like Jack up the 'bean stalk', to the abode of gods. Turning to Buddhist imagery we find a remarkable image of Meru. As we can see on the next page, the Meru pillar is strikingly similar to the human skeletal system, the bones.

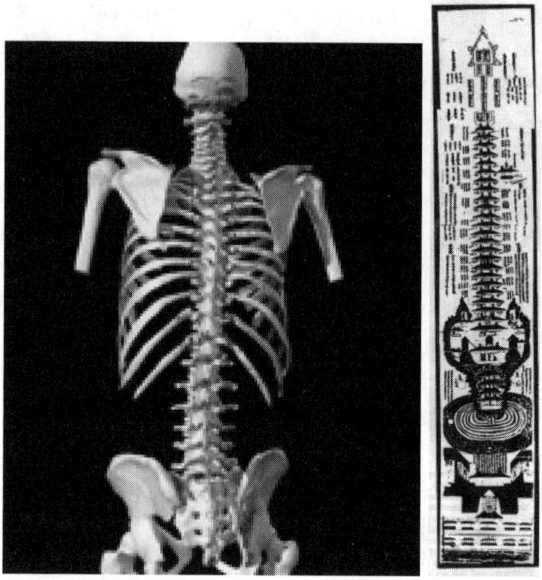

Genesis, the first book of the Old Testament, says we were created in God's image. When the Meru drawing is compared to the human skeletal system it reveals our bones represent the ladder of stairway to heaven.

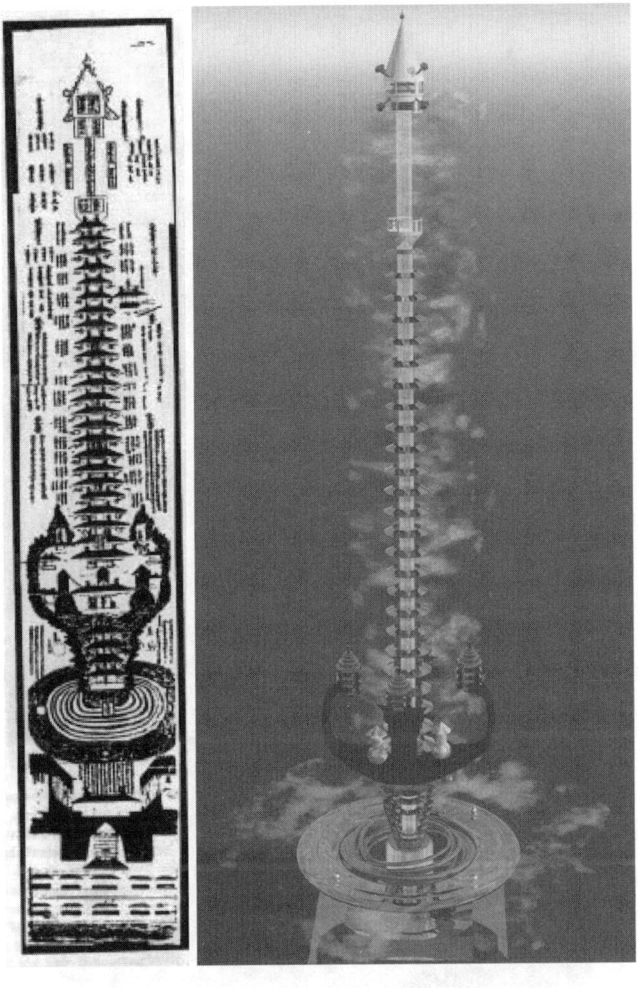

Meditate on this. Meru from a second century Chinese manuscript. A rendering of this object in 3-D by digital artist Jack Andrews.

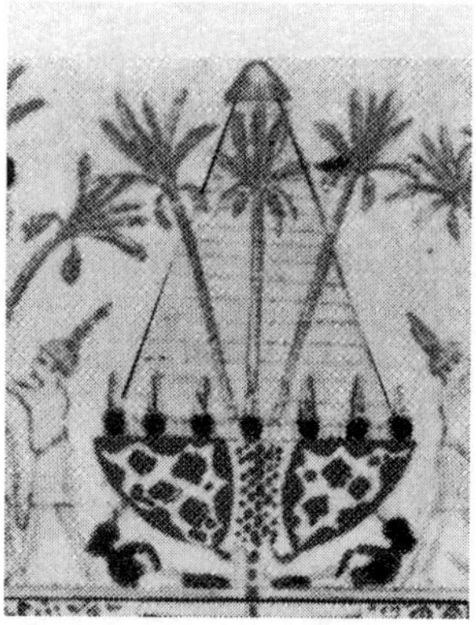

The ben bens or cones atop the towers are a virtual match for one another.

Followers of *Bon-Po* shamans of Tibet's pre-Buddhist, shamanistic religion, revere Mount Meru as the center of their religion. Located in the center of Shambhalla it is a gateway between the lower worlds and the higher worlds. As I have written in several articles published in *Atlantis Rising* magazine and available at my website, williamhenry.net, the Meru diagram resembles a particle accelerator. Physicists envision constructing giant, space-based accelerators to open holes in space. As such, Meru can be thought of as a conduit through which ascended humans ('mystical fish') ascend to the heavens.

One can see that the Meru drawing is an axis that resembles an antenna. It is a 'Fish Tower'. So too is the temple bones of the human body. MM's connection to the Fish Tower brings us to the possibility that she knew the secrets of this ladder or Stairway to Heaven. I will have much more to say about this possibility momentarily.

MAR, MER, MARY, MERRY, MERY, MERI

As noted, *Mer* is an Egyptian word for both "waters" and "mother-love". The Greek name 'Mary' is from the Egyptian 'Mery' meaning 'beloved'. Today, *merry* means cheerful. Synonyms are vivacious, lively and blithe, which is the word from which comes *bliss*. In between the Greek Mary and the Egyptian Mery was the Hebrew 'Miriam' (Meer-yahm), the name (title) of the prophetess and sister of Moses and Aaron in Exodus 15:21. It meant: "wished for child," "bitter" or "rebellious". Resonant Egyptian names include Meryamon (Beloved of Amon) and Merytaten (Beloved of Aten).

In her book, *Jesus and the Riddle of the Dead Sea Scrolls*, Barbara Thiering reveals that the Magdalene was called *Mary* as a *title*, not a name. This tradition is upheld to this day in the Catholic faith by nuns who are called Sister Mary, such and such.

The name 'Miriam' was applied to Essene women who were *prophetesses*. In Greek it became Maria, Mary. The title, notes Thiering, *was used of all women in the order who were the brides of the David kings.*

This title connects Mary Magdalene to an ancient tradition of Mary goddesses who held or preserved sacred wisdom... especially that related to the Fish Tower. Before she was initiated by Jesus she had already mastered the school of Isis and Istar.

Even at the time of Jesus and Mary Magdalene Mary was not a personal name. It was a title of distinction (like 'Jesus Christ', which is a title meaning 'Anointed Savior'). This explains the confusion among the three Marys (Miryams or Maryams) who play such prominent roles in the Gospel story. In Egyptian form the title Mery Magdalen is Beloved Tower or Beloved of the Fish Tower. The Meru Pillar, I propose, is a prime example this Tower.

The Mary, the Magdalene, was a priestess. That much is certain. But now, the question becomes where (or what) is her temple tower? We will endeavor to answer this question in the next chapter.

4.
MAGDALENE =153

Shedding further light on the 'Fish Tower' of Magdala is the contemplative Magdalene scholar Margaret Starbird. In her volume *The Goddess in the Gospels* she makes a fascinating study of the numbers coded by the number coding of the Greek version of Mary Magdalene's name. Using *gematria* or "numbers theology" of the Hellenistic world, numbers were coded in the New Testament that were based on the ancient canon ('sacred rule') of sacred geometry derived by the Pythagoreans centuries before. In Greek gematria the Greek epithet "h Magdalhnh" bears the number 153, a profoundly important number. This number indicates that Mary Magdalene was the "Fish Goddess" among early Christians.

There is also a deep connection between the number of the fish, 153, and the tower or church. In Micah 4:8, for instance, the stronghold of the infant church is called the Tower of Flock. The Hebrew word for "Tower of the Flock" is "Migdal Eder". From the phonetic similarity of the two titles it is claimed that Mary Magdalene was the Migdal Eder, or tower of the church. Some believe prophecy declares that one day she will have a special place of dominion within the restored Kingdom: "And you, O (tower of the flock) the stronghold of the daughter of Zion, to you shall it come, even the former dominion shall come, the kingdom of the daughter Jerusalem." (Others believe Jesus is the Tower of the Flock.)

153 is the end product of threes. 51 times 3 = 153. Three being the triangle number, the digital root number, the Trinity number.

Archimedes (*c*. 287-212 B.C.) in his treatise *On the Measurement of the Circle* uses the number ratio 153:265 as a mathematical shorthand for the "measure of the fish" or the *vesica piscis* (more momentarily). It is presumed that any ancient reader skilled in mathematics would have immediately recognized the higher meaning encoded in any story featuring this number.

Christian Sacred Geometry scholar David Fideler notes in *Jesus Christ: Sun of God* that 153 is associated with the symbolism of the sun god Apollo at *Delphi*, the most famous oracle of ancient Greece. Delphi was revered throughout the Greek world as the site of the *omphalos* stone, the *navel* or *womb* center (*Meru* means center) of the universe.

According to Greek legend, Apollo, the Sun god (*Sol* god or *Soul* god) who founded the great Temple at Delphi, usually took the form of a serpent. In the bible he is Apollyon, the "angel of the bottomless pit" in Revelation 9:11. However, it was in the guise of a *dolphin*, that Apollo led thither a crew of Cretan mariners. (In Ireland the sun god is called *Fin*.) Upon reaching *the sands of Krisa* (= the brain sand of the pineal and the Christ Mind?), Apollo leapt from the vessel (the skull?) like a star, whilst sparks of light (glow rays) streamed from him till their radiance reached the heavens. Hastening to his Sanctuary, he lit a fire and returned to the astonished mariners in his earlier form as a beautiful youth. He taught that if they chose the right words, the right thoughts and the right actions their name would be known throughout the world as the guardians of Apollo's shrine. In the inner *hestia* or hearth of the Temple of Delphic Apollo an eternal flame burned.

This "god" was likely embodied as an individual, or more likely, as a group of individuals who formed a school of scholars. One later master of this school was Pythagoras of Crotona. It is widely believed by students of esoteric Christianity that the Essenes were organized to retrieve and revive the works of Pythagoras (and Apollo). This body of knowledge included works from the Egyptian and Babylonian Mystery Schools, as well as the Eleusianian Mysteries and the Mysteries of Isis at Thebes.

As this number system predates Christianity it is hypothesized that Mary's epithet 'Magdalene' was chosen to resonate with concepts previously assigned to the number 153, including the vesica, the omphalos, the god of light, the eternal flame and the "womb-fish". By following this path we recognize her as an initiate of Pythagoras.

153 IN ENGLISH

Inspired by the gematrists I looked for insight into 153 using the simple English gematria code A=1, B=2, C=3. For instance, GOD =7+15+4 =26, THE = 20+8+5=33, etc., "The Kingdom of God" = 153 (33+73+21+26). So does "The Water of Life" = 153. (A remarkable list of 1717 153s is provided at http://asis.com/~stag/153list.html)

Catch this, 153 is also the number of fish caught by the apostles in John 21:11. "I'll make you fishers of men," proclaimed Jesus.[Mat. 6:33] What did these fishers do? For one thing they built a church. As the story of the building of the tower-church in *Hermas* reveals, the Early Christians interconnected the ideas of church and tower. The Good Christians, in turn, connected the church-tower with a circle or ring , and hence with the Round Towers.

Three tower watermarks of the Good people. Note that the one on the left is ringed and has the letters ***T*** *and* ***R*** *at its top with the symbol for a star atop them. The* ***T*** *surmounted middle tower appears to be constructed of square stones (called ashlars) ala the stone tower of* Hermas.

A study of the circle-ring-magdala-tower word connection gives us the following: church comes from *kirk*, or *circe*, meaning *circle*. The word *spire*, used to describe the antennas atop churches, is the root of *spiral*. One of the surnames of Apollo was *Tortor* (he is *Taur, Thor* or *Thoth*). All of these gods knew the Way, the path, the *thor*ougfare to the heavens. They *tra*versed this path. In Gaelic *tor* is a conical hill or castle, like Glastonbury Tor. The word *tower* is the same as the French *tour*, which also means a *circle* or *wheel.* The famous *Tour Magdala* of Rennes-le-Chateau in Southern France is the 'Tower Magdala' (Tower Tower). It features a circular *turret* and may properly be called a Fish Tower. *T'ra* is the Egyptian word for fortress. *Tara* is the Buddhist goddess of compassion.

E = SOLOMON'S KEY

And now to complete this circuit we note that there was a world-famous "E" inscribed over Apollo's Oracle at Delphi. Because this letter is the fifth letter of so many alphabets, the Greeks considered it to be equivalent to the number 5. The five points of E caused it to be regarded as equivalent to the five-pointed Pentagram , the symbol sacred to Venus and known as *Solomon's Key.*

The star pattern of the pentagram may explain why the five-pointed E was esteemed to be the *letter of Light.* In 1905 Einstein's equation, $E = mc^2$ re-affirmed this connection in the collective mind. *E* represents units of energy, *m* represents units of mass, and c^2 is the speed of light squared, or multiplied by itself. Because the speed of light is a very large number and is multiplied by itself, this equation points out how a small amount of matter can release a huge amount of energy, as in a nuclear reaction. Is it by design or coincidence that the letter E formed the *Key of Light*?

In *Myth and Symbol in Ancient Egypt* Rundle Clark notes that during the Middle Kingdom the *bennu* bird, the heron, became the 'soul' of Osiris and *the symbol of the planet Venus* – the morning star. The heron delivers the vital essence from the 'Isle of Fire', which Clark calls 'the place of everlasting light beyond the limits of the world'. This is where the gods were born and where they were sent into the world. Hence, *the Key of Life of the heron and its message of light and life and Solomon's Key are the same.*

John Michell, an authority on ancient sacred science, proposes this five-pointed star with a dot and with the Hebrew letters J,R,S,L,M, is an ancient emblem for Jerusalem. In *The Temple at Jerusalem: A Revelation* he says that the dot at the center is Gulgotha. As we recall, Gulgotha means 'the head', 'the stone' and 'the gate'. It is an oracular center, another Meru gateway between heaven and earth. Significantly, the pentacle was the logo for Pythagoras' Mystery School. It represents perfect attunement with the Word or Life Force.

The pentagram spills over into legends of Jerusalem's Temple of Solomon, which sits atop Mount Moriah, retold by Michell. He describes the Temple as an instrument of a mystical, priestly form of alchemy by which oppositely charged elements in the Earth and atmosphere were brought together and ritually mated. The product of the union was a 'spirit' that blessed and sanctified the people of Israel. The marriage itself was technical, potentially dangerous and involved physics and astronomy.

I propose the science practiced atop Moriah (like Meru) also involved chemistry, anatomy, physiology, astrology and cosmic rays from the galactic center.

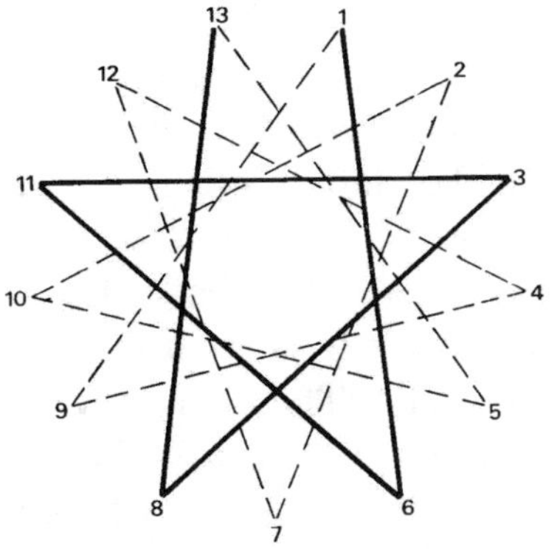

In Refgue of the Apocalypse *Elizabeth Van Buren observes that the highest point of a five-pointed star opens to reveal a hidden thirteen-pointed star. Points "1" and "13" are formed of point "1". This reveals the way to the mystic center (Meru, Tula).*

Astoundingly, one of the great secrets guarded by the Templars is that this symbol referred to a *temple in the stars* above Jerusalem. A similar 'stargate plan' has been perceived in the area of Rennes-le-Chateau in Southern

France where five mountains form the shape of a pentagram. In the plan of this temple is Solomon's Key to forgotten knowledge. This is made even more interesting when Greg Rigby's research into the Gothic cathedrals as markers for the seven stars of Ursa Major is added in. It is traditional that Ursa Major points to the pole star Polaris. Rigby aligns Rennes-le-Chateau with the position that would represent the Pole Star.

The mystery phrase, "*Et in Arcadia ego"*(normally translated "I am in Arcadia") associated with Rennes-le-Chateau also plays an important role in this line of thinking. Arcadia is the Greek name for paradise. It is the 'home' of Hermes. His tablet, it is believed, were hidden in Arcadia. In this context, it is interesting to note that the Latin prefix "arca" means "a chest or box" (it is the root of the word *arcane*). What is kept in this box? Well, arcane secrets. Whose secrets? The secrets of the Arcadians or *Arkades*, who name also means "People of the Bear." These "Bear people" are the people of the Great Bear, Ursa Major. Legends attached to Rennes-le-Chateau suggest that buried in this area is a "casket" or "chest" that plunged to earth from the Great Bear. Significantly, the earliest Sumieran sign for the Great Bear, where it was called the "Plough", was the sign "AR", which is a pentagram.

One final note. Numerous authors insist that the area of Rennes-le-Chateau, which is home to the famed Church of Mary Magdalene refurbished by Berenger Sauniere, is the entrance to the underworld. In *Blue Apples* I proposed it is perhaps even a star gate. In the next chapter we will explore Mary Magdalene's revelation concerning this gate.

5.
THE FISH GATE

"And Mary answered and said to the Savior,'Now we know, O Master, freely, surely, plainly, that ***thou has brought the Keys of the Mysteries of the Kingdom of Light****, which remit the sins of souls that they may be cleansed and be transformed into pure light, and be brought into the Light."*

Pistis Sophia

According to Gnostic Christian belief recorded in the *Gospel of Mary*, written sometime in the second century and recovered in the 20th century, Mary Magdalene is presented as *the* Christian authority. In Grail vernacular she is the 'ultimate fisher person'. She is 153, 'the Tower'. Her high position is due to the perception that she was the closest to Jesus in life, his beloved, and received a special revelation, perhaps a blessed flash of illumination, from the risen Jesus that was hidden from the other apostles. The fact that Jesus had secret teachings he gave only to those who he had given healing power is clearly indicated in Matthew 13:10-11 and Mark 4:10-12 & 34. The exact nature of these teachings is unknown. However, Mary Magdalene is the key figure associated with them. They are straight out of the Egyptian mysteries of the heron.

The *Gospel of Mary* says MM was given a special transmission of knowledge (*gnosis*). This transmission came after Jesus' resurrection and concerned the nature of matter, of salvation, and of the soul's journey through the darkness of the astral planes to reach the realm, kingdom or empire of light (which may well be the center of our galaxy).

Mary's revelation is in the form of a Gnostic dialogue. As Jesus' chief apostle in life Mary now questions the risen Jesus. The first question Mary asks is how one sees a vision. Jesus replies that the soul sees through *the mind*, which is the conduit between the soul and the spirit.

At this point the text breaks off. Sadly, four crucial pages of this dialog are lost. Only the beginning and end of the revelation are extant.

When the text resumes Mary is in the midst of describing Jesus' revelation concerning the rise of the soul.

After recounting her illumination to the disciples Mary falls silent. Andrew is the first to speak. He refuses to believe her story. The hot-tempered Peter flies into a jealous fit. He questions if Jesus would really have revealed these secrets of a woman. Levi ('love') is sympathetic to Mary and plays the role of peacemaker. This confrontation is repeated in *The Gospel of Thomas*, *Pistis Sophia*, and *The Gospel of the Egyptians*. To the modern mind there's a word for Peter's behavior and his sexist attitude. One moment, let me fish for it. Oh yes, there it is: *pathetic*.

Mary Magdalene is clearly possessed of a superior spiritual teaching (The Pure Word = 153), one *sympathetic* to Jesus (The True Light = 153), and one that Jesus did not intend for certain of the apostles to know. A tantalizing reference to the nature of Jesus' true teaching is provided in the *Pistis Sophia*. Jesus tells Mary:

"***Do not cease seeking day or night, and do not let yourselves relax until you have found all the Mysteries of the Kingdom of Light, which will purify you and make you into Pure Light and lead you into the Kingdom of Light.***"

Additional clues to the secrets of this special revelation and the means to transform oneself into a being of pure light in order to enter the Kingdom of Light is, conveniently, encoded in the number 153. As noted, 153 is identified with the almond-shaped symbol  called the *vesica piscis*, which we will now take a moment to discuss.

To begin, this symbol, called the 'fish' or the "vulva," always has attributes of feminine regeneration. The vesica is the Egyptian hieroglyph *Ru*, meaning 'birth passage', 'doorway'. It is found in the word *ute-rus* or uterus, the gate through which the WORD is made flesh and bone, as well as *Me-ru*, the Tower of the East. It was a very ancient, even archetypal symbol for the Goddess. It was called the "holy of holies" and the "inner sanctum."

The vesica piscis is the same as the mouth-shaped Egyptian hieroglyphic of *Atum-Re*, the Sun God who comes from the Abyss. It is also the same as the fish symbol of Jesus . In his book *Sacred Geometry*, Robert Lawlor notes the relationship of the 'mouth' symbol and the path of a vibrating string. Both have a flattened, vesical form. Intriguingly, this football-shaped form is the Mayan hieroglyph meaning 'galaxy'.

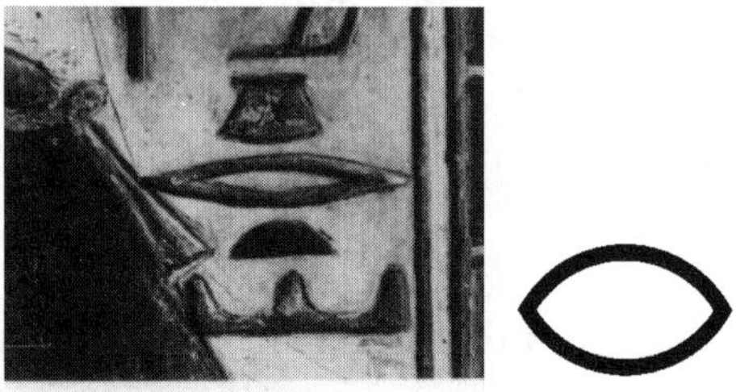

The Egyptian 'mouth' symbol of Atum-Re (left). The Mayan symbol for the Milky Way and love (right).

Interestingly, one of the 12 gates of ancient Jerusalem was known as the fish gate (2Chr33:v14-Neh3:v3-Neh12:v39-Zeph1:v10). The fish were brought in this gate into Jerusalem from the Sea of Galilee and the Jordan River. According to Jewish tradition, the Messiah will enter Jerusalem through the Eastern Gate, also known as the Golden Gate. To prevent this, the Muslims sealed the gate in the year 810. It has remained closed for 12 centuries. By English gematria Seek The Entrance = 153. The one that truly raises an eyebrow is Use The Fish Gate = 153.

A second great eyebrow raiser is the fact the *vesica piscis* is called the Vessel of the Fish. It was well known as *Yoni* in the ancient world. Yoni is an ancient Indo-Aryan word that means "Divine Passage," notes mythologist Barbara Walker in *The Woman's Dictionary of Symbols and Sacred Objects*. In India, Meru is the yoni.

The yoni originally referred to a passage of stars that the child passed through. It therefore makes perfect sense why the term also came to be used by ancient physicians to refer to female genitalia.

"With an intentional double entendre," notes Barbara Walker, "the mandorla was sometimes piously interpreted as *a gateway to heaven*," says Walker.

This gateway is found in Christian paintings depicting the Transfiguration, the Ascension, the Last Judgment, the Harrowing of Hell, and in symbolic portrayals of the evangelists and Jesus in Majesty (Magesty). The Virgin Mary and the major angels were also shown enclosed in a mandorla or Fish Gate. Two examples are shown here. One portrays Mary delivering Jesus from this female-genital emblem. The other is the famed twelfth-century panel in Chartres Cathedral, which shows "Christ of the

Apocalypse" within the gateway or the mouth of the fish .

Summing up, Magdala means 'fish tower' and the title Magdalene is the mystical fish number 153 by gematria.

The symbol of the fish, the almond-shaped vesica , , is a fish mouth. The fish, in turn, is a symbol for a gateway, particularly for a (star) gateway through which souls pass. I can't resist stating the obvious. Something fishy is going on here.

As a priestess of the Fish Tower, meaning the priestess who presided over the well or fountain of life, MM possessed the teaching which transformed us into mystical fish. (This well is located at the center of our galaxy.)

A *midrash* teaches that a miraculous 'well' accompanied the Hebrews throughout their journey in the wilderness, providing them with water. This 'well' was given by God to the Miriam to honor her bravery and devotion to the Jewish people. In a new and popular ritual some Jews place a "Cup of Miriam," filled with water, beside the customary "Cup of Elijah" (filled with wine) during the Passover Seder. The cup represents the "living waters" of Miriam's well and serves as a reminder of the Exodus from Egypt when manna fell from the sky like rain.

We will explore MM's connection to manna in a later chapter.

THE KINGDOM OF LIGHT

Let's return to Jesus' statement to MM in the *Pistis Sophia*:

"***Do not cease seeking day or night, and do not let yourselves relax until you have found all the Mysteries of the Kingdom of Light, which will purify you and make you into Pure Light and lead you into the Kingdom of Light.***"

This is an astounding statement I am certain the reader will wish to study in detail. It is vital to note that the idea of purity is not novel to Christianity. It's Egyptian and Babylonian.

In Utterance **513** (an anagram for **153**) from the Egyptian Pyramid Texts, for example, we read: '***Be pure: occupy your seat in the Bark of Re***: row over the sky and mount up to the distant ones: row with the imperishable stars, navigate with the Unwearying Stars'.

'The Bark of Re' is the Ship of the Gods. It is a fact that virtually all of the great gods of myth sail in a ship, though no one has yet offered a theory to account for the many unusual traits of this celestial vehicle, which is constantly portrayed as a dual-headed serpent ship moving across the waters of the sky.

The dual-headed serpent ship of the Egyptian gods. The stairs  *of the ship of the gods represented the Primeval Hill, the Mountain of Light or the Pure Mound of God.*

The Egyptian scene depicts a pillar or tower of water that rises from the cosmic waters. This is remarkably close to the description of the Tower that arose from the waters in the *Book of Hermas* and became the Church. This connection is made explicit in early Christian art as a soul ship, the craft of the fisherman. Today, the main part of a church's interior, the place where the people worship, is called a "nave," from the Latin "navis" – ship. The main part of the Egyptian ship is a stairway (to heaven). The purification instructions or mysteries that enabled us to board the ship of the gods is nowhere to be found in modern Christianity.

Top. Ra rides the ship of the gods into a gate of stars. Bottom. A modern depiction of a stargate. The comparison of the shape of the ship of the gods with the shape of a wormhole is wildly suggestive.

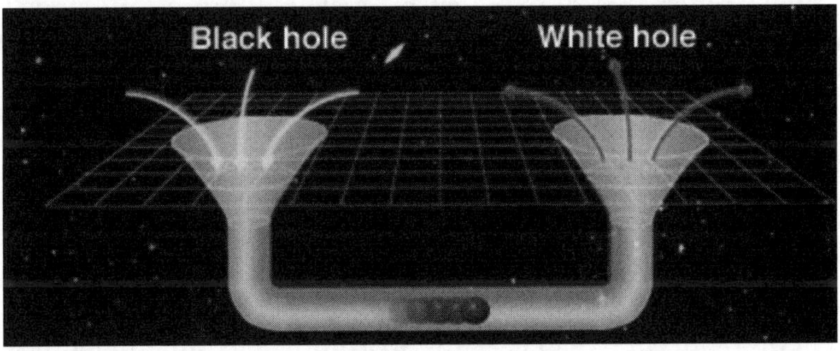

We are reminded that Jesus spent 15-18 years in the temples of Egypt, Iran, Iraq and Central Asia, likely in search of the secrets of how a human is transformed into a being of pure light. In the 20th century documents were discovered in Central Asia that belonged to the

Manicheans, the devotees of the Persian Master Mani who derived his teaching from the Magi and the Christians. In a teaching called the "Parinirvana of the Prophet" Mani is the Apostle of Light who takes off his armor and puts on a royal garment. When he sat down in a Ship of Light he received the Divine Garment, the diadem of Light, and the beautiful garland. And in great joy he flew together with the Light Gods along the Column of Glory, *the path of the Light*, (to) the *meeting-place of the Gods*.

That's a Garment of Light, a Column of Glory (called the *Perfect Man* by Manicheans), and a Ship of Light.

Put on your Cathar shades 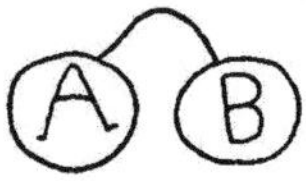

. Look up to the night sky. Look at the Big Dipper, for instance. Can any human reach this dipper just by just walking a few steps? General relativity explained a mechanism to contract this huge distance into few meters. Albert Einstein called this mechanism 'bridges' in space-time. Today, scientists call them wormholes. A wormhole would act as a shortcut connecting two distant regions in the universe.

In fact, as I am the first to recognize, the Egyptian ark of the gods resembles a modern *stargate* or *wormhole*. Theoretically, physicists view wormholes as time machines that may open gateways to parallel dimensions. They are the subjects of intense scientific research in America and Europe.

A ring ⊙ *of life.*
www.nasa.gov/centers/glenn/multimedia/artgallery/art_feature_001_CD1998_76634.html

As in this example from NASA, the concentric rings symbolize a two-dimensional expression of a three-dimensional experience: that of traveling through interstellar passageways called *stargates* or *wormholes*. This hypothetical spacecraft with a "negative energy" induction ring was inspired by recent theories describing how space could be warped with negative energy to produce hyperfast transport to reach distant star systems. In the 1990s, NASA Glenn Research Center lead the

Breakthrough Propulsion Physics Project. NASA's primary effort to produce near-term, credible, and measurable progress toward the technology breakthroughs needed to revolutionize space travel and enable interstellar voyages.

In the past few years the scientifically rooted concept of wormholes and star gates, also called the Einstein-Rosen bridge, have become popular topics of such television shows as *Star Trek: The Next Generation* and *Sliders* and movies such as *Stargate* and *Contact* which feature ancient stargate technology for opening wormholes in space/time.

The Age of Aquarius – symbolized by a human pouring water from a jar -- is that of our ascension to the stars. It is the Stargate Age.

THE DIVINE PASSAGE AND SOLOMON'S KEY

This idea of the Divine Passage or gateway is central to Gnostic belief. In the second century AD, the Gnostics picked up on Plato's idea and described the sphere of Earth being surrounded by a 12-angled pyramid. These 12 angles are described as "eyes", "pipes," and even more fascinating to our story, as "holes" in the Earth. In the human brain what do we find? *Twelve Cranial Nerves.*

Plato had good company in his belief about the 12-angled Earth. According to one account, Hippasus, a follower of Pythagoras, was drowned at sea for revealing the secret of the 12-angled Earth. This secret was alluded to by the logo of the Pythagoreans, the pentagram or pentagon,  which composes the 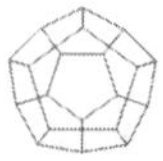 . Harold

Bayley says this is the famous Seal with which King Solomon (*c.* 1100 B.C.) is said to have worked his amazing marvels. In Egypt, the five-pointed star in circle was the symbol for the *Duat*, which has literally been interpreted as a "stargate," the entrance to the Underworld. Venus is the morning star which precedes the sun out of the Underworld. Among Solomon's mythical feats with this key 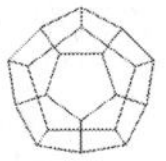 was the manufacture of the gold used to line the cube-shaped Holy of Holies (the Oracle) of his Temple by alchemical means.

Intriguingly, in *Myth and Symbol in Ancient Egypt* Rundle Clarke noted the concept of the Duat as both a place in the "otherworld" and an earthly location, which was also located in Sumer, specifically at Enki's temple site at Eridu. He interpreted it as a midway station for souls.

The Duat, 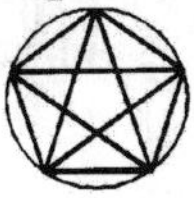, or Hidden Place, was sometimes conceived as a completely enclosed Circle of the Gods, formed by the body of Osiris. At the head-point there was an opening to the skies symbolized by the goddess Nut, through which the imperishable star (symbolized by the celestial disk) could be reached (see below).

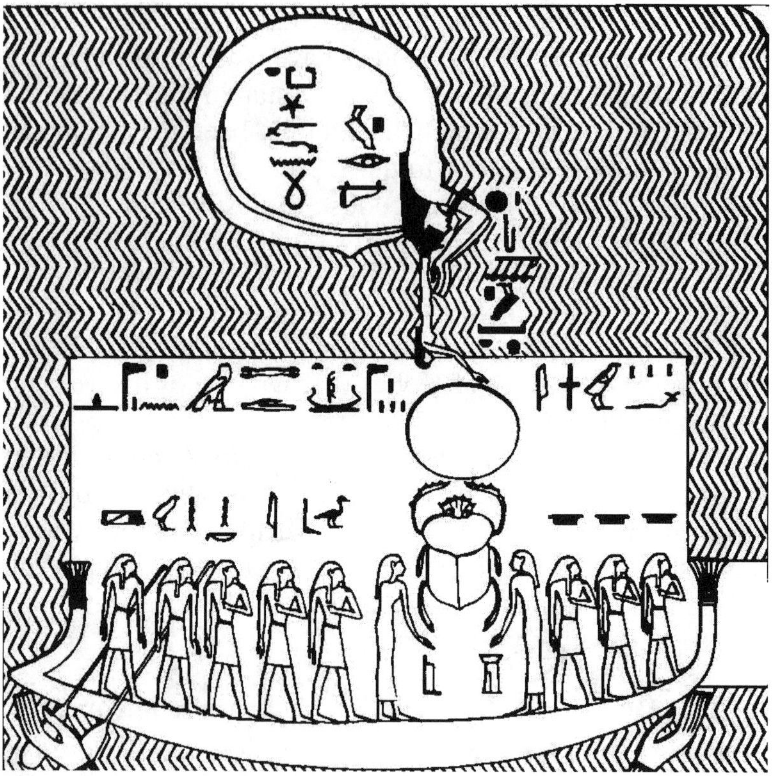

The gods ride upon their ship. Turning the image upside down, one can see Nut (the sky) who receives the ring of the Sun. She is standing on the head of Osiris who, with his body, encircles the Duat.

6.
MYSTICAL MAGDALA AND FISH CODE CLUES

"...and a threefold cord is not easily broken"
Ecclisiastes 4:12

Jane Schaberg, Professor of Religious Studies and Women's Studies at the University of Detroit Mercy provided a most intriguing link between Mary and Magdala in her book *The Resurrection of Mary Magdalene*. She notes that Migdal or Magdala has a very high place in women's *mystical* and *literary* traditions for its connection to the daughters of Job, who died there. Rabbinical tradition claims they lived there, too.

This tradition, recorded in the *Testament of Job*, a first century document that may have circulated with the *Hermas* is highly important and incredibly exciting. As we will see, the story of Job's daughters reveals ancient Magdala had an otherworldly connection. In fact, as a literary reference 'Magdala' may have meant something like 'Wonderland' or 'Oz' means today. That is, a magical place associated with knowledge of extraordinary beings that dwell in an otherworldly locale accessed via a (worm) hole in space-time or via whirlwinds. Here's the story.

Job is the son of Jacob's brother, Esau. He had a lot of family history to work through. His father, the eldest son of Isaac and Rebecca, was tricked into selling his birthright (ruler ship of Israel) to his twin brother, Jacob, for a mess of pottage. He tried in vain to regain his blessing. Jacob went on to experience the Ladder to Heaven, during which he traveled into the heavenly realms and returned to earth declaring the site of his experience a *terrible place* and the "gate to God." Jacob then set-up a pillar to mark the spot (called *Luz*) and poured *oil* upon it. Afterwards, he founded the 12-tribe nation of Israel.

According to all midrash, Esau also became a very significant character in world history. It is Esau who is regarded as the forefather of Rome and the Roman Empire. The fierce enmity between the Romans and the Jews is traced to the struggle between Jacob and Esau.

Job was mixed-up in the early conflicts and most likely suffered from having to bear the cross of the family name of Esau, which came to metaphorically stand for anyone who was tricked into a worthless bargain.

In the opening of the *Testament of Job* the patriarch is feeling ill. Perceiving that his stewardship was nearly over Job gathered his ten children, whom he considered the 'chosen ones'. "In all the land there were no women so beautiful as Job's daughters," says the Book of Job.[42:14-15] Dove, Cinnamon and Horn of Kohl were the meanings of their names. In the *Testament of Job* the sisters were called Day, Kasia and Amaltheia's Horn.

He called his daughter and said to her, "take the signet ring, go to the chamber and bring me the three golden boxes so that I may give you an inheritance." And she went away and brought them. And he opened them and brought forth "***Three bands, shimmering, so that no man could***

describe their form since they are not from earth but from heaven, flashing with bright sparks like rays of the sun."

One of Job's daughters complains that this isn't much by way of inheritance. "We won't be able to sustain our life from them, will we?" She asks.

The three Mary's of the New Testament ring of Job's three daughters and the three golden boxes.

And Job replied to them, "not only will you sustain life from these, *but these bands will also lead you* ***into the better world, to live in the heavens***.

In fact, according to Job, the Lord gave him these cords.

The name of each sash corresponds to the wisdom or magic it acts as a conduit for when the person wears the sash: the "Spirit," the "Creation of the Heavens," and "The Paternal Splendor" (*Testament of Job* 46:1 – 51:4).

When Day put on the cord she went out of her body, put on a new heart and never again cared for earthly things. Then, she sang angelic hymns in *the* ***language of the angels***.

Her sister's heart was also transformed the moment she put on this sash. She too no longer wished for worldly things. And when she opened her mouth she suddenly spoke the language of the rulers (archons). And when she sang her hymns, the *Testament of Job* tells us they were loaded with insight into the workings of the heavens.

The same singing and speaking the language of the angels happened when Job's third daughter, Amalthea, put on the shimmering sash. These sashes and their oddities caught my attention as they reminded me the three rays of the Bon and of the fluer-de-lis. Significantly, the Knights Templar wore three-fold cords or sashes around the waist by that connected them to a strange idol (a head), which, among other charges, led to their persecution. It is claimed the Templars possessed the secrets of Jesus and may have protected the descendents of Jesus and Mary Magdalene (more later).

THE ARCHONS

The primary key to perceiving the mystical knowledge enfolded in *The Testament of Job* is the Archons. These provocative beings are featured in one of the most astonishing books in the Nag Hammadi collection the *Hypostasis of the Archons*. It reveals that the Gnostics, including Mary Magdalene, studied the existence of an immaterial world inhabited by demigods called *archons* and *eons*, beings that were half human and half divine. According to John Lash's interpretation of Gnostic literature, these beings came from the galactic center.

The Hypostasis of the Archons says the evil archons clothed man in a material body, a casket or tomb (of flesh and bone). They contrived to keep Adam and Eve, along with their Divine Particles trapped in matter, enslaved forever in the wheel of reincarnation as tillers of the Garden of Eden. In this way humans serve food for the rulers (more on this subject momentarily).

Although the various Gnostic cosmogonies differ slightly in details, they share the core concept of the duality of worlds. In all Gnostic systems, the "true God" resides in the "realm of Light," while the soul, or "*divine spark*", is imprisoned in a body on Earth in the evil "realm of Darkness." The soul is enclosed in seven "vestments" or "soul-garments". The only escape is to acquire self-knowledge and to ignite the divine spark.

Are these 'malachim' from the Baghdad Museum the archons?

Our divine spark or "solar drop," perceived by some as a drop of molten gold or as a tapering flame (in ceremony *illuminati* were given a lighted taper, notes *Webster's*), is called the "indestructible drop" in Tibetan yoga. As beings of light our soul drop is both a wave or ray and a particle • or a drop. I believe it is referred to in the popular children's song, "Doe, a deer a female deer, ***ray a drop of golden sun***..."

The Seven chakras or energy centers dot the spine. These seven notes correspond to the seven vestments of the soul. These are considered to be the seven energy bodies that animate the flesh in yoga philosophy.

In *Tower of Alchemy*, alchemical teacher David Goddard notes theosophical writings compiled from the masters of the Far East in which the soul drop is considered a "Seed atom" or a "nucleus" that resides within the center of the subtle energy bodies. It is the essence of our soul, possibly ejected from the center of the Milky Way galaxy, and washed ashore like a fish out of water here on Earth, a bright blue apple dangling from the Orion arm of the galaxy, and looking for the wormhole that will return it to the Source. It popped in. In a flash it can pop out. From incarnation to incarnation the soul drop grows a physical body. While incarnate it attempts to grow (through breath) a body of light to ride the ship of the gods. Think of the cocoon transforming into a butterfly. This is the goal of the Magnum Opus, the Great Work, alchemy (more later).

Along with the archons the *Hypostasis* also describes a veil that exists between the world above and the realms below. "And the shadow came into being beneath the veil; and that shadow became matter; and that shadow was projected apart." With the application of the veil thus began a program of mind-body control-- or soul enslavement which involved keeping humankind distracted by material problems and concerns, imprisoned by its own fear of death, of mortality, and ignorant of its true, divine nature.

Hence the soul became "entangled in the darkness of matter," confined to bodily identification, ruled by a Church and condemned to endless, repeated reincarnation (or reincarceration), without possibility of parole, of graduation to goldhood or godliness.

The 'soul drop' in its 'Mustard Seed'. Image by Dana Augustine.

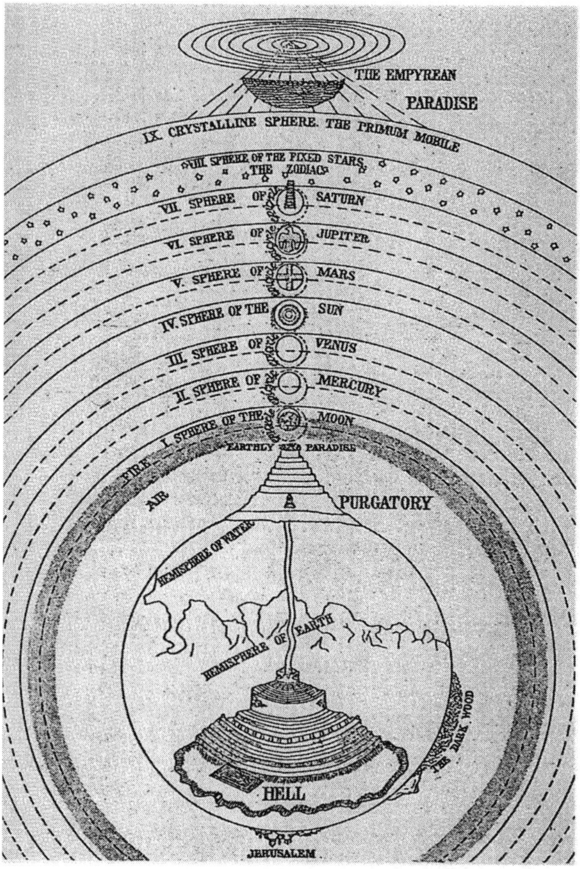

In Dante's Divine Comedy (1307-1321), the soul on its passage rises from the realm of Hell, which projects spherically onto the earth, via the mountain of Purgatory and nine spheres. At the top is Paradise, where the soul finds its home in the white rose of heaven, illuminated by the divine light.

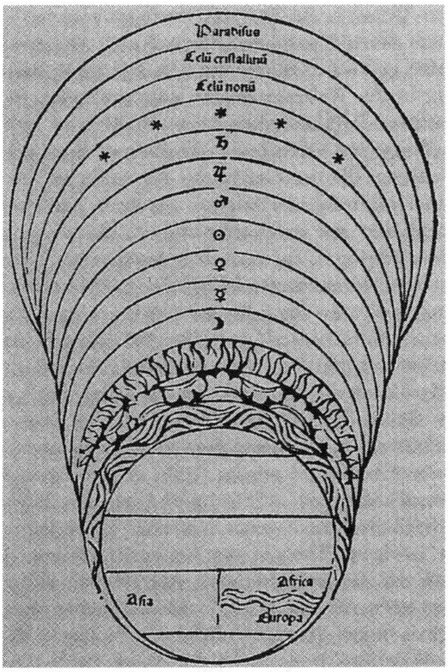

The writing of the Neoplatonists on the celestial hierarchies influenced renderings of the Christian cosmos.

Primarily the illumination Jesus provided Mary Magdalene concerns the secrets of the divine particle's origin, the nature of the matrix in which it is trapped, and the means by which it can 'ascend' to its destination, the Merkaba. Its destination is union with the Deity in the Empire of Light.

The only way to acquire this knowledge is through divine revelation. A messenger from the Empire of Light brought this *gnosis* to humanity. The Gnostic texts make clear that this messenger is Jesus, usually called "The Savior."

The knowledge delivered by this messenger is comprised of "mysteries" which enable the spirit of the illumined to pass through the astral barriers that impede its path to the Empire of Divine Light. Once the spirit has received *gnosis*, it is prepared after leaving the body to shed its soul-garments in its quantum journey through the halls and holes of the universe and to return home to unite with the intelligent and Divine consciousness substance from which it originated.

As we will explore further, the spirit's shedding its soul-garments is similar to Mary Magdalene's having seven demons ejected from her by Jesus in Luke 8:2. In the Gnostic texts the *Gospel of Mary* and the *Pistis Sophia* Mary Magdalene is presented as one of the few people in Jesus' life to receive the flash of *gnosis* he delivered from the Empire of Light. Hence, she is one of the few people to receive the secret of the alchemical transformation of the human into an angel.

7.
MARY MAGDALENE AND THE MERKABA MYTHS

The Gnostic gospels well document that Mary Magdalene certainly behaved like the other famous women of Magdala, the three enlightened daughters of Job. She traveled (or tripped) the astral plane. She negotiated the realm of the archons (and possibly knew their language). She revealed knowledge of the workings of the heavens.

Not only could Job's daughters astral travel, speak the language of angels (or archons) and describe the workings of the heavens, what is more they could see and celebrate the whirlwind or heavenly chariot that came for the soul of Job. His three wise daughters became authors of *Merkaba myths*, or mystics of the Merkaba. In Hebrew mysticism the *Merkaba* is the vehicle of light in which the divine spark travels the heavens.

THE FISH GATE – ELIJAH = 153

Importantly, *gilgal*, the root of Gulgotha, is the name of the place where Elijah crossed into heaven in a *whirlwind*[II Kings 2:1] (with 50, the number of the Anunnaki, sons of the prophets watching).

With the 50 watching Elijah took his mantle, his miracle cloak, and wrapped it together, and smote the waters. Suddenly, they divided. Next, *there appeared* a chariot of fire, and horses of fire, and parted them both asunder; and Elijah went up by a whirlwind into heaven.[II Kings 2:11]

After watching Elijah disappear, Elisha took up the mantle of Elijah and he too parted the waters and 'went over'! Seeing that he possessed the power or spirit of Elijah the 50 accepted him. [II Kings 2:14-15]

A literal reading of this episode tells us that through the power of Elijah's cloak or garment a hole in space opened. The power of this garment is transmittable.

Visionary prophets such as Elijah, Ezekiel and Enoch had experienced this *Merkaba* 'chariot' or ship of light. The Merkaba is an interdimensional vehicle described in Buddhist texts. This craft, said to be made of counter rotating fields of light, is capable of carrying the consciousness directly to higher dimensions. The Merkaba is a product of breathing "prana" (or energy, the source, akasha, God, Buddah, Allah, Mother Nature) and careful meditation. Jesus had trained Mary Magdalene in its mysteries, secrets and the means to attune her soul to it. This is a theme that we will encounter through this work. It will require that we familiarize our selves with the influence of Babylonian and Egyptian spiritual beliefs and concepts on Early Christians. For instance, in the Sumerian seal of the two priests clad in fish suits Enki, lord of wisdom, hovers above a radiant tower in a ring or a disk, i.e. a Merkaba.

The *Testament of Job*'s account of these three wise women and their remarkable abilities implants in the literary tradition the idea of the language of the angels and Merkaba mysticism at Magdala. By following the symbolism of these accounts some astonishing speculations to the possible knowledge Mary of Magdala would have acquired can be proposed

The probability that MM knew the secrets of Jesus' chariot of spirit, the whirlwind or Merkaba seems as likely as it is revolutionary in its implications.

SHE TALKS LIKE THE ANGELS TALK

Magdala's connection to the Merkaba myths and the Language of the Angels and Mary Magdalene's connection to its secrets demands that we investigate this further. Much is known about this language in alchemical circles. In his *Mysteries of the Cathedrals* the highly revered French master alchemist, Fulcanelli, calls it the language of the gods and the Language of the Birds. He claims it was knowledge of this language that Jesus revealed to his Apostles, by sending them his spirit, the Holy Ghost.

Remember, a *dove* symbolizes the Holy Spirit. The language of the angels is also called the Language of the Birds, likely because the Latin *aves,* or bird, is phonetically the same as *avi*, angel, *ava,* apple (the symbol of forbidden knowledge), and *ova*, life.

As I noted in my book *The Language of the Birds*, the Gnostics taught that in the Garden of Eden stands the holy *Tree* of Life. One tenet of the Bird Language is that names and place names are intentionally placed in stories to point to specific knowledge. This code equates words that sound alike in different languages, connecting word concepts by sound *in English.*

Though it sounds bizarre, the phonetic resonance of ancient words in English reveal astonishing literary and historical synchronicities or meaningful coincidences between seemingly unrelated subjects that point to the interconnectedness of all creation.

For instance, without the vowels the mystical word 'tree' is 'tr', which is pronounced *ter*, the primary sound in words such as *terrific*, *terrible*, *enter*, *terra, terror*, *tear*, *tara*, *tyre*, *tire*, *tar, tour, taur, tor* and *tower*. High in this tree's branches sings a bird – a dove or a heron. Listen for the voice of the bird, for when you are properly aligned with Heaven and Earth, she will tell you all things. Her name is *Sophia*. When 'in tune' or resonating with Sophia we bring magic into our lives, and an effortless flow of synchronicity. We flip from the outer world to the inner world. It begins with a search for the inner meanings of words, as opposed to strictly focusing on the outer meaning.

The English language is a living, breathing entity created in the early 14th century. It has been growing and expanding ever since, flowing from culture to culture constantly absorbing words from other languages. That is why English today has a vocabulary of over one million words. Other languages have far fewer words because they wish to keep their language pure.

Made official with the publication of the King James Version of the Bible by Sir Francis Bacon, English as a code language has facilitated the technological and spiritual explosion that has placed us, at this moment, on the brink of building not just rockets, but stargates to the stars.

English is the official language of the Internet, the web that is unifying humanity and preparing us for our elevation.

Of course, 'scholars' label such talk babbling, nonsense. Funny, nonsense is what the word babble and 'babel' means today. Originally, it meant 'gate' or 'ladder'. After the destruction of the tower of Babel the Hebrew scribes changed the meaning of the word to confusion, nonsense. A 'babbler' would thus be an apropos description of a person who refers to the gate. Funnier yet, "a babbler" is a term used in Acts 17:18 to describe the Apostle Paul in Athens. *Strong's* says it came to be used as noun signifying a crow, or some other bird.

A crow! Did the Apostle Paul -- the babbler -- also speak the Bird Language?

Acts tells us Paul went to Athens where he debated in the synagogues with the Jews, and with the devout persons, and in the market daily. Then certain philosophers, Epicureans and Stoics, encountered him. They wondered what this babbler would say. They listened to his tale about this strange god named Jesus and his resurrection.

I can empathize with Paul. A 'scholar' of ancient languages once called me a 'babbler' during a written debate in which I noted my use of the Language of the Birds as a research tool. Instead of taking 1.53 seconds to do a Google search to see that the Language of the Birds has been around a very long time and is connected to Jesus, Elijah and others, this scholar assumed I invented this language and inferred I had a mental problem because I got my information from birds! Later, in my paper, I outlined the principles of this language system. He advised his readers not to read these paragraphs!

I live in Nashville, Tennessee, which for over one hundred years has been known as 'the Athens of the South'. It's the 'the buckle of the *babble*, excuse me, *bible*, belt.' "*Three cords* and the truth" is a common Nashville songwriter's expression for the craft of the songwriter. Ironically, like its ancient namesake Nashville is filled with 'false idols' today, and I don't' mean the country music stars that work and live in Nashville's beautiful green hills. Just like Athens in Paul's time the Athens of the South has a scale replica of Athena's Parthenon complete with a 42-foot tall gilded statue of Athena. Nashville also has a 2,200-foot long magician's rod and a Temple of Mars. Actually, these are my favorite places in town. They are magnificent working temples.

THE BIRD LANGUAGE AND THE TOWER

In *The Language of the Birds* I detail the ancient belief in an original pre-Flood language spoken by the angels and taught to Adam and Eve in the Garden of Eden. It was the language spoken before the Tower of Babel episode during which Nimrod built a *tower* or *gate* that reached into the heavens. Deciding against company, Yahweh, the Old Testament slave master, destroyed the Tower and separated humanity by language. As noted, after the Babel episode the Hebrew scribes changed the meaning of the word babel to mean 'confusion' or 'nonsense'.

As the book of Genesis recalls:

And the lord came down to see the city and the tower, *which the children of men had builded. And the lord said,* *behold, the people is one, and they have all one language and this they begin to do:* ***and now nothing will be restrained from them, which they have imagined to do****.*

Go to, let ***us*** *go down, and there confound their language, that they may not understand one another's speech.*

This episode marks a terrifying turning point in the bible. It tells of an extraterrestrial force, the Lord (probably *a* lord), and his squad of ladder to heaven demolition specialists, who descend from the sky, dismantle humankind's stairway (or stargate) to the stars, scramble our communications and withhold profound knowledge from humanity. With the Stairway to Heaven in place *nothing is impossible for humanity.* What's earth life like without it? Well …

All of human endeavor centers on re-acquisition of the knowledge that makes all our wildest dreams possible for us and enables the rebuilding of this Tower gate of Babel. This includes the Language of the Angels. With this gate in place humans are able to talk with the angels, and also to walk the stars with the celestials.

This knowledge, I believe, was characterized as the knowledge of the workings of the heavens referenced in the book of Job. Others consider it forbidden knowledge. An apple symbolized it in the Garden of Eden story.

MAGDALA = WONDERLAND?

Saying Mary is from Magdala clearly meant something profound to the scribes who penned the New Testament. It linked her with the metaphysics present in Magdala. Today, 'wonderland' is a catch phrase for a parallel dimension in the literary mind. Back then it appears to me that Magdala meant the same thing in magical Jewish literature.

If the mystical Magdala literary connection holds, we may link Mary Magdalene as a master of this metaphysics. In my opinion, this means that Mary's role in Gnostic literature is well defined. She was an Early Christian Alice in Wonderland.

I believe the meaning of her name, Magdala=Tower, was a literary reference to the Round Tower that led to the land of the angels. It is also known as the Stairway to Heaven.

NEBUCHADNEZZAR'S TOWER

One biblical round tower well worth taking a momentary diversion to discuss here is the image of gold constructed by the Babylonian king Nebuchadnezzar.

The image is a massive three score (60) cubits high and six cubits wide. This means it is a tall tower.

A cubit is 18 inches, making the image 540 inches high (three score or thirty times 18 inches high). 540 inches is 45 feet high, about the size of a four and a half story building!

Nebuchadnezzar could not make this gleaming image or tower work. This was a major failure. Like the tribal leader David, who ruled Jerusalem five hundred years before him, the king had planned to unify his kingdom, and the golden image was the unifying force. He tried using music to get it to work. He demanded that when the people heard the music play they were to fall down and worship the golden image (as if this act would impress the lifeless heap). If they didn't they would be tossed into a burning fiery furnace.

Nebuchadnezzar acknowledged that Daniel had immense prophetic gifts, including the ability to interpret dreams. In chapter four of Daniel, he is asked to interpret a dream in which Nebuchadnezzar saw:

'***a tree in the midst of the Earth, and the height thereof was great. The tree grew, and was strong, and the height thereof reached into heaven, and the sight thereof to the end of the Earth***'.

There was *great fruit* in this tree and the birds of Heaven lived in its branches. From this tree the king saw a "*watcher*" and a "holy one" from Heaven emerge. They told him to destroy the tree, and leave its 'stump' in the Earth.

This was a confusing dream to the king, but not to us. The "watchers" is another name for the Shining Ones. It is also the Egyptian name for "divine being" or "god" NTR, or *neter*, which means "one who watches". Neter-neter land is the name of the place in the stars where these beings dwell. Sumeria, another earthly land of the Shining Ones, was known as the land of 'ones who watch'.

Ultimately, as Nebuchadnezzar's story continues, the king captured three wise Jews from Solomon's Temple in Jerusalem. Unfortunately for Nebuchadnezzar, they refuse to worship the hulking image or the god of the Babylonian king. What is more, the three insult Nebuchadnezzar by betting the king that their god will save them from the fiery furnace.

Clearly, the three wise men from the Temple of Solomon possess crucial knowledge that Nebuchadnezzar needs to make this golden gadget work. He was successful in firing up the fiery furnace component of the 'image'. But beyond that he was stuck. He needed the 'open sesame'.

What is this tower, this golden image of which I speak? This holy object is likely the Axis Mundi, the Pillar of God.

In the story from Daniel the three wise men refuse to spill the beans to Nebuchadnezzar, what is undoubtedly the 'open sesame'. Furious, the king orders that the three be cast into the 'fiery furnace'.

Before entering the furnace "The three men put on *their coats, their hats and their other garments*, and were cast in the midst of the burning fiery furnace" says Daniel 3:21.

"Their coats, their hats, and their other garments," you say? This is an immensely meaningful statement.

Why put on any clothes at all if your body is about to be translated into a toasted marshmallow by the fiery furnace?

These garments turn out to be more than just standard-issue loungewear at the Temple of Solomon or the garb of hostages in Babylon. That is, if they turn out to be anything like the coat, the hat and the other garments the goddess Mari is wearing in *The Goddess with a Vase* discovered at her temple at Mari in 1934, which we will discuss in the next chapter.

Mari is shown wearing her Shugurra helmet ('a hat'). Literally translated *Shugurra* means 'that which makes go go far into the universe'. It is possible this is also the "helmet of salvation" described in Ephesians 6:17.

What happens to those who don the "armor of God" get-up and walk through the fiery furnace? Where do they go? Through the black hole?

This detail is omitted. However, after the three wise men from Solomon's Temple entered the fiery furnace, Nebuchadnezzar and all the king's men cautiously approached the lethal furnace. He asks that the three men appear to him. When they do, the king (and I'm certain all the assembled) stands utterly astonished. He's expecting nasty flame-broiled corpses. Instead, he sees the three wise men are in perfect condition!

"Did we not cast three men bound into the midst of the fire?" asks the baffled king.

He certainly did. To add to the high strangeness of this event, *a fourth person* now accompanies them!

However, this is not just any man. Nebuchadnezzar believes this fourth man is an angel. Not just any angel either. The fourth man is like the Son of God!

Is this Jesus, the Son of God? Is Nebuchadnezzar telling us the three wise men returned from their stargate travels with Jesus in tow six hundred years before his appearance in the New Testament?

It is quite conceivable because, understandably, at this point Nebuchadnezzar was convinced: the god of the three wise Jews is *the* God. He proclaims that if anyone speaks against this God, he will cut them to pieces, and their houses will be made into dunghills. Next, he promoted the three wise men.

The Bible does not say what happened after this Son of God arrived. I believe, however, that tremendous knowledge must have been gained from his appearance.

ORIGINAL LANGUAGE = 153

Back to the Bird Language. A primary lesson of the Language of the Birds is that Nature is connected. It is the fear-based logical, religio-scientific mind of humankind that separates. By learning this language we become more fully reconnected and resonant with the matrix of Earth life. The Language of the Birds is a way of life. It teaches us to work with nature's forces and to explore the relationships between all the wonders of her creation.

With this language, promise mystics, we can heal our world and ourselves, transforming it from wasteland into a garden or a paradise.

In this study we will focus on the repetition of one particular word of power: *Magdala* or *Magdalene*. We will hunt the world's literary traditions for names and place names that resonate with Magdala.

In fact, I believe Jesus implored us to pay attention to this name. Prior to his crucifixion experience, Mary Magdalene embalmed Jesus. After, Jesus declares: "I say to you, wherever the message is proclaimed in the whole world, what she did will also be spoken of *in memory of her*."

What, exactly, are we to remember about Her? Her actions? How about her *name*: Magdalene = Tower = Babel. Is this Tower what is important to remember?

LORDS GATE CODING = 153

Following this pun, it is highly strange, and incredibly significant here, that when Nimrod gathered the people of Babel to build the Tower or Stairway to Heaven they did so to make a *Name* for themselves. Hence, the building of the Tower to Heaven and the building of a Name are linked. I believe what Jesus is asking us to remember is that the name and place name Magdala or Magdalene refer to knowledge of the 'Stairway to Heaven'. Further, I believe he wishes for us to recall that, long ago, a nasty being destroyed our Tower and our connection to the stars. Jesus had come to fix this. Unfortunately, he encountered blockage from know it all priests.

There is, I propose, a very important and overlooked connection between Mary Magdalene's anointing oil, the Tower or Stairway of Babel, Mer-ka-ba mysticism and the crucifixion of Jesus.

8.
MARY MAGDALENE AND MARI

Let us return to the proposal that MM came from Syria. While we cannot definitively say that the Illuminator came from this land, no more than we can say for certain that Jesus came from Galilee, there are many correlations between MM (and Jesus) and the gods and goddesses of Syria. Mystery and intrigue awaits us as we explore these correlations and discover their striking similarity.

Ancient Syria was the home of the goddess ***Mari***, also known as ***Mari-Ishtar*** or ***Istara*** who was worshipped at Mari 150 miles upriver from Babylon. ***Mari-Ishtar,*** from whom we derive ***Easter*** is the Akkadian counterpart to the Sumerian ***Inanna*** and to the Semitic goddess ***Astarte***, the goddess most commonly known simply as a goddess associated with the planet Venus. Noble by birth. Wise by choice. Dressed to kill. Coiled and battle ready for both peace and war. This goddess commands respect.

As early as 3,500 B.C. Inanna was worshipped as the great goddess. Her many titles resonate with figures who came after her, including the Virgin Mary and Jesus: 'Queen of Heaven and Earth', 'Morning and Evening Star', 'Light of the World', 'Righteous Judge', 'Forgiver of Sins', 'Holy Shepherdess'. She gave birth to a son who was named 'the Shepherd', 'Lord of the Sheepfold', 'Lord of the Net', and 'Lord of Life'.

Numerous authors have noted and marveled at the astonishing reoccurrence of ancient Sumerian images in the Old and New Testaments. Especially interesting is the powerful resemblance between Mari and Mary Magdalene. Mythologist Barbara Walker even says MM imitated Mari. Others claim neither goddess existed. They are beings from the literary twilight zone, part of a category of 'things that never happened, but always are'. Never here, but ever near. Like Never Land and Wonderland Magdala, MM's home, is purely mythical.

The holy temple of Mari was discovered in 1933 on the eastern flank of Syria, near the Iraqi border. A Bedouin tribe was digging through a mound for a gravestone that would be used for a recently deceased tribesman, when they came across a headless statue. After the news reached the French authorities currently in control of Syria, the report was investigated and digging on the site was started on December 14, 1933 by archaeologists from the Louvre in Paris. Discoveries came quickly, with the temple of Ishtar being discovered in the next month. The excavation by the French archaeologist Parrot of this rare example of a Mesopotamian palace found with its costumes and archives virtually intact has been one of the keys to the unraveling of the history of the Syria/Mesopotamia region from the mid-third millennium to the eighteenth century BCE.

In 1936 a French archaeological expedition to Mari uncovered a vast archive of some 25,000 cuneiform tablets. They reveal that Mari was the center of a vast network of trade routes ranging from Crete to Elam, from Cappadocia to Megiddo.

Importantly, the Jewish, Christian and Muslim patriarch Abraham once lived at Mari. Born in *Ur* around 1900 B.C. Abraham lived first at Haran where he spent his time gathering a mysterious substance and souls. After God commanded Abraham to leave Haran, the Bible says Abraham took Sara, his nephew Lot, and "all their ***substance*** *that they had gathered*, and ***all the souls that they had gotten*** *at Haran*," and they went forth into the land of Canaan. He followed the Euphrates through the land of Sichem to the kingdom of *Mari* and its fabulous capital city.[7]

Abraham found Mari inhabited by a Semitic tribe called *Amorites*. Coincidentally, their name *Amorites* rings of *Moreh* or *Meru*, the key tone of this investigation. Amor derives from the Akkadian *amurru* and Sumerian *martu* ("westerners"). Amurru's symbol was a spade or hoe called a *marru* (or meru?). It is represented as a tall pillar (or tower?). It is spotted in the scene on the next page that shows ancient gods hovering in a craft. Mounted to a dragon it may be thought of as a beast. I believe it matches the 'image of the Beast' of Babylon constructed by Nebuchadnezzar *c.* 600 B.C. A 'fiery furnace' is featured in the book of Daniel along with this Tower of the Beast. Three wise men from the Temple of Solomon put on coats, hats and other garments, entered this furnace and returned with the son of God in tow. I believe this is a record of a stargate event. The three wise men traveled to the home of god in the stars and brought him to earth. The image on the bottom of the next page is highly instructive of this event, portraying a 'fiery furnace' and gods hovering above in a whirling craft.

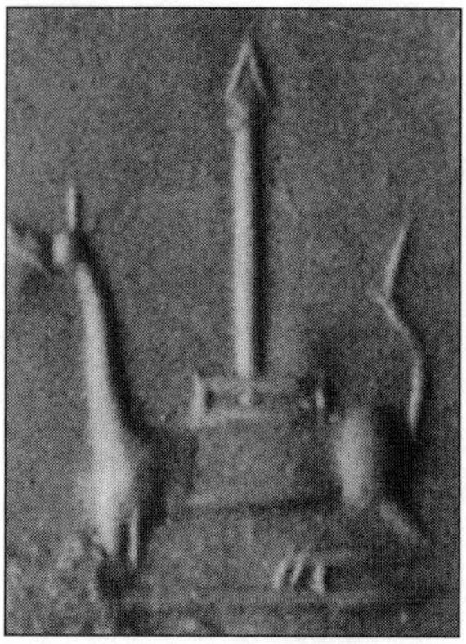

The Pillar or Tower of Amurru (or Meru?).

Detail of a Sumerian cylinder seal showing Amurru pillar on left-hand side. Is this the 'beast' of the book of Daniel?

Is-Tara lifting the healing serpent/kundalini. The serpent resembles a sine wave or a vibration. This 'Tower' resembles the Amurru pillar. One wonders if this could be a model for the Tower of Siloam. Before Mary Magdalene was initiated by Jesus she was likely an initiate of Ishtar's school.

THE LADY WITH THE VASE

Discovered by the French archaeologist Andre Parrot at Mari in 1936 was the astounding life-size statue of the goddess Ishtar or Mari shown here.

French archaeologists stand beside the life-size statue of 'The Mother of Life' excavated at Mari in 1934.

The statue bears no inscription, so archaeologists have labeled it 'Goddess with Flowing Vase' and dated it to the 18th century B.C. As can be seen in the detail on the next page, the inlays have been gouged out of the eyes, and her nose has been badly damaged. She wears a massive helmet. With both hands she tilts vase from which flowed the 'water of fertility'. Later, the Greeks called this vase the *aryballos* and used it *to contain oil and perfume*.

Goddess with Flowing Vase.

Her robe is called *pala* or 'miracle' garment. Streaming down her robe, the water would have clothed the lower part of he body with a rippling, translucent veil of water imparting the idea that she had either risen from the water or lived in it, like a mer-maid. This appears to symbolize the glow-ray fied body attributed to MM.

Her helmet is called *Shugurra*, which literally translated by Zecharia Sitchin means, "that which makes go far into the universe." This translation makes we wonder. Did she astral travel like Job's daughters and MM? Or, was she traveling through the stargate opened by a Tower?

As a priveleged child of Syria did the young MM model her life after Mari or emulate the greatest of all Syrian 'energies', 'sacred principles' or enlightened beings?

May we even speculate that MM had even been groomed to personify Mari, preparing her body, mind and spirit to become a royal companion to a savior and to receive his immense gifts?

I lean toward the latter conjecture for the reason that Jesus was simultaneously bred and prepared to become her companion, the Christ. I do not think this was a coincidence, so we'll spend a moment exploring this thesis.

JESUS AND MELCHIZEDEK

Jesus was a "priest forever after the Order of Melchizedek" (Epistle to the Hebrews, 5:6), the ultra-mysterious and messianic Old Testament priest and King of Sion who ruled Jerusalem at approximately the same time that Mari was worshipped in Syria.

While some believe Jesus was born in a shed among animals, the genealogy recorded in the book of Matthew traces the royal bloodline of Jesus Christ through his human parents to show his birthright as King of Israel and descendant of both David and Abraham. As a youth, the future King Jesus was taken to Egypt to prepare for the impending emergence of his kingdom, the Empire of Light.

Esoterically, it is taught that Christ is an office, like that of a president. 'The Messiah' and 'the Christ' are titles of individuals who hold the "energy" of this office. Some claim these individuals are sent from other high and far away realms to guide and support humanity. Others believe that at any given time there is a Messiah-in-training and another in office incarnate on Earth. It makes sense to me that his spiritual companion and radiant co-ruler, MM, would have been similarly prepared.

As noted by Robert Feather in *The Secret Initiation of Jesus at Qumran*, Dead Sea Scroll scholar Margaret Barker maintains that Jesus was not only a priest of Melchizedek's order, but also that he patterned his life on him. He may have flat imitated him.

Melchizedek's special area of expertise included the communion ceremony and apparently the Stairway to Heaven. The bible goes to great pains to make the explicit point that Lord Melchizedek, the King of Sion and a forerunner of Jeuss, initiated Abram in the Grail mysteries (Genesis 14:18) , which are symbolized by the bread and wine (later Jesus performed this ceremony). After this Abram became the new and improved *Abra-H-am* and Sara became the enhanced SaraH.[Genesis 17:5]

Mystics claim the addition of the *H* signified Abraham's acquisition of the "breath of God" or "soul of God." Simultaneously, Sara became Sarah, suggesting she too received this "breath" or "soul."

The *H* represented the transformation of Abraham and Sarah from humans to something more than human. This same transformation has been subliminally attached to the mythology of Jesus. Who has ever heard the expletive "Jesus *H*. Christ!" and not wondered what it meant or where it originated?

Lord Melchizedek at his Grail communion table with whirling bread and wine flanked by Abel and Abraham. A mosaic from the seventh century, Ravenna

In Hebrew mysticism this *H* ladder is called the *Sephiroth*, the Mystical Tree. It features ten qualities as set forth in the *Sefer ha-Zohar*, the Cabalistic *Book of Splendour*. Cabalists called all ten collectively the *Merkaba*, or "chariot of god." Recall that Merkaba mysticism is the literary 'business' of Magdala.

The H, I propose, symbolizes the ladder or stairway to heaven and indicates their access to the gate of God, the Tower (the Babel or Magdal), knowledge of which is breathed into the disciple. H is the 8th letter of the English alphabet. The picture of Cheth, the eighth letter of the Hebrew alphabet, shows two pillars united by one crossbeam, resembling a ladder or doorway. Cheth means "a field," something perceived, or that can be cultivated – in short, spiritual perception.

So, when Abraham and Sarah received their H they received a spiritual initiation that transformed their perception and may have prepared them to see the Merbaka (like Job's daughters).

Interestingly, Feather provides a convincing body of revolutionary archaeological evidence and textual references that suggests Melchizedek was actually the Egyptian King of Light, Akhenaton, who reintroduced the ancient religion of Light called Aton.

Feather further states that the first Christians revered the memory of Akhenaton and his wife, Nefertiti, and wanted to associate Jesus with them. I came to a similar conclusion in my *Stargate 2012* lecture presentation only I was coming from a different angle. I had concluded that MM was acting the role of Nefertiti. I'll have more to say about this connection later in our exploration of the anointing oil Mary Magdalene provided to Jesus.

SHAKTI

Following this line of thinking we may think of 'the Magdalene' as a (magical) office, as well. It is interesting in the extreme that the name *Mari* is seen as the same as *Maya*, the mother of the Egyptian god of alchemy, Thoth, and Buddha. Maya is also a Hindu term for supernatural power, as well as illusion or unreality. Maya is the means to 'pierce the veil'. It is the root of *Matrix.*

The concept of Maya is related to *Shakti*, in Hinduism the name given to the female consorts or spiritual partner of male spiritual masters or deities *(Shiva).* In the Gnostic gospels it is clear that MM is the 'tower of the flock' who played the role of the Messiah's interpreter, conduit to the Matrix, and consort or *shakti*. The idea of Shakti is prominent in Tantra where the *Kundalini* energy is directed toward attaining higher consciousness and liberation from ignorance, suffering and rebirth (the aim of the Early Christians).

The Kundalini ("coiled up") energy is regarded as a goddess or feminine energy. The *shakti* personifies the female who has 'pierced the veil' and 'knows' the dynamic, manifesting *feminine* energy that creates the universe, and also the male static, unmanifest aspect of the divine reality. The symbol for this male-female duality is Mercury's caduceus rod (often topped by a *dove*). In my view, it represents the meeting or union of male and female, Heaven and Earth, Heart and Brain.

Inanna standing on two lions and holding the caduceus of entwined serpents in her right hand; cylinder seal, c. 1850-1700 BC.

The raising of kundalini ('the anointing of the dove'), referred to in myth and scripture, as the raising of the serpent ultimately triggers latent feminine knowledge (symbolized by the forbidden fruit) that leads to altered states of consciousness and enhanced human powers (known as *sidhis*, pronounced 'shee').

The raising of kundalini is also referred to as Pranic Awakening. Prana is interpreted as the vital, life-sustaining force in the body. One symbol for Prana is the Egyptian *ankh* or Key of Life. This fits as kundalini is also interpreted as a vibrational phenomenon that initiates a period, or a process of vibrational spiritual development (Sovatsky, 1998) It is interesting that the symbol for *living wasters* , so closely resembles a serpent.

9.
ONE NIGHT IN CAPERNAUM

According to the biblical account, Mary Magdalene's relationship with Jesus began near the end of his life. She learned of the famous magician and exorcist who had been thrown out of Nazareth, nearly escaping being stoned, and was living and healing masses of people in Capernaum (ka-per-na-um), near Magdala[Luke 4: 16-30], where he also multiplied the 153 fishes [Luke 5:5-7].

One night Jesus found himself sitting down to meat (and probably plenty of wine) at the home of one of the Pharisees (a class composed of mostly Jewish intellectuals and scribes). One can imagine the Pharisee quizzing Jesus about how a person could eat the heavenly bread and have eternal life. From the very beginning Jesus told the Jews that God required them to believe in him as the God-sent Messiah[6:29]. He repeatedly states that those who believe in this God-sent stuff have eternal life (6:35, 40, 47). As history records, the Jews would not believe in him and still await the Messiah.

A lowly possessed woman,[Luke 8: 2-3] described as a sinner, brought in an alabaster box of valuable ointment or balm. She stood at his feet weeping and began to wash his feet with her tears and to wipe them with her hair. She kissed his feet and anointed them with her balm.[Luke 7:36-39]

Astounded, the Pharisee questioned Jesus' credentials as a prophet. As a 'sinner' this woman was likely ostracized and deemed untouchable by the other Jews of Galilee, as it was believed that her affliction was transmittable. What's he doing allowing her to touch him?

The traditional Christian interpretation of this story is that Jesus forgives this woman of her sins. Her faith saved her.

Was this woman Mary Magdalene? That depends. Was Jesus anointed once or twice? Scholars can't agree on either question.

There is no indication in the text that the unnamed woman is Magdalene, but tradition has linked her with Magdalene. The following chapter of Luke immediately introduces "Mary, called Magdalene, from whom seven demons had gone out..." Luke 9:1-3

The source of the confusion appears to stem from the belief that Magdala was a wealthy city the Romans destroyed because of its moral depravity (naturally) and its participation in the Jewish revolt. Moreover, in the Talmud, the word Magdalene is derived from the expression "curling women's hair," which some declare to mean "adulteress" (a definition which many question). Even though the penitent woman of Luke 7 is not specifically identified as Mary Magdalene, the adulteress "from whom seven devils had gone out" of Luke 8, one could easily draw the conclusion, as did Pope Gregory.

When Pope Gregory made (some say invented) this connection in the sixth century he added to it the notion that Mary was a prostitute. Mary Magdalene as the repentant prostitute who found forgiveness with the Lord was born. Although the Roman Catholic Church withdrew from this mistaken linkage at the Second Vatican Council (1969) it survives strongly in folk Catholicism.

The link between the sinner woman and Mary Magdalene has produced tragic results that extend well beyond the fact that it highlights the utter fallibility and bias of the men of the Church when it comes to interpreting the bible. In fact, it is often asserted these men deleted certain texts from the bible to insure that men would run (or is it *ruin*?) the Church. More tragic is the two thousand years of social de-evolution it has brought. Before Gregory's time women held high positions in the religious affairs. After, women were delegated to the side, deemed not as holy as men. As noted, this is the *pathetic* church, which is not sympathetic with the original Christian teaching rendered by MM.

As the 21st century dawns this situation is changing for two reasons:

1. We have recently come into possession of the archaeological facts, source texts and secondary scholarship required to grasp the foundations upon which the Christian religion was formulated.

2. Simultaneously, and for the first time since the recorded events took place, we have reclaimed the spiritual knowledge required to interpret the technology described in the code-language of ancient religious myth.

Hence, there is a growing library of revolutionary new books that is sparking a renaissance in Magdalene studies. A circle of scholars including Karen King from Harvard's Divinity School are revising the history of women in the Church and are taking a serious look at the woman of substance we call Mary Magdalene. Many now believe she was even present at the Last Supper. Oh boy! Let there be light!

There are actually four mentions in the Gospels of Jesus being anointed. The instance found in Luke when Jesus' feet are anointed by the sinner woman would appear to be a separate instance, some time during the second year of Jesus' revolution.

The other three appear to be the same account of a singular event (Matthew 26:6-13; Mark 14:3-9; John 12: 1-8). Mary Magdalene anointed Jesus' feet a second time, and in the house of another Simon, this time Simon the Leper. This time, Mary Magdalene's anointing was in order to embalm the body that was soon to be hung on the cross.

After their meeting Jesus exorcised Mary of seven demons with the Holy Spirit. Consequently, she emerged fully transformed and prepared, unlike others before her, to embrace the Empire of Light.[Matthew 12:28] She became his number one, the Magdalene. She shared a relationship with Jesus that no bishops, archbishops, priests, Popes, or kings could ever dream of.

The exact manner through which Jesus performed this cosmic cleansing is unknown (and like his secret teachings seldom discussed in modern Christian circles). However, the Pharisees claimed he was a black magician who operated as nothing more than an agent of Beelzebul, the lord of the underworld. It takes one to know one, as they say. The hypocritically self-righteous Pharisees claimed that Jesus was just a little to familiar with demons.[MT 12:24-28]

Early Christian art portrayed Jesus wielding a magic wand to perform his miracles. Might this have been Jesus' method of exorcism too? (Please see Appendix.)

The inherent symbolism of the number seven in the ancient world has led many to believe that this procedure had more to do with aligning Mary Magdalene's seven *chakras* or energy centers with the pure energy of the Holy Spirit than it does with removing actual "demons." When Jesus communicated the Holy Spirit to the disciples after the crucifixion he did so by breathing it upon his initiates.[John 20:22]

As Reiki practitioners can attest, a master healer can breathe energy symbols into a person's energy field and activate latent spiritual capabilities that cleanse and purify body, mind and spirit, transforming one into a healer. Jesus' travels in the Far East are cited as the likely places where Jesus learned these techniques. Of course, modern science disputes the existence of such a life force energy. It is fair to say that if Jesus were alive and practicing today he too would be labeled a quack by science. "Show us the studies!" they would shout at him.

Freshly cleansed, purified and empowered from her transformative experience in Capernaum, MM, the

Magnificent, accompanied Jesus from her home in Magdala to Jerusalem. She watched his dangerous showdown with the hated Roman and Jewish authorities, witnessed his crucifixion and entombment, found his tomb empty and was the first to experience the risen Jesus. She is mentioned first among all the Marys in the New Testament. And designated "Magdalene," the woman cleaned of sin.

In the next chapter I will continue our discussion about sin, but from a very different perspective I'm certain than many have previously considered this subject. I'll begin with a survey of the traditional Christian thoughts about sin, a word mentioned 642 times in the bible, and then connect it with alchemy.

10.
SIN WAVE

"And ye *shall serve the Lord Your God, and he shall bless thy bread and they water, and I will take away sickness from the midst of thee."*

Exodus 23:25

The Bible declares from beginning to end that we are all sinners. "There is none righteous, no, not one," says Romans 3:10. It goes on to state in verse 11 of the same chapter, "There is none that understands, there is none that seeks after God."

Go down to verse 23 and we find these words, "For all have sinned and come short of the glory." Go over a couple of chapters to Chapter 5 and in verse 8 we read this, "But God commendeth his love toward us, in that while we were yet sinners, Christ died for us."

In the first epistle of John, God assures us, "If we confess our sins, He is faithful and just to forgive us our sins and cleanse us from all unrighteousness."

What is sin? Sin is defined as the estrangement from god.

Sin means to violate a law of God or a moral law. Sin is moral evil (as opposed to good). Sin is a morally bad act.

Sin is any thought or action regarded by theologians as a transgression of God's will or contrary to the law of God.

Therefore, sin is rebellion against God.

In the Old Testament sin is set forth as an act of disobedience; [Gen., 2: 16-17; 3: 11; Is., 1: 2-4; Jer.: 2, 32] as an insult to God; [Num., 27: 14] as something detested and punished by God; [Gen., 3: 14-19; Gen., 4: 9-16] as injurious to the sinner; [Tob., 12: 10] to be expiated by penance. [Ps. 1: 19] In the New Testament it is clearly taught by Paul that sin is a transgression of the law; [Rom., 2: 23; v, 12-20] a servitude from which we are liberated by grace; [Rom., 6: 16-18] a disobedience punished by God. [Heb., 10: 26-31] John describes sin as an offence to God, a disorder of the will, [John, 12: 43] an iniquity. [I John, 3: 4-10]

In the Christian tradition the origin of sin is traced to Adam and Eve who disobeyed God. Because of their disobedience, sin entered into the world and because of sin, humankind was separated from God. You see, God is pure, perfect and Holy and cannot be joined together with sin. For example: if you lie, you have sinned. Why? Because God has said not to lie. [Exodus 20:16] If you do what God has forbidden, then you have sinned. In addition, if you do not do what God has commanded, you sin.[James 4:17] Either way, the result is eternal separation from God. [Isaiah 59:2] Sin is lawlessness[1 John 1:3] and unrighteousness.[1 John 5:17]

Sin leads to blindness[John 9] and death.[Rom. 6:23]

We do not die of disease, cancer, heart failure or stroke, as modern medicine claims. The bible says we die of sin.

Everyone is a sinner. Everyone dies. No one is immune. By the bible's logic, I know I am a sinner because I am aging. I am dieing. I can tell this because my hair is turning grey at the temples. My back occasionally aches in the morning. I am dieing. Therefore, I must be a sinner. But I'm not alone.

Paul, in the book of Romans, discusses sin. He shows that everyone, both Jew and Greek, is under sin.[Romans 3:9] He shows that sin is not simply something that is done, but *a condition of the heart.*[Romans 3:10-12] This heart condition leads to death.

In the Sermon on the Mount Jesus teaches that sins come from the heart.[Matthew, 15: 19-20] Christian preachers preach that through a change in heart the Lord can clean us up and make us feel like a new person! They tell us that it does not matter what we have done; 2,000 years ago God sent His Son, Jesus Christ to come to this earth and die on the cross to pay the penalty for your sin.

The bible says: "For God *so loved* the world that He gave His only begotten Son, that whoever believes in Him should not perish but have everlasting life."[John 3:16]

In Ephesians Paul says that we are "by nature children of wrath"[Eph. 2:3] Yet, "while we were still helpless, at the right time Christ died for the ungodly".[Romans 5:6]

It makes no difference how much or how little you've sinned, or what sin you committed, you still fall equally short of God's perfection. There's no middle ground.

The Bible says: "For all have sinned; all fall short of God's glorious standard."[Romans 3:23]

In other words, even though you are separated from God because of your sin, God made a way for you to come back to Him. And, He is offering this salvation to you as a free gift. All you have to do is receive it is to admit your spiritual need, "I am a sinner." Second, you must believe that Jesus Christ died for you on the cross to take away your sins. Thirdly, you repent. In other words, be willing to turn from your sin. Finally, you must receive, through prayer, Jesus Christ into your heart and life.

THE HEART OF THE MATTER

I do not believe in these conditions.

Instead, I believe the bible is describing the functioning of our mystic anatomy, particularly that of the heart.

What is required to overcome sin is belief and love. Both develop in the heart, and the heart is the House of Eternal knowledge, as the Prophet Mohamed said: "Consult your heart and ***hear the secret*** ordnance of God, discovered by the inward knowledge of the heart which is faith and divinity."

Astounding new medical research has discovered an independent wisdom inherent to the heart that is not governed by other systems of the body. The heart has neural cells similar to those found in the brain pointing to an innate logic to the heart. The heart is 'autogenic', it has its own intelligence (*gennii*, genius). It does not require a signal from the brain to beat, meaning it truly is separate, independent. The impulse to beat originates in the heart muscle itself in a small bit of specialized tissue called the *sin*o-auricular node, embedded in the wall of the right auricle. New research reveals this is not dependent on ANY external stimulus, and no other part of the body controls this function. You can be brain dead and your heart can still maintain the cells. When the heart stops beating the bones of the temple begins to crumble.

HEART INTELLIGENCE

Christ is a tone or vibration that alters our heart, mind and soul or heart/mind/soul. Some of the most prestigious doctors and researchers in the medical community are providing the details of this alteration process. The research is focused on the heart's amazing properties and influences over other bodily systems. It is making the connection between science and spirituality. "Heart Intelligence" is a phrase used to describe numerous attributes of the electrical and magnetic energy waves radiating from the heart that influence functions and systems, including the brain. When the waves of these energy fields are "Phi coherent" or in phase with Phi relationships, specific beneficial results occur within the mind and body. Phi is a number, approximately 1.618, known as the Golden Proportion, the Golden Ratio, the Golden Mean and the Divine Proportion. The progression or development of the whole of nature, from the subatomic to the supergalactic, follows this ratio. Temples such as Athena's Parthenon are books in stone containing volumes of knowledge about this ratio. The human body/temple is a template in-formed by Phi.

The Golden Mean spiral  and the whirlwind of phi-losophy that surrounds it has been called a doorway that weaves the ethereal and material dimensions together. It is the ratio of the Golden Man exemplified by Leonardo daVinci's famous drawing, *Vitruvian Man*. Exploration of the concepts associated with Phi lead to the "Door of Love" in the heart.

The Golden Mean is intimately tied to the number 5 (phive) and the five-pointed star or Solomon's Key. I find it most interesting that the Golden Mean is used as a symbol or an analogy for spirit in the material, and as an analogy for the thread that ties the material and ethereal dimensions together. This thread sheds new light on the Christian equation of the vine with Christ. The vine bears the grape (the enlightened hearts) that opens the door to other dimensions. Parallel dimensions can be likened to a cluster of grapes all stemming from a healthy *Golden-Mean vine*. (For more on the mysteries symbolized by the cluster of grapes please see my analysis in *Cloak of the Illuminati* or *Stargate 2012* DVD.)

Continuing, when the thud, thud, thud of the heart (s)wells the lungs at its 'snail's pace' tiny sacs called *alveoli*, which resemble clusters of grapes, are filled, manifesting a high-pitched *whine*. In Hebrew the literal name of Jesus derives from *Yehoshua*, a word that originally meant "breath", "protection" and "peaceful." In other words, it describes the breath of life. As J. Nigro Sansonese points out in *The Body of Myth*, when the Angel of Annunciation tells the Virgin Mary "thou shalt call his name Jesus: for he shall save the people from their sins," a double-entendre results between a literal sound, that of the breath, and the approximation of that sound, *Yehoshua* (transliterated in the Vulgate as *Jesus*).

Within the core of our heart, I propose, is a connection to the heart of the Milky Way, the Great Cosmic Mother of the Sun. Recent images of the galactic core reveal that it resembles a cluster of grapes. As we connect with the energies of the galactic center, through the Phi thread/vine, we begin to embody a revitalizing cosmic energy. This, I believe, is what is meant by Jesus' miracle of turning water into wine. It is a reference to the transmutation of the waters of our body into wine, a heavenly substance. It begins by attuning, uniting, marrying or (Mari-ring) our consciousness to the Golden Man.

Interestingly, for thousands of years the *clockwise spiral* ideogram  has been strongly associated with *water*, *power* and outgoing *energy*. Starting from the middle it forms a '*G*' (the Mayan term for 'love'). Its mirror (twin) image, or inversion, the spiral in its *counterclockwise rotation* , also a 'G', appeared at approximately the same time. It is an Egyptian hieroglyph for *thread*. A similar Chinese ideogram means *return* or *homecoming*. The Tibetans painted the thread on the walls of their homes and gave it the meaning *home*, the place one returns to.

The counter clockwise spiral  *of our Milky Way.*

There are fascinating Mayan parallels to Egyptian, Gnostic and Cathar hieroglyphics. They used a G with a cross, the stairway to heaven, mounted to it . Its meaning, 'cross or stairway to the Milky Way', is easily interpreted in light of Mayan symbolism. Presented here we see a G that spawns a ladder or flight of stairs . In *Secrets of Maya Science/Religion* Maya ceremonial leader Hunbatz Men says the G stands for the concepts egg, love, Milky Way and zero. A distinct G shape characterizes spiral galaxies such as our Milky Way. How did the Mayans know galaxies are 'G' shaped? Probably, the same way Jesus knew.

Following this vine of research explains why the Gnostics portrayed the crucifixion of Jesus as serpent on a pillar. This serpent is a symbol for a *sin*e wave, a vibration, that is lifted from the heart to the brain that causes sin to vanish. This image matches the Egyptian hieroglyph 'shed', , which means 'shine'. As the book of Hebrews says, without the *shedding* of blood there is no remission of sin. It is clear from our investigation that the shedding of blood is the shining or purification of the blood.

16th century Gnostic thaler.

Some of the results of shedding the blood include: The reduction and neutralization of the stress chemicals adrenaline and cortisol, increases in immune system efficiency. The benefits? Increased longevity. Increased spiritual capacity. Increased intelligence.

When the waves of these energy fields are "Phi tuned", they are associated with emotional states that are generally perceived as open, receptive, or loving.

With these thoughts about Heart Intelligence in mind let us return to our discussion about sin.

THE BABYLONIAN DOCTRINE OF SIN

In 1905, while Einstein presented the world the gift of the theory of Relativity and Sir Flinders Petrie explored the temple of Hat.Hor/Ishtar in Egypt (which we'll discuss momentarily), Julian Morgenstern published an amazing book in Germany on the ancient Babylonian religion. *The Doctrine of Sin in the Babylonian Religion* provides astounding insight that brings new clarity to the concept of sin. As the publisher of the book, Paul Tice, observes in the introduction to the reprint of book, "the recognition of sin and trying to avoid it in ancient Babylon is ironic because Christianity in general considers Babylonia to have been one of the most sinful and depraved societies to have ever existed."

To begin, religion in Babylon was originally the relation existing between the gods and men. Men did not worship the gods. As in Egypt, they *worked* for them or as Gardner says they 'work-shipped' them.

The duty of man was to bring pure food to the gods. This food consisted of bread and wine. Many frescos from Egypt show priests offering food to the gods. The least impurities in this food caused the sacrifice to be defiled, aborted. It is perhaps for this reason that not every priest could offer sacrifice, the pure food, or participate in the divine service, the serving of the food.

Similar requirements were likely met by any layperson fortunate enough to sacrifice to the gods, and may have included those involved in the Work itself. This is inferred by the fact that the food had to be pure. In order for the food to be pure those manufacturing it had to be pure as well. The worker had to be ritually clean, otherwise the Work would not be accepted.

Therefore, Morgenstern concludes, since it was man's duty to sacrifice (work), it was first of all his duty to keep himself ritually pure. Any neglect of these duties was sufficient for the food to miss the mark and to cause the anger of the gods. This was sin. Sin was thus originally the transgression of the ritual laws of the Work. Poetically speaking, sin means to 'miss the *merc*', to miss the alchemical teaching of the Merc gods, including Mercury, Hermes, and Thoth.

The usual method, notes Morgenstern, by which the gods visited their anger upon man for not working was through sickness. Sickness was therefore an indication of sin, not doing the Work.

Sickness was a state of impurity, unfitting man for participation in making or serving the food of the Gods.

Sickness was, therefore, not only an indication of, but in itself, sin.

Sickness was caused by evil spirits (we now call germs?), the messengers of the gods' anger. They entered the doomed man's body, and firmly seated there, carried on their work of evil, undisturbed. Their presence was therefore synonymous with sickness and uncleanliness; consequently also with sin.

In time, says Morgenstern, the evil spirits ceased to be looked upon as messengers of the gods' anger; became independent of them; the inveterate enemies of their creature, man.

A sick man, one possessed by evil spirits, or possibly germs, was unclean and distasteful to the gods, i.e. a sinner.

Therefore, says Morgenstern, in the Babylonian religious literature the expressions, sin, uncleanliness, sickness, possession by evil spirits, are pure synonyms. They denote an evil or vile state of the body, the result of the divine anger (the opposite of love). It unfitted or disqualified man for participation in religious ceremonies; making him an out cast, a fish out of water.

Thus we read: Mayest thou be freed from transgression, wickedness, curse, sickness sighing, witchcraft, spell, charm, evil machinations of men.

And again: "Uncleanliness has come against me, to judge my cause, to decide my decision; Tear out the evil sickness of my body; Destroy all evil of my flesh and my sinews; May the evil in my body, my flesh and my sinews on this day come forth, and may I see the Light.

Of the evil spirits it is said: They put a woeful fever in his body; A ban of evil hath settled in his body; An evil disease they have put in his body; An evil plague hath settled in his body; An evil venom they have put in his body; An evil curse hath settled in his body...Which have been put in the body of the sick man..."

These later passages describe a vaccination of some sort, putting the germ in the body so that it can repel it. Together with the earlier passages they prove that sin, evil, sickness, possession by evil spirits, witchcraft and misfortune are all the same thing in the Babylonian religion; something material, that has entered the body of the sinner.

THE CRAFT: THE ONLY CURE FOR SIN

The curing of sickness, the expulsion of evil spirits, and the expiation of sin, are identical, and must be so treated. The treatment is the Work, the Magnum Opus, the Craft.

Consider these words penned long ago by the prophet Isaiah, "Come now, let us reason together, saith the Lord: though your sins be as scarlet, they shall be white as snow; though they be red like crimson, they shall be as wool. [Isa. 1:18] (The colors white and red are the colors of mushrooms and alchemy.)

Omitted, however, was a full explanation of sin in the light of the Craft.

As servants of the gods, the completion of the Work and the consequent transformation of the human out the evil or sinful status (realm), ignited the divine nature or particle within the body. As Morgenstern states, "It made the human, for all purposes, gods of inferior rank."

Therefore, to overcome sin meant we became gods or were *apotheosized*. Viewed in this light when MM overcame sin she became a goddess. We can now say that performing the Great Work made her a Pure One with a Pure Heart. It prepared her to walk the stars with the Lord.

In *Tower of Alchemy* David Goddard says those who perfected the Divine Work are easy to spot. When spiritual practitioners have achieved a relatively high level of development, their etheric bodies are transformed into gold. They have developed, to a certain degree, the GOLDEN BODY. The gold first manifests externally, then it gradually manifests inwardly into the physical body. This is why some saints of different religions are sometimes depicted with a golden garment or a golden body. It also explains the golden coffins of Egyptian pharaohs.

The alchemists' furnace, the athanor, was given the shape of a tower to signify that the Craft involved a process of transformation and ascension. Practitioners of Alchemy build their *Tower* of the Art. Goddard notes in *The Tower of Alchemy* that the "thought form" of the inner tower or castle has been used by alchemical adepts for centuries.

It is my premise that Mary Magdalene and Jesus cannot be understood without the acknowledgement that (s)he embodied the chief elements of a suppressed, older religion and ancient wisdom tradition called *theurgy* and that this was what brought both of them into conflict with the religious authorities of Rome.

Jesus and MM were *theurgists* (from *theo*, 'God', and *ur* 'light'). Theurgy, according to R.T. Wallis, "is a system of ritual purification based on a magical view of the universe and derived from the *Chaldean Oracles*". Mainly assembled in Alexandria, Egypt two millennia ago, theurgy contains elements of Persian, Greek, Babylonian and Egyptian religions mingled to form a new elixir for the soul. It was taught in Athens until the fifth century AD.

These specialists in the holy initiated students in profound secrets that led to the soul's salvation. The stairway to heaven and the doorway symbolized salvation. They wielded supernatural powers to influence events and to reunite followers with God or Ultimate Reality. 'Mystic' was the term applied to those who had made this ultimate cosmic connection. Jesus became the embodiment of the "way," or "path" or "door" to enlightenment and the example, or target, of the "perfected man". He achieved the goal of all human psychophysical and psychospiritual evolution.

GOD MAKING

The term *theurgy* means not only "divine work" but also perhaps "god-making" or "making gods of men", and was intended as a contrast to *theology*, which merely talks about the gods, and *theoria*, the purely philosophical intuitive contemplation advocated by Plotinus.

I have noted many times that despite the diversity of bibles, the KJV, NewKJV, and the New American Standard, and now the New New American Standard (can you believe that!) and the hundreds of variations of the modern Christian faith (Catholic, Baptist, Methodist, Protestant, Lutheran, Church of Christ, Reformed Baptist, etc.) there is actually only two forms of Christianity: the religion *about* Jesus and the religion *of* Jesus.

The religion *about* Jesus is the descriptive story of a being who came to earth, healed the sick, preached a message of love, was persecuted by the religious and political authorities of his time and who died at their hands, but promised to return. This is Christianity for the masses.

This story line not only fits Steven Spielberg's movie *E.T.*, but also echoes that of nearly all the world's sixteen crucified saviors who preceded Jesus. (I'm not sure of what to make of Mr. Spielberg's story. Is he inferring that Jesus is a reptilian extraterrestrial?)

In the sequel to the story *about* Jesus he was crucified, died, was buried, *rose* from the dead (an event witnessed by Mary Magdalene), and returned to Heaven, where he is now residing, awaiting the appointed end time set for his second coming to raise the dead, judge all men, destroy this world and produce a new one. Christians can hardly wait for this to occur.

Then, there is the religion *of* Jesus ***and*** Mary Magdalene forbidden by the Catholic Church and many of the derivatives thereof. This religion is epitomized by the statement attributed to Jesus in *The Books of the Savior*, also known as *Pistis Sophia* (Faith-Wisdom), in response to a question posed by Mary Magdalene. With tremendous wisdom Jesus provides a mission statement to MM for how to spend our lives:

"*Do not cease seeking day or night, and do not let yourselves relax until you have found all the Mysteries of the Kingdom of Light, which will purify you and make you into Pure Light and lead you into the Kingdom of Light.*"

These 'cleansing mysteries' are nowhere to be found in modern Christianity. In ancient times, the cleansing or purification mysteries, this activation or 'attunement', was at the heart of the Essene teachings. The Essenes saw themselves as the holy ones in the brotherhood of "The Sons of Light." Everyone else was evil, called "The Sons of Darkness," or the "men of the Pit." All were to participate in "The War of the Sons of Light with Sons of Darkness."

Interestingly, without the vowels the words sin, sine, sing, sign, Sion, Sun, and Essene are the same: SN.

The etymology of the word Essene is a mystery to bible scholars. However, from the above word plays and puns we can derive a very good idea of its origins. It refers to an essence produced in the brains as the result of a sine wave from heaven

The Essenes called themselves Therapeutae, "healers," claiming that their austere lifestyle gave them the power to cast out demons of sickness and even to restore life of the dead. Considering this, Christ raising Lazarus from the dead seems a typical Essenic miracle. This miracle is the performance of the Great Work.

According to the definition offered by Father John Rossner, the magi were "specialists in the holy" who acted as 'Mid-wives' in the birth of the "God-Men" from the "Old." These magicians did not practice or demonstrate this craft merely for entertainment purposes or to cause sensations. They did so to provide a demonstration of the means to overcome suffering and to display the powers of the fully functioning human being.

THE MESSIAH AND THE CRAFT

In addition to sin, Morgenstern provides critical explanations for the Babylonian seal of Enki we examined a moment ago. He explains this is a purification ceremony. He says the officiating 'fish' priest is the *masmasu*, the purifier. This title was given to Marduk, the son of E.A., the great wise sage of ancient Sumer, who is hovering in the disk.

Ahura Mazda in his winged disk or craft.

Importantly, this is one of the many examples of the gods of Light, the Illi, flying in such a craft, celestial disk or *winged ring*. Another depiction, shown here, is on the doorways and on the walls at Persepolis in Iran. These are almost certainly taken from the Babylonian ideas of the Anunnaki.

Scholars have usually interpreted this god as Ahura Mazda, who is also known as 'the God of Light', holding the ***ring of Cosmic Sovereignty***, , with his hand raised in a gesture of blessing. Talk about a powerful term. Cosmic Sovereignty is the term applied to the Divine State withheld from 'sinful' humanity and, for that which we all seek.

Ahura Mazda is often interchanged with Enki. This makes sense, as the wisdom of E.A. was the technical means to elevate, through the asipu principles, an ordinary human to the level of the gods. It is Merkaba metaphysics.

The priest who performed these Babylonian purification or baptismal ceremonies, says Morgenstern, was called *asipu* or masmasu. Masmasu was probably derived from the Sumerian MAS-MAS. *Mas* is quite close to *Maz*, as in Ahura Mazda or Masda.

Mas is strikingly similar to the Egyptian *Mes*, the root of the Hebrew *Messiah*, as well as *Mos* or *Moses* and the suffix of Her-MES. The ME (pronounced *May*) were the tablets of civilization brought by Enki. They most certainly link with the Emerald Tablet of Hermes.

May, we recall, is also the name of a pillar or tower of mysteries in pagan belief. Its alternate name is *Mag*.

The state of uncleanliness and sin, from which the masmas (Messiah) released the sick man, was called mamitu. This word had two meanings, "bann" or "exorcism" and "state of evil or uncleanliness.

A synonym for mammitu, notes Morgenstern, was *iltu*, 'to bind' and denoting "the state of being bound." Phonetically, *mami* is similar to mummi or mummy, the Egyptian term from a body bound or wrapped. In a moment, we will see that this was called the KRST or *Karast* garment. It lifted one out of sin and transformed one into a god.

In fact, before the *baru* priest could perform his holy work, says Morgenstern, he had to fulfill certain qualifications. He had to be of noble, priestly, blood, a descendent of Enmeduranki. He had to be of perfect bodily growth and thoroughly knowledgeable in his priestly duties. The key to decoding the ability of the baru priest is to identify Enmeduranki.

En-me-duranki was a sage of Eridu. Some scholars believe he is the Sumerian equivalent of the biblical Enoch. Enmeduranki, means the 'Master of the Divine Tablets of the bond Heaven-Earth." These ME tablets had been preserved and hidden by the Anunnaki before the Flood. They were recovered and Enmeduranki became knowledgeable in them.

"The learned savant who guards the secrets of the gods will bind his favored son with an oath before Shamash and Adad... and will instruct him in the secrets of the gods." "Thus was the line of priests created, those who are allowed to approach Shamash and Adad."

The mullilu or 'purifiier'.

Let us now return to the towers in the seals. Morgenstern informs us that *Mul ilu* was the name of the sacred tower or utensil. This is the term applied to the cones emitted from the utensil, as well. Mullilu means *purifier*. Mul, interestingly enough, is the Sumerian word for star, making the "star of light" one possible interpretation of this utensil. Starlight, we may presume, is the purifier.

The technical term for purifying the place where the purification ceremony was to be held was sabatu. Sometimes, instead of merely sprinkling with holy water, the whole body was washed or baptized. Sabba is a word that means baptize.

The need for some means to expel the evil spirits from the body was very urgent in Babylonian thought, notes Morgenstern. Their presence meant continual sickness and suffering, and eventual death. Life required their removal.

Morgenstern says the chief means by which this was accomplished were fire (light) and water. They were the great purifiers. Water refers to the celestial waters. The god of light, Marduk, was looked upon as the son and chief messenger of E.A. against the evil spirits.

A study of Sumerian titles of some of the most important gods of the ashipu ceremony is illuminating. Marduk was called "controller of the siptu", and DINGIR-SILIG-NAM-TI-LA, or "controller of life." He was "***the reviver of the dead***," a state apparently brought about by the asipu.

E.A. was "lord of life", and his companion, the earth mother goddess Ninhursag or Damkina, "mistress of life."

It is easy to see that these concepts were cut and pasted wholesale into the Christian tradition and applied to Jesus who became the reviver of the dead and the chief means by which sin was overcome. What was omitted, or downplayed, was the role of the Fish Tower in this process.

Earlier, we noted that Nebuchadnezzar built an *image of gold* that stood three score (60) cubits high and six cubits wide. This was a Round Tower.

The bible subtly records that it was the people of Daniel who could make this Tower work. Old Testament scholars universally agree that Daniel was compiled over a long period of time and does not represent the visions of one particular person. Daniel ('God is my judge') was not a personal name. The question who or what then is *the* Daniel takes on paramount importance.

In her *Woman's Encyclopedia of Myths and Secrets*, Barbara Walker answers this question by saying 'Daniel' was a title used to distinguish a group of people, "a person of the Goddess Dana or Diana". Dana was Jacob's daughter, his 13th child. Her name means 'light of An'.

There's your trouble. That is exactly the same meaning as the Celtic Tuatha De' Danann ('Children of the Goddess Diana'). In Irish history, the mystical Tuatha De' Danann, are described as heaven-sent 'gods, and not-gods'. They are compared with the Sanskrit *deva* (shining one, god) and *adeva* (Devil), which became *daeva* (devil) in Persian. The Old English *divell* (devil) can be traced to the Roman derivative *divus*, *divi*: gods.

In *Bloodline of the Holy Grail* Laurence Gardner says Mary Magdalene, as the *Miriam*, was the Head Sister of the Order of Dan. Her order appears to be the continuation of the mysterious Shining Ones or Illumined Ones who possessed the secrets of the great Tower.

11.
TEACH THE BREAD OF LIFE = 153

It must have been quite a sight for Mary when she first beheld Jesus. Described by Luke as a gluttonous man, a winebibber and a friend of publicans and sinners (Luke 7:34) he apparently attracted large crowds, like a modern celebrity. It was adios reality when he appeared. The people of Capernaum literally crawled over one another to see the magician perform miracles and healings and to hear his vision of the divine New Age and the Kingdom or Empire of Light to come.

The Jewish elders confronted Jesus in the synagogue at Capernaum and demanded that he produce the 'bread of God'[Psalm 78:24, Exodus 16:15], the manna that miraculously rained from heaven and fed the Israelites in the wilderness during the Exodus.[John 6:31-59] This magical substance suddenly disappeared after the Israelites entered Canaan. There was a strong Rabbinic belief that when the Messiah came he would rain manna from heaven once again. This was the great work of the master Moses. Now the Jewish leaders were demanding that Jesus produce this celestial substance as proof to his claim to be the Messiah. He responded with his discourse on the bread of life in which he disclosed that it was not Moses who manufactured this substance, but God.

Jesus was born in Bethelehem, the 'House of Bread'. As an adult, Jesus connects himself to manna when he describes himself as: "**The bread of God is he which came down from heaven, and gives life unto the world.**" John 6:33

Later Jesus added (or someone added for him),

"**I am the living bread which came down from heaven: if any man eat of this bread, he shall live for ever: and the bread that I will give is my flesh, which I will give for the life of the world.**" John 6:51

This bread is referred to again in Revelation 2:17. Jesus says:

"**He that hath an ear, let him hear what the Spirit saith unto the churches; To him that overcometh will I give to eat of the *hidden manna*, and will give him a *white stone*, and in the stone a new name written, which no man knoweth saving he that receiveth (it).**"

Jesus states that he possesses a technique for bringing this substance – the white manna stone or snow-like crystal -- out of the Milky Way. He can open the heavens and bring to Earth a supply of this pure food. He is further stating that he is the embodiment of this substance. THE STONE OF GOD = 153.

As Mary Magdalene was the first to see the risen bread/manna/Christ outside the tomb on Easter morning she seemingly had knowledge of this matter. It also appears she assisted in an obstetric operation. She assisted in the birth of the risen bread/manna/Christ… substance.

After the Resurrection, MM sailed to France where she is further connected to this substance. In the *Ecstasy* portrayals of Mary Magdalene from Provence, notes Gardner in *The Magdalene Legacy*, Mary is portrayed in the company of angels, who were said to have fed her a mystical form of bread.

VITAL LINK MANNA = 153

In *Montsegur and the Mystery of the Cathars* Jean Markhale adds an important detail concerning this bread. He notes that the Cathars of Southern France, who venerated Mary Magdalene, recited the Lord's Prayer in a heretical form. This prayer was revered as the prayer spoken by the angels before the crystal throne of Christ. Instead of *daily bread*, the Cathars said ***bread beyond substance***. Markhale believes this was because to the Cathars material bread (or other food) was a diabolical creation, like everything else in this realm. However, it is possible it is related to a heavenly substance, the mystical bread of the *Ecstasy* portrayals.

Jesus' crime was explicitly stated on a placard placed above his head on the cross by Pontius Pilate. Written in Greek, Latin and Hebrew the placard read: INRI. Exoterically, this is translated as "*Jesus the Nazorean, King of the Jews*." This declared the official capitol charge against Jesus -- declaring himself the one and only savior and challenging the sovereign authority of Tiberius Caesar

-- and at the same time mocked him. *This* is the "King of the Jews?"

In the wisdom tradition INRI means; "*By Fire Nature is Renewed Whole*," pointing to Jesus' role as a bringer of higher frequency knowledge or 'fire'. The Rosicrucians altered the meaning of INRI to IGNE NITRUM RORIS INVENITUR or "the baptism or cleansing power of dew is only discovered by fire." Jesus was considered the 'bringer of the dew'.

It is vital that we understand as much about this distinctive substance as possible. This stuff is obviously IT as far as Jesus was concerned. Briefly examining it here will serve to introduce us to the tremendous insight and knowledge potentially possessed by MM and for which she was called the Illuminator.

MANNA

What's a manna? It's an ethereal substance from the stars, described in Exodus 16:31 as bread, small, round, white and sweet, which sustained life. Manifesting in the morning along with *dew* it *dove* out of the Milky Way at night and turned to a crystalline form on Earth in the morning. It is considered to be interchangeable with the Holy Spirit, which is symbolized by a *dove*. Interestingly, in *Holy Blood, Holy Grail* Baigent, Leigh and Lincoln note that Magdala is called the "Village of Doves" .

In the Egyptian Papyrus of Ani *manna* is referred to as *What is this?* or "*what is it*"? The Greeks called it 'golden rain' and associated its appearance with Pallas-Athena, the goddess of wisdom and one of the role models for Mary

Magdalene. Manna in Greek means 'mother'. It is called the "white dew" and the "white dove" (*duv*). It is *ben, bon.*

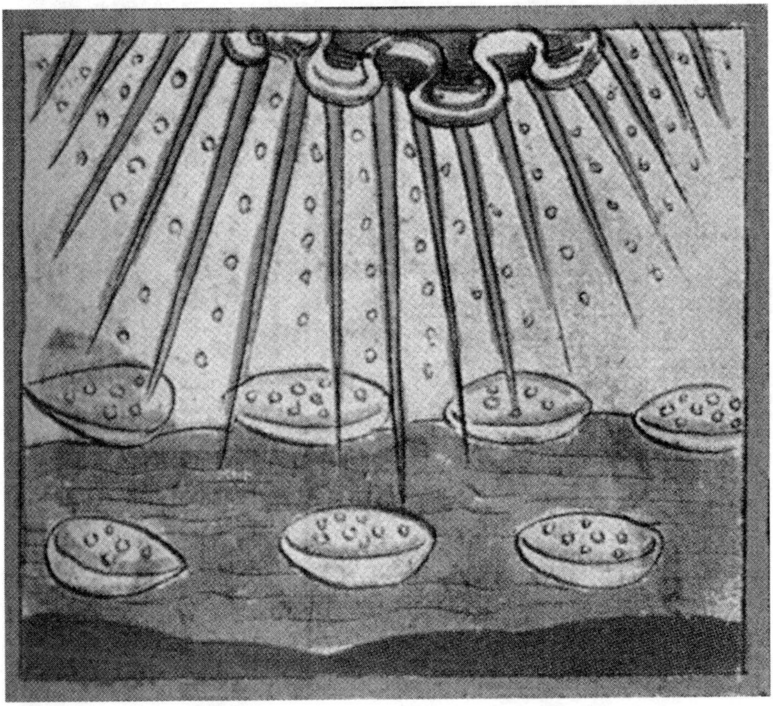

"Blessed of the Lord be his land, for the precious things of heaven, for the dew," says Deuteronomy.

Vulcan, the god of alchemy, seeking to free Jupiter (the Greek Zeus) from his headaches with an axe, releases Pallas Athena, the goddess of wisdom, form his skull. Golden Rain, manna, falls upon her. Her birth is celebrated annually by the festival of the "Golden Rain" in which gold coins are scattered. In Earth Under Fire, *Dr. Paul LaViolette proposes that Zeus signifies the Galactic core. Athena, who springs from Zeus' head, he says, signifies the outburst of cosmic rays violently emitted from the Galactic center during a starburst event.*

Where there's a mother there is a father. In Jesus' story this is Joseph. Like another important figure in our story, Joseph of Arimathea, Jesus' father was considered a *ho tekton*, a term often interpreted to mean 'carpenter'.

Once again, the works of Laurence Gardner, especially *The Lost Secrets of the Sacred Ark* and *The Magdalene Legacy*, come in handy. In his collected woks he's given rise to a new understanding of *ho tekton*; One that links the Josephs with the manufacture of this Christ substance. He says a *ho tekton* is a "master craftsman" or "master of the craft". Previously, craftsman was thought to mean 'carpenter' or 'wood worker'. However, Gardner connected the Josephs' craft with *The* Craft. Alchemy. They were alchemists who produced ('made', 'identified', 'crafted') bread. In the East 'wood' is the fifth element called *quintessence*. It is light. In *Blue Apples*, I profiled Jesus, the wood worker, as a word worker, light worker or alchemist.

When Morgenstern's analysis of sin is factored in it suggests this substance enabled us to overcome 'sin', to become pure, and to walk with the gods. Many voices in my lecture audiences note that manna resembles the substance of Frank Herbert's sci-fi novel *Dune*, in which a spice mined from the planet Arrakis (Iraq-is?) enables one to fold space and to span light years of space-time while standing still.

Gardner cites the incident recorded in the Old Testament book of Exodus 32:20. Here we are told that Moses burned the Golden Calf worshipped by the Israelites while he was away on Mount Horeb, and made from it a powder called 'bread' which he mixed with water and gave to the Israelites (THE WATER OF LIFE = 153). Gardner describes a roaring, smoking furnace in an alchemical laboratory or workshop in the Sinai where the sacred *mfkzt*, the enigmatic white powder of gold was produced from the golden calf. By way of ingestion (as *conical* bread-cakes or by water immersion) this substance was the "giver of life", says Gardner. Again, he provides the incredible details of this incident in *Lost Secrets of the Sacred Ark.*

The identity of the golden calf is known and important. Egyptian sculpture shows the calf-eared goddess Hathor painted in gold. She was the 'golden calf-woman' worshipped at Denderah, the temple called "the House of Bread." Incredibly, the Israelites were not only worshipping Hathor at Sinai, they were also making bread or manna. In *Mystery of the Cathedrals* Fulcanelli says this 'sacred cow' is a symbol of alchemy. I'll have more to say about the golden calf in the next chapter.

As noted, Gardner proposes this craft must have been revived during Jesus' time as he reveals that his wealthy uncle Joseph of Arimathea was a master of the craft. Joseph of Arimathea is one of the more mysterious figures in the New Testament. It is his newly hewn 'tomb' from which MM sees the risen bread or manna/Christ appears. It is not difficult to see this smith's 'tomb' as a *crucible*, an alchemical furnace that baked 'christ', the bread or manna. Interestingly, the Round Towers of Ireland are thought to be chimneys.

In legend, Joseph is a quite remarkable figure - his exploits (in various literary traditions) include:

- Founder of the first Christian Church in England.
- Keeper of the Holy Grail, the transformed ('illumined') blood and water that spurt from Jesus' body.

• Uncle of Mary, Mother of Jesus

• Merchant involved in the tin trade between the West coast of England, and the Mediterranean - took the boy Jesus to Cornwall and/or Somerset in England sometime between the ages of 12 and 30.

• Ancestor of Sir Lancelot and Sir Galahad of Arthurian fame.

Most importantly, as far as we are concerned, he accompanied Mary Magdalene to Provence. This brings up an interesting speculation as to the identity of the 'angel' mentioned earlier who fed Mary Magdalene the 'bread' of the angels. It was Joseph of Arimathea.

It is easy to see that these two worked together. The manufacture of this substance would have been the final training event designed to pull together all the knowledge the Jesus studio had accumulated. It culminated in the making of the bread of the angels. Now, they were ready for the next step... acquiring the vibration or Ring of Cosmic Sovereignty.

12.
THE ALABASTRON

My insertion of the word 'crucible' in relation to the tomb of Jesus in the last chapter was inspired by Mircea Eliade's book *The Forge and the Crucible: The Origins and Structures of Alchemy* in which he documents the rise of alchemy in the ancient world and the impact it had on human consciousness. A **crucible** is a cup-shaped piece of laboratory equipment used to contain chemical compounds when heating them to very high temperatures.

That cup-shaped crucible sounds like the Holy Grail many an author has quested for. What is important to us is the substance it contained: the Holy Blood, apparently produced from imbibing the holy bread of the angels.

In Grail lore, either Joseph of Arimathea or Mary Magdalene captured the transformed blood and water spurting from the side of Jesus' body as it hung on the pillar. In the Appendix we'll explore the mysterious Templar graffiti at Domme, France that shows a pregnant woman holding a rod or wand.

Another container is mentioned in the story of Mary Magdalene, the *alabastron* – the box with anointing oil.

This mysterious *alabastron* appears to have some form of miraculous qualities. In this box, or "vessel of light or life," was kept the anointing oil -- a *balm* made out of an appropriate flower, supposedly spikenard (that originally grew in India).

An astounding fact is that the alabaster for this box came from the 'lost' city of Alabastron, the Roman name for Akhenaton's holy city, Akhetaton.

Nefertiti with ointment jar receiving the key of life. MM and jar (right).

The anointing (or "embalmment") of Jesus ranks as one of the most important events in the Gospels. The event happened when Jesus and his disciples were in Bethany. The time was two days before the Passover, the day before Jesus' triumphant entry into Jerusalem on an ass, which was followed later that week by the Last Supper and the Crucifixion. Jesus and the disciples visited the house of 'Simon the Leper', a mysterious figure who has never been identified. While they were feasting, a woman having an *alabastron*, meaning an Egyptian crystal unguent jar, vase or box – containing "exceedingly precious ointment' came up to Jesus and poured its contents on his *head*.[Matt. 26:7] The disciples were outraged, protesting that this was a waste of ointment and money. In response, Jesus makes an astonishing statement: 'For in that she poured this ointment upon my body, *she did it to prepare me for burial.* Verily I say unto you, Wheresoever this gospel shall be preached in the whole world, that also which this woman hath done shall be spoke of in memory of her."

THE HOLY HARLOT

We are asked to believe that Mary Magdalene's embalming of Jesus was a spontaneous act. This is utterly ridiculous. She was likely a highly trained spiritual practitioner. The nature of her training is even recorded in history and lore that says she was a *harlot.*

This word *harlot* originally referred to the patronesses of the goddess Ishtar, who appears in the Bible as Ashtoreth, Asherah, or Esther, the Queen of Heaven. [Jeremiah 44:19] This goddess is Isis. A related word is *harine*. Moses' brother Aaron was called **Harun** or **Haroon** in the Qur'an. The place of ***herons***, I have proposed, is the center of the Milky Way galaxy.

Babylonian scriptures called Ishtar the Light of the World. The crucifixion and resurrection, and escape from the underworld of this Sumerian goddess (also known as Ishtar), is told in cuneiform tablets inscribed c. 1500 B.C.E., attesting to a very old tradition. We'll discuss Ishtar further in a later chapter.

Above all, we are told, *the anointing oil was used for*

the installation rites of all Hebrew kings and priests. This raises the provocative theory that Mary Magdalene's anointing of Jesus was the performing of an ancient Israelite ceremony of anointing kingly candidates in order to enhance their physical powers, protect them from danger and increase their connection to God. This ceremony took place in the Temple of Solomon in Jerusalem, a site that we will investigate momentarily. In this ceremony the spirit of God would enter the new king enabling him to become the 'Anointed of Yahweh'.

Anointing set sacred things apart from secular. The anointment of sacred objects was an ancient tradition in Israel: Exodus 30:22-33, where Moses was instructed by God to anoint the meeting tent and all its furnishings with specially prepared oil. At the beginning of his shamanic career, Moses discovered the angel of the Lord in flames of fire from within a bush atop Mount Sinai. As I noted in *The Healing Sun Code*, 'Sinai' is a metaphor for Meru, the spinal cord.

NARD

Mary Magdalene's box (skull) contained a sacred substance commonly referred to as 'spikenard' or 'nard'. Spikenard lengthens the time that the brain chemical GABA (gamma-aminobutyric acid), a natural relaxant, circulates through your system. When applied topically, spikenard's relaxing components are absorbed through the skin. It's used today as a seduction cream and to enhance sensual experience.

In my opinion, the spikenard component of Mary's oil is a carrier for another substance. It is also a clever literary ruse by the editors of the New Testament to conceal a far more profound substance. Calling it nard settles it for many. It takes them off of the trail of the real anointing oil.

The basis for this speculation is the discovery of an ancient practice revealed by Franz Koecher, whose translation of pharmacological texts left by ancient Babylonian physicians was reported in *The Chicago Tribune* (July 23, 2005, Section 1, p. 15).

To the consternation of scholars, many of these recipes called for the excrement of animals – dog poop, pig droppings and other barnyard excrement – as key ingredients. Modern pharmacologists snubbed their ancient predecessors, chalking the inclusion of the ingredients to the ignorance of the ancients.

But Koecher found that the dung in the ointment – so to speak – actually was a diversion by the ancients.

He discovered the physicians listed use of animal excrement simply as codes for actual secret plant ingredients that they didn't want their patients (or competitors perhaps) to know, so that the patients couldn't make their own medicine. He discovered the equivalence lists, about 100 coded plant names.

EMBALMING THE SAVIOR

The story of Mary "embalming" Jesus with oil is akin to Isis embalming Osiris, the Egyptian savior. Isis, the companion of Osiris (the Egyptians did not have a word for 'wife'), along with the god of alchemy, Thoth, resurrected

Osiris after his rival and brother, Set, broke, cut, divided, immolated his body into fourteen fragments (similar to the body of Christ symbolized by the bread broken in the Christian sacrament). Isis sought these pieces and found them (all except for his phallus *which was eaten by a fish*, so the story says), and bound them together with a woven purple cloth that magically reconstituted his body. All depictions from the time of the Osirian religion show him tightly wrapped in this shroud.

Isis sending rays to the embalmed Osiris.

The "embalming" of Osiris prepared him for his journey aboard the ship of the gods. This ship is shown beneath him. It closely resembles the shape of modern wormhole.

KARAST

There are too many similarities in the story of Osiris and Jesus and Isis and Mary Magdalene. As the early 20th century Egyptologist E.A. Wallis Budge writes in the preface to *Osiris & The Egyptian Resurrection*, "The central figure of the ancient Egyptian Religion was Osiris, and the chief fundamentals of his cult were the belief in his divinity, death, resurrection and absolute control of the destines of the bodies and souls of men." That's the role Christianity assigns to Jesus.

Gerald Massey was an early 20th century poet and Egyptologist who stirred great controversy over his interpretation of Egyptian words and his criticism of scholars. "It is unfortunate and humiliating to us as a nation," wrote Massey, "that Egyptology and Assyriology in England should have first fallen into the hands of devout believers in biblical 'history'. Such statements of truth put him in the line of fire of bible-believing scholars.

In *Ancient Egypt: The Light of the World* Massey brings a key piece of poetry to this quest. He notes that the name of Osiris' shroud, and therefore the name of the perfume/balm was KRST, Karast. He further states that the Egyptian word for mummy is *ges*, which signifies to wrap up in bandages. This word, *ges*, or *kes*, to embalm the corpse, is a reduced or abraded form of an earlier word, *karas*. The word *krs* denotes the embalmment of the mummy, and the *krst*, as the mummy, was made in the process of preparation by purifying, anointing, and embalming.

"The resurrection of the human soul in the after-life was the central fact of the Egyptian religion," writes

Massey, "and the transfigured, re-erected mummy, otherwise called the Karast, was a supreme symbol."

Scholars have difficulty following and documenting some of Massey's poetic interpretations of Egyptian hieroglyphs, including as noted, that of *krst*. Still, this idea resonates.

For instance, "Karast" is how Christ is pronounced with a thick Tennessee accent. Some people here in Nashville pronounce the name of the NFL team, the Titans, so that the 'i' sounds like 'Tot-ans' (rhymes with 'hot-ans'). The 'i' in Christ is pronounced the same way, so Christ is pronounced 'Ka-Rost' or 'Krosst', but it is understood that they mean Christ.

If, in fact, the Greek word *Christ* ('anointed'), *Christos, Krstos*, or the Latin *Chrestus* comes from the Egyptian *Karast* ('oil') this would further fuse Christianity with the religion of Osiris and date the origins of this ceremony enacted by Jesus and Mary Magdalene to at least 10,000 B.C.

During the process of anointing, writes E.A. Wallis Budge in *The Mummy*, it was said, "O Asar (Osiris) the thick oil which is poured upon thee furnishes thy mouth with life". It is also said that the anointing is done *to give sight to the eyes, hearing to the ears, sense of smell to the nostrils and utterance to the mount.*"

To embalm the body thus was to caress (k-r-s) it lovingly and the embalmment was a mode of enlightening or making the Christ *(karast)* the Anointed.

Esoteric Christianity is dedicated to the revelation of the secrets that enable one to 'put on the new clothes'. Drawing upon the sacred traditions of India, Iran, Egypt,

Greece, and mystical Jewish teachings the first Christians, the Nazarenes, led by Mary Magdalene, formulated a teaching whereby the average ("fallen") individual ignites his divine self and is transformed into a cosmic being. This was symbolized by the putting on of a new cloak or mantle, the Christ body.

The Hermit Zosimus Giving a Cloak to Magdalene
1320s Fresco, Magdalene Chapel, Lower Church, San Francesco, Assisi

In the book of Genesis a special configuration of clothing called the "robes of skin' (*Gen.* 3:21) is mentioned. This refers to the 'lost" body or garment of Light. Philip says "There is no other way for a person to acquire this quality except by putting on the perfect Light." (76:25)

Restoration of the body of light in Philip, therefore, comes about through clothing oneself in the garments of "water and fire" (baptism and chrism), which, unlike the earthly garments, prepare the soul for ascent.

In *Cloak of the Illuminati* I linked this power garment with ascent via a ladder or stairway to heaven.

This restoration of the Christ body can most clearly be seen in the Gnostic text *Hymn of the Pearl* [*Col.* 3:10] where the prince sees in the angel of light, which comes to meet him the reflection of his own true Self, or alter ego, which had been preserved in the upper world. Perhaps a somewhat gnostic Paul spoke of "putting on the new man, who is renewed...after the image of his creator."

IN THE TOMB

It is important to note the description of what transpired after the crucifixion. It is said that Nicodemus came and brought "a mixture of myrrh and aloes, about *a hundred pound*," and "they took the body of Jesus and bound it in linen cloths with the spcies as the custom of the Jews is to bury". [John 19: 39-40] This again, says Massey, denotes the making of the *Karast*-mummy = the Christ body.

Dr. Charles Muses, a mathematician, philosopher and computer scientist, who died in 2000, claims in his 1985 book *The Lion Path*, that the Egyptians had developed a technology in which tones, lights, and an as-yet unidentified plant are used, to "open a rusty valve", or trigger the production of large pulses of hormones similar to the ecdysone (ecdydsterone), produced by *larval* forms of insects, which allows the adult form to emerge. In this way, they would allow the gestation or mutation of a *non-molecular body* – a new skin -- that would allow the survival of consciousness beyond physical death. Just as every chrysalis has embossed wings on it, wrote Muses, so too, does every mummy case have folded wings on it (see Abydos symbol). *Larva* means 'a ghost' or 'specter'. It is the earliest stage of insect development, after it is hatched and before it is changed into a *chrysalis* or *pupa*, the stage in between the larval and adult forms.

These sacred tones (the Holy Grail) are used to allow us to shift through the veil of creation into the realm of pure unity of matter and energy. THE TONES OF GOD = 153. Traditional shamanic peoples around the world say the Blue Stone or Apple is actually how our soul travels to the inner realm and it is inside of a *quantum egg* or in an "*interphasic state of existence*" (able to jump through time and cross great distances or even to use this skill locally).

A preliminary stage between the human body and this non-molecular body was what I term the Cloak of the Illuminati, which is the Garment of the Oracle found in the example of the *Pallium* conferred upon or transmitted to Elisha by Elijah just before he *rose* into the heavens in a "whirlwind", *c.* 800 B.C. This is the *Pala* garment of Mari.

In Egypt, Akhenaton's Disk worshippers of ATON (or ATEN) symbolized the ideogram for the word '*rise*' is ***three rays*** or beams of light falling from a disk .

As Muses points out, in this drawing *from the tomb of Tutankhamun* (Akhenaton's successor) we see the *three rays* or *beams* of Star-Power energy entering the forehead of the pupal Osiris. The word *sba*,  "star" (which resembles a star fish) also means "door" and, with the determinative  for "walking," it meant "passing through a star-door," said Muses. The *ba* or winged soul shown under this glyph in the figure indicates that it was the soul's passage through these doors that effected the Osirian transformation or metamorphosis into the immortal state and its glorified body."

Osiris receiving rays. From the Second Shrine of Tutankhamun.

We know that a sound can cause a human to enter a state of bliss or stupidity. Those who donned the Cloak knew the secret of the pitch or frequency of God = Solomon's Key that transmuted an ordinary human into a star walker.

The process of preparing, embalming and Christifying the mummy obviously survives in the *Chrisome* or *krisum* of the Roman Catholic Church. Also called the Chrismal, Chrismatory, *The Catholic Encyclopedia* defines *Chrisome* as a term "Formerly used to designate the sheath, or cloth-covering (*theca*) in which relics were wrapped up." The Latin *chrismale* was also applied:

- to the pall or corporal
- to the vessel for the Blessed Eucharist
- to the cere-cloth covering the table of the altar
- sometimes to *the long white-hooded robes in which the newly-baptized were clothed* (cf. Roman Ritual, II, cap. ii, n. 24), and which they wore from Holy Saturday evening till Low Sunday — called consequently *Dominica in Albis*. This garment, however, was more commonly known as the *chrisome*, and resembled in shape the modern alb, except that it had a kind of hood for the head. Its representative is now the *vestis candida* still used at baptism.

In present-day usage the words *chrismal* and *chrismatory* are taken indiscriminately and almost universally to refer to the vessels that are employed to hold the oils that are solemnly consecrated by the bishop.

While the terms of this oil and the Christ garment have survived lost is technique for manufacturing them. This belonged to Mary Magdalene.

13.
THE MYSTERY OF PERFUME

I'd like to return to Moses' meeting in the flames with God on Sinai. Where there's flames of fire there's smoke. The French word *perfume* or *parfume* means "through the smoke." Here is another connection to Mary Magdalene, the perfumer.

In an article on the schism between ancient perfumery and its modern counterparts Raed Rady observes that what most people do not realize is that, from the very beginning, the whole issue of perfumery was enveloped in secrecy. The art began in Egypt several thousand years ago and was mastered by about 2500 BC (although it started much earlier). It was practiced by a certain type or a certain order of priesthood who were alchemists. In fact, one of the modern Arabic terms for Egypt is "Al Khem", the source of our word *alchemy*.

The Egyptian system of perfumery, says Rady, was very complicated, precise and specific at the every level of existence. Yet, in this complexity, he proposes there was total unification. As an example, he says an important point for our understanding of perfumery was the lack of distinction between what we would call today cosmetics, perfume, body care products, bath products, food flavoring, food preservation, religious ceremonies, magic, pharmaceuticals and medicines. All of these aspects were combined together and related to the practice of the priesthood for healing. *This was perfumery.*

Furthermore, notes Rady, it is important to realize, that at that time, healing referred to all aspects of the human being. There was again, no distinction between a physical, emotional, mental or spiritual ailment. Perfumery was practiced in order to achieve spiritual perfection *not* physical perfection. That was only achieved by perfecting the lower bodies of the physical, emotional and mental layers of the human being.

Mainly perfumery was practiced in the temple of Hathor/Ishtar at Denderah, which was the source of all the products created. We recall that Hathor is the cow-eared goddess, the 'golden calf', who was pulverized into powder by the Israelites.

Standing in Hathor's perfumery at Denderah is an eye-opening experience. One sees color depictions of gods operating giant tubes mounted to TET pillars. The same scene is duplicated in the crypt and in the Temple of Isis that stands behind Denderah.

We note that the bulbs emerge from lotus flowers. In Egypt Senshen (S-N-SHN = 'ascension') is another name for the lily or lotus flower. (Guardians of the Grail, p. 161) Is it possible that this cryptic scene had something to do with ascension?

In *A Woman's Encyclopedia of Myths and Secrets* Barbara Walker quotes Aristides, a Roman who was initiated into the Mysteries of Isis-Hathor, spoke of a mystical experience during which he saw, coming from Isis, "a Light and other *unutterable* things conducing to salvation."

The Crypt at Denderah. Photo by author.

Aristede's statement is all the more interesting considering Hathor's temple at Denderah was called 'the house of bread'. As mentioned, the Bethelehem, the traditional birthplace of Jesus, is a Hebrew word, meaning house of bread or house of Laham, a goddess. Strangely, bread and perfume go together at Denderah.

What is the meaning of the serpent in these jars at Denderah? In several of my previous books I have upheld that the serpent that is lifted is a symbol for a sine wave, a vibration. (In fact, I believe Denderah is a pun on Ten-terah or Tantra.) This serpent sings a song of life, bathing the atmosphere around it and feeding those who come into contact with it with spiritual energy. This spiritual energy, in turn, activated latent abilities within the mind-brain-body system. This, I proposed, is what happened at Siloam. The serpent energy enlightened the blind. One early Jewish sect called themselves Naassians ('serpent worshippers') and for them the snake or serpent was the Messiah.

With this sine wave coursing through our hearts and brains secretions are released. The heart sings Phi tunes. An epiphany is experienced, literally the appearance, manifestation, coming to light of God or the Divine Head.

In his book *Freemasonry of the Ancient Egyptians*, Manly P. Hall describes the immensely advanced cerebral abilities that high-initiates would acquire through initiation by such a sine wave. Hall tells of Pythagoras and the supernatural effect he had on strangers. When they met him on the road people 'fell upon their knees before him, overcome by some mysterious force which he emanated'. Appolonius of Tyana, a messianic figure of the first century, apparently displayed this same force. When hearing of a riot among the people, the prophet stood silent in front of them and, by the force of his personality and power of his words, he quelled the crowd. As an initiate of Pythagoras, we may speculate that MM had the same power.

MUFKZT

According to Gerald Massey in *Light of the World*, *Mafekh* or *Mafkhet* is one title of Hathor, the Golden Calf. She was the mistress of the mines, he says. The precious metals were called *mafkat*. Mafekh, he adds, is an Egyptian name for the turquoise and other treasure of the mines of Hathor, as well. Laurence Gardner has presented evidence that the Egyptian name for the 'bread of the angels' is also *mfkzt* (sometimes pronounced *"mufkuzt")*. This is identical to Massey's name for the head of Hathor, but with a 'z' added.

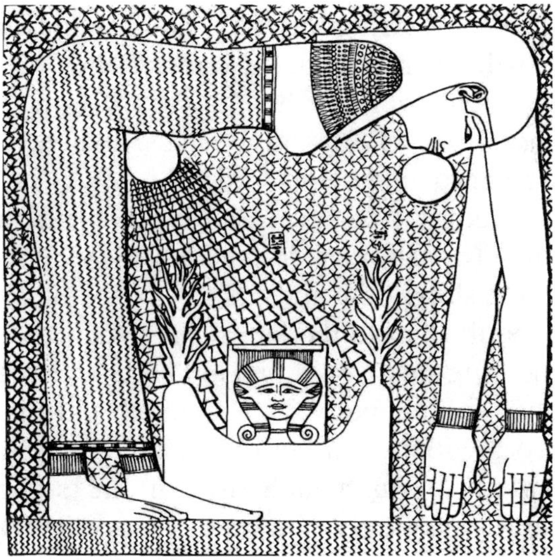

Particles of solar radiation bathe the head of Hathor, with the cow's ears, that rises from the gate.

Gardner proposes that the Israelites inherited from the Egyptians an ancient process for manufacturing a magical powder, called *mufkit* (literally, *what is it*?), that fed the light bodies of the pharaohs. We have been referring to this body as the *Karast* body.

One Egyptologist who takes issue with Gardner's *mfkzt* analysis is indigenous Egyptian scholar Abd'El Hakim. As Egyptologist Stephen Mehler tells the story in *From Light Into Darkness*, when he presented the words *Melfkat* or *Mefkat* to Hakim for interpretation the Egyptologist dismissed Gardner's translation as incorrect, stating that the term Gardner is referring to would be *Maskat*. This would refer to powdered metal, but a powder that was used to adorn the eyes in ancient Khemit. This was the source of the word *mascara*, says Hakim. Besides, he notes, Egyptian words that refer to gold begin with *neb*.

Here, we return to Massey. He says that "not only is the risen mummy (or sahu) called the karast, Osiris as the lord of the bier, the ship of the gods, is the *Neb-karast*, which he says is the equivalent to the later Christ the Lord. Another way of rendering this would be Golden Oil, Golden Christ or possibly 'golden body'. The latter definition is in perfect accord with our earlier discussion about sin and the transformation, through alchemy, of the sinner into a golden one. Interestingly, the Sanskrit word *samskara* or *sa-mskara = sa mascara* has a meaning that approximates the English "sin." (Of course, 'mushroom man' James Arthur, would have assuredly noted that with the change of an 'a' for a 'u' and the addition of an 'i' the word mascara is *muscaria*, the name of the psychedelic mushroom.)

So who is correct here? Massey and Hakim? Or Gardner?

If Gardner's *mufkzt* does actually mean mascara, this certainly could change the complexion of his thesis.

However, the mufkzt = mascara equation would align the creation of this substance – the bread -- with the idea of perfume – the mist -- which we have seen is a general term that refers to the creation of all ‘perfume’ substances for healing and is the specialty of MM.

THE ‘Z’

Checking Gardner’s books, however, I cannot find where he uses the word *melfkat* or *mefkat*, as suggested by Mehler. Gardner uses the obtuse *mfkzt*, with that dreadful z.

Now, it is vital to note that the ‘z’ in this term is not really a ‘z’. As Gardner informed me in person and in correspondence, it is an approximation of a squiggly line.

“The ‘z’”, he said, “is a phonetic symbol that looks like a lower case handwritten ‘z’.” He once drew this on a napkin for me. Later, he emailed it to me. Here it is: ʒ .

Apparently, Gardener noted, it is pronounced like an “a” - so it’s actually “m-f-ka-t”. I quote: “Hence, the middle section is ‘ka’, as in ‘vital spirit’. In this particular phonetic structure, the “m’ symbol is equivalent to “in” or “inside”. “f” = “his” -- and “t” = bread. So the whole is: “Inside his vital spirit bread”.

Got it?

This celestial substance or food was said to awaken the imbiber’s powers of perception, awareness and intuition. In fact, it did even more than that. According to Gardner, it lifted an ordinary person to the angelic levels. This gives entirely new meaning to the Lord’s Prayer, which as recorded in Matthew 6:9-13, states 'Give us this day our daily bread'.

Again, this is the bread fed to Mary Magdalene by the angels (or Joseph of Arimathea) in France.

We should know that no direct evidence, no samples, of this bread said to have been recovered from the ancient world have ever been analyzed. Gardner talks about 50 tons of this powder being discovered in the Sinai by W. M. Flinders Petrie in 1905. However, consulting Petrie's record of this expedition, he says he found 50 tons of ash. Again, actual samples of this powder/ash have yet to be tested.

Still, I find it fascinating, as Gardner notes, that the name "Ormus" is also used to describe the mfkzt powder. Modern science, says Gardner, now classifies this *Ormus* powder as an Orbitally Rearranged Monoatomic Element. A monoatomic element has one atom per molecule; a diatomic element has two atoms per molecule. ORMUS researcher Barry Carter notes that elements in this configuration are superconductors at room temperature and exhibit other quantum physical behaviors at a visible scale. Some of these quantum physical behaviors include:

- Anomalous responses to gravity
- Superfluidity
- "Tunneling" through solid objects.

Carter notes that one fairly recent discovery in biology and physics is that a certain small structure in every cell, called the microtubule, exhibits superconductive and tunneling behaviors at body temperature. In theory, this means that anywhere we can think we would like to go, we can travel there not only spiritually, but physically, and take our physical body with us.

It is thought that this bread and water is the same as that shared by Jesus on Mt. Herod with James, Peter and John. When Jesus was transfigured before their eyes, a column of light came out the top of his head. That *mfkzt*!

In Zoroastrian thought and in Gnostic texts, Ormus is synonymous with the principle of light. Ormus was also the name of an Egyptian sage and mystic, a Gnostic "adept" of Alexandria (Egypt), and who in A.D. 46 was converted to a mystical form of Christianity symbolized by a rose + cross.

Right on cue, the Templars adopted Ormus as one of the subtitles of their Order, not Baigent, Leigh and Lincoln in *Holy Blood, Holy Grail*. This subtitle was supposedly used until 1306 – a year before the arrest of the French Templars. The Temple devise for Ormus  was and is thought to be an acrostic or anagram which combines a number of key words and symbols, including to my eyes, the Egyptian hieroglyph for the heron, , and the astrological sign glyphs for Scorpio ♏, which points to the galactic center, the place of herons. One key word is *ours*, which means "**bear**" in French. This makes it sound as though this substance is connected to the Bear People.

In the Sumero-Babylonian language *orm* means "worm" and "serpent." *Or*, of course, is gold.

A wormy, wavy or squiggly line, , which reminds me of a horizontal version of Gardner's , is often used to represent the creative force of the universe, as well as *water. The expression OM* or , *O-mmmm*, represents the vibrating or 'living' ring, the waters of life. Is this the water with which Moses mixed the white powder?

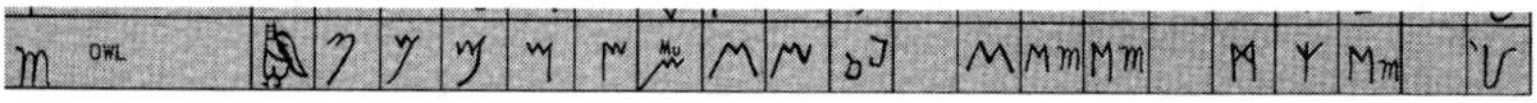

This alphabet chart from an old bible shows some interesting variations on the letter 'M'.

When captured or jarred up it seems that  becomes , the symbol for "the hidden god" (occult in Latin). In Egypt this was *Amon* or *Amen*, one of whose hieroglyphs  was a serpent in an oval, mirroring the filament in the jars from Hathor's crypt. It meant a pregnant belly, says Barbara Walker in *The Woman's Encyclopedia of Myths and Secrets*

It looks to me like the Bear People found a way to bottle the tones of god.

AMEN
TONES OF GOD = 153.

14.
SOLOMON'S KEY

Mary Magdalene was with Jesus when he returned to Jerusalem from Capernaum. She witnessed his violent reaction when he learned that Caiaphas, the high priest of the Temple of Solomon, perched high atop Mount Moriah, had authorized trading in the Temple. In reaction, Jesus assembled a commando force of disciples, many of whom had received advanced spiritual training like Mary Magdalene. Their mission was to cast out these merchants. Unfortunately for Jesus one of his men, Barrabas, murdered a man during the raid. Jesus' last days had begun.

Solomon is considered one of the wisest of the wise. He worshipped the goddess *Asherah* or *Ashtoreth*, both names for Is-Tara or Mari. (In addition, *Asherah* is cited as a source for *Osiris*). One of the great mysteries of Solomon's Temple is the incredible discrepancy between Solomon's Temple I (950 BC) and Solomon's Temple II, built on the pad of the former temple by Prince Zerubbabel after the Israelite's Babylonian Captivity in *c*. 575 B.C. This second Temple was subsequently enlarged during the time of Jesus and Mary Magdalene by King Herod the Great who conducted major construction works from 37 B.C. until his death in 4 B.C. On the First Temple the height of the Porch is 30 cubits.[9 I Kings 6:2] On Solomon's Temple II it is a towering *120* cubits (60 meters) high,[10 II Chronicles 3:4] and it is overlaid with pure gold! A cubit was originally equal to the length of the forearm from the tip of the middle finger to the elbow, or about 17 to 22 inches. 120 cubits is approximately as tall as a 20-story building. Accounting for this huge discrepancy has given biblical scholars headaches for centuries.

Here is how scholars have reconciled the differences:

1). The discrepancy is ignored – the most popular way of "explaining" Bible difficulties.

2). The chronicler (probably the prophet Ezra), was under the influence of the prophetic bravado and exaggerated the Porch's height in order to inflate the Jewish national ego.

3). The verse contains a typo. A scribe intended to write 30 cubits but wrote 120 instead.

4.) The discrepancy is dismissed as a "textual" error.

None of these explanations pass the "red face" or "straight face" test. This leaves the fourth explanation. Maybe the Porch was a Tower and it was truly 120 cubits high, after all. Indeed, the Temple tower soared toward heaven... just like the Tower of Babel. Masons certainly seemed to think so, anyway. In the following depictions from a Masonic bible the massive tower can be seen.

RESTORATION OF KING SOLOMON'S TEMPLE, BY JOHN WESLEY KELCHNER.

Solomon's Temple from an old Masonic bible.

This discrepancy makes an enormous difference. It leads us to ponder why such a tall tower was necessary on the Second Temple but not the first. For hubris? For defense? For observation? Did it function as a beacon that could be seen for miles around? This Tower *is* the mystery of Solomon's Temple. Strangely, it is rarely discussed in writings about the rebuilt Temple.

Exploring these questions is vital as the Temple of Solomon is one of the key settings in the Gospel story of Jesus and Mary Magdalene. And with the intriguing Magdala = Tower connections we have explored, the enormous Tower of Solomon takes on further significance. In fact, the Tower or Magdala of Solomon (let's call it for what it was) was a special place for Jesus. It was in front of the south entrance to the Temple that the preacher from Nazareth overturned the merchants and moneychangers' tables.

In John 10:23 we are told directly that: *"Jesus walked in the temple, in Solomon's Porch."* And what, exactly, did he do there? What did he see? I shall shortly present evidence upon which to base an answer.

In Luke 4: 9 the devil brings Jesus to Jerusalem, and *set him on a pinnacle of the temple, and said to him, If thou be the Son of God, cast thyself down from hence.* Again, it would make a huge difference if this pinnacle towered 20 stories over Jerusalem, instead of a mere two stories.

According to Josephus, the Temple's immenseness presented a marvelous appearance. Josephus says, "Its fineness, to such as had not seen it, was incredible; and to such as had seen it was greatly amazing." I bet it was simply majestic. I'll also bet it resembled a giant nuclear cooling tower from a distance.

The monumental "porch" or "portico" was located on the east side of the outer court of the Temple, and it rested on a massive Herodian retaining wall (which incidentally can still be seen in part at the present Temple wall area). The immense retaining wall that supported it was 130 feet high resting in the valley below and made of marvelous stones.

The stones of Moriah were revealed in 1996 when the clearing of centuries of rubble revealed an astonishing discovery on the Temple Mount. *Someone* by some unknown means had placed on this spot three cyclopean stone slabs:

- one 42 feet long;
- another 40 feet long,
- and a third over 25 feet long.

The largest of the three weighs an incredible 1,200,000 pounds, or about 600 tons! The smaller two stones weigh 570 and 355 tons each. Even today we do not have cranes capable of moving such massive blocks. Yet in ancient times someone living in Jerusalem quarried these rocks at a quarry archaeologists claim was three miles away. Then they cut, dressed and moved these stones into place. Who could have done this? And how? Further, why would they have done this? What spiritual (or any other) activity could possibly have required such a massive platform? What did Herod intend for this temple to *do*?

It is important for us to find out as it was at this enigmatic stone pad and great Temple Tower that Jesus was seen often, speaking and teaching the people or just walking, as in John 10 during the festival of "lamps" or chanukkah, which commemorates the re-dedication of the temple and of God to His people. Later, after His death his disciples gathered here often.

It was in the cloisters of the Temple that the Levite gurus resided and it was here that the doctors of the law met to hear and answer questions.

During their last visit to Jerusalem with Jesus, the apostles (probably including Mary Magdalene) admired Herod's temple:

Jesus left and was going away from the temple when his disciples came to him to call his attention to its buildings. "Yes," he said, "you may well look at all these. I tell you this: not a single stone here will be left in its place; every one of them will be thrown down." (Matthew 24:1-2) (Mark 13::1-2) (Luke 21:5-6)

He was correct. The Romans burned Jerusalem and destroyed Solomon's Temple II in 70 AD. The Temple and its great Magdala Tower where Jesus taught was no more.

Six hundred years later the Prophet Mohammed was miraculously transported from his home in Arabia to this very spot in Jerusalem where he was lifted into the heavens on a 'white horse'. Why did this ascension happen here instead of at Mecca?

We shall return to the mysteries of this awesome, and today highly protected, dot of real estate in the next chapter. As we will explore, in the tunnels beneath this site the Templars recovered knowledge legends say belonged to

Jesus and Mary Magdalene and that catapulted them into global prominence.

15.
THE TEMPLARS AND THE SKULL OF GOD

The Bible tells us Solomon's Temple was built to house the Ark of the Covenant, the golden box built by Moses at the foot of Mount Sinai per Yahweh's instruction and maintained by the Levites. The golden box was supposed to have rested upon the *stone pillar* that Jacob set up at Bethel after entering the *terrible* Gate to God and the Gate to Heaven in his famed experience with the Ladder to God.

The manna was called the Shewbread or "Bread of the presence of God", and was set out on a golden table in front of the Ark of the Covenant.

One eyewitness to the mound Moriah in Jesus and Mary Magdalene's time was Josephus. In *The Wars of the Jews* he reported that Herod's rebuilt Solomon's Temple was built of white marble, covered with heavy plates of gold in front and rising high above its marble-cloistered courts-themselves a succession of terraces-the temple, compared by Josephus to a snow-covered mountain. He says this temple appeared to strangers, when they were coming to it at a distance, like a mountain covered with snow; for as to those parts of it that were not gilt, they were exceeding white. "*When the sun came up it radiated so fiery a flash that people had to avert their eyes as if looking directly into the sun.*"

Speculation has abounded for centuries as to the exact nature of the treasure recovered by the Templars from this site. The spotlight was shone on this secret when the Catholic Church turned against the Templars in the fall of 1307.

Of all the mysteries concerning the Knights Templar, the strangest of them all has to be the charges leveled against them by the Church and Pope Clement V on August 12, 1307. This list was compiled from two primary sources, partly from the king's spies who had infiltrated the Templar Order, and partly from the confession of an alleged Templar defector, say Baigent, Leigh and Lincoln in *Holy Blood, Holy Grail.*

Armed with this list of heresies King Philip V of France acted against the Templars, issuing sealed and secret orders to his seneschals (a group as ruthless and efficient at mass murder as the Nazis SS). Philip planned it so that the orders would be opened everywhere simultaneously and executed at once. At dawn on Friday, October 13, 1307, all the Templars in France were arrested by the king's men, their possessions were seized and their preceptories placed under the king's authority.

In the ensuing days word began to creep through the grapevines of France of the gruesome torture of the Templars at the hands of Philip. Many were burned or imprisoned. Strange confessions were extracted and even more bizarre accusations were made. The Templars were accused of denying Christ, of repudiating, trampling, and spitting on the cross.

The most baffling of the charges against the Templars to some investigators is the accusations surrounding the 'bearded head' that the Templars worshipped known as 'Baphomet'.

46. That the brothers themselves had idols in every province, viz. Heads; some of which had three faces, and sone one, and some a man's skull.

47. That they adored that idol, or those idols, especially in their great chapters and assemblies.

48. That they worshipped it.

49. As their God.

50. As their Savior.

51. That some of them did so.

52. That the greater part did.

53. That they said that that head could save them.

54. That it could produce riches.

55. That it had given to the order all its wealth.

56. That it caused the earth to bring forth seed.

57. That it made the trees flourish.

58. ***That they bound or touched the head of the said idols with cords, wherewith they bound themselves about their shirts, or next to their skins.***

59. That at their reception the aforesaid little cords, or others of the same length, were delivered to each of the brothers.

60. That they did this in worship of their idol.

61. That it was enjoined them to grid themselves with the said little cords, as before mentioned, and continually to wear them.

62. That the brethren of the order were generally received in that manner.

63. That they did these things out of devotion.

64. That they did them everywhere.

This list poses many questions. For instance, were the cords of the Templar the same three cords given to Job's daughters? And what was the 'idol' of the Templars?

Further, what was the 'head' revered by the Templars? What kind of a head or skull can produce riches?

When the Templars were asked about this head, they either said it was a Christian martyr woman, or it was *the model of the speaking head that the pope Sylvester II made.*

Pope Sylvester II (d. 1003) was believed to have possessed a golden head called *Meridiana*, which spoke to him in oracles. It could answer any question posed to it with a yes or no answer, like a modern day computer. Meridiana was also reputed to have been a female demon who had appeared after he had been rejected by his earthly love, and with whose help he managed to ascend to the papal throne (another legend tells that he won the papacy playing dice with the devil).

A Spanish magician known as the Black Moor programmed the oracle head. The Black Moor is also said to be the author of *King Solomon's Key*, an important occult text that had influenced Nostradamus and Doctor John Dee. Sylvester II died in 1003, in a bizarre murder plot just before ending the dark ages. The giant oracle head has not been found. References still exist in the Vatican library.

The Keys of Solomon, says Eliphas Lévi (d. 1875), a master of the Rosicrucian interpretation of the Kaballah, are religious and natural forces expressed by signs and symbols. I take stock in the words of Levi. He attended seminary at Saint-Sulpice, the occult center of the Catholic

Church in Paris, but was expelled for teaching doctrines contrary to those of the Roman Catholic Church.

The Ring of Solomon, another component of the Key (both are synthesized in the Seal of Solomon) is said to encode all the science and faith of the Magi in one symbol. Lévi says the Seal of Solomon, his Keys and his Ring are tokens of supreme royalty.

I find it highly intriguing, if not likely, that the 'Black Moor' who penned *King Solomon's Key* is a pun name for the 'Black Mare', the Black ('hidden', 'secret', 'occult') Mary. The Black Mary is Mary Magdalene.

This makes sense.

Subjected to interrogation by the Inquisators a number of knights referred to something called 'Baphomet'. In addition, a knight under interrogation mentioned another curious relic, a reliquary in the shape of a woman's head... It was hinged on top, and contained what was described as a great head of gilded silver, most beautiful. Inside were two head-bones, wrapped in a cloth of white linen, with another red cloth around it. A label was attached, on which was written the legend 'Caput LVIIIm" (Head 58M). The bones inside were of a small woman.

Enter Eliphas Lévi, who is perhaps best known for his work regarding the alleged deity of the Knights Templar, the Baphomet.

Lévi considered the Baphomet to be a depiction of the absolute in symbolic form. His treatment of the Baphomet Mythos is best seen in his illustration of the Baphomet shown below, which he used as a front piece to one of his many books. According to the author Michael Howard, author of *The Occult Conspiracy*, Lévi based the illustration on a Gargoyle that appears on a building owned by the Templars; the Commandry of Saint Bris le Vineux.

Lévi believed that if one rearranged the letters in Baphomet by reversing them you would get an abbreviated Latin phrase:

TEM OHP AB

He further believed that this would represent the Latin "Templi omnivm hominum pacis abbas" or in English "The Father Of The Temple Of Peace Of All Men". This he felt to be a reference to King Solomon's Temple (Solomon means 'peace'), which Eliphas believed had the sole purpose of bringing peace to the world.

As Manly P. Hall observed, the name *Solomon* may be divided into three syllables (chords?), *Sol-om-on*, symbolizing *light* and *glory* collectively and respectively. The Temple of Solomon is, therefore, the "the House of Everlasting Light'. It was considered a house of initiation. The Templar skull that could perform miracles spit these secrets of Everlasting Light.

Of particular interest here is the alchemical symbol known as the *caput mortem* or 'dead head' of the alchemists and secret 'skull' or skill of the Johannite Templars  , who upheld John the Baptist as the true messiah.

By following the puns and the historical evidence what the Templars actually possessed was a *skill* from an ancient *school* that was symbolized by a *skull*. What I believed they possessed was the secrets imparted by Mary Magdalene. If these three dots of the dead head correspond to the three cords Job gave to his daughters then we may hypothesize that the knowledge the Templars recovered concerned the means the transform our hearts, the Language of the Angels (or Birds), the Language of the Archons and knowledge of the heavens.

Some historians have suggested that the name 'Baphomet' was a word play on the name '*Muhammed*', and claim that the Templars were actually Muslims. The authors of *HBHG* state that the Templars had a "sustained and sympathetic contact with Islamic and Jewish culture." This is very important, as it enabled them to gain access to some of the methods and mysteries of Eastern mysticism.

The ideas that the Templars gleaned from Islamic culture were threatening to Roman Catholicism. Templar Masters, claim the authors of *Holy Blood, Holy Grail*, often employed Arab secretaries, and many Templars, having learned Arabic in captivity, were fluent in the language.

In my opinion this does not resonate.

On the other hand, the name 'Baphomet' does ring of the Arabic '*abufihamet*'. As J.S.M. Ward observes in *Freemasonry and the Ancient Gods*, abufihamet means 'Father of Understanding' or 'Father of Wisdom'. Interestingly, 'father' in Arabic is taken to mean 'source'.

Ward continues saying, "If this is indeed the origin of Baphomet, it would therefore refer presumably to some *supernatural*, or *divine principle*. But what might have differentiated Baphomet from any other supernatural or divine principle remains unclear."

Another researcher who surmised that Baphomet may be a code term for a body of wisdom was Dead Sea Scroll scholar Dr. Hugh Schonfield, author of numerous books on Essene mysteries. When he was near completion of his book *The Essene Odyssey* some striking information about the Knights Templar made a timely appearance. The book was *Holy Blood, Holy Grail.* Though Dr. Schonfield rejected the proposals of Mssrs. Baigent, Leigh and Lincoln he did credit these authors with turning up information which conjuncted with his own research into the Essenes. In particular, he noted that the evidence of links with Essene lore suggested that the Templar reports of a bearded head that spoke them and invested them with occult powers might have a foundation in fact.

Dr. Schonfield decided to treat what he termed 'the obviously artificial name' Baphomet as an Atbash Cipher. In the Atbash Cipher, the first letter of the Hebrew alphabet is exchanged with the last. As Schonfield writes in *The Essene Odyssey*, "Setting down Baphomet in Hebrew characters...by Atbash converted immediately into (*Sophia*), the Greek word for Wisdom."

The centuries old secret was revealed for the first time, claimed Schonfield.

In his excitement he continues, saying that the bearded male head referred to by the Templars is the head of the cosmic figure of the Adam Kadmon (Sky Man). In Hebrew, this head is denominated as Chokmah or *Wisdom.*

As Schonfield notes, the Greek Sophia represented as a woman rather than a man. He was not surprised to find in Templar hands, according to Inquisition records, a *casket* surmounted by "a great head of gilded silver, most beautiful, and constituting the image of a woman."

Schonfield concludes that the Templars must have had access to Gnostic mythology, which in turn is traced to extremely ancient cosmologies. He notes that in the Bible there is an echo in *Proverbs* viii, where Wisdom (feminine), like the masculine Logos (Word) of the Gospel of John, was in the Beginning with God, and beside Him when he created the Earth. In the Gnostic systems Wisdom (Sophia) was captured by the Powers of the material world and forced to prostitute herself. It was to redeem her, and thus "restore all things," says Schonfield, that the Archetypal Man appeared on Earth.

In the Gnostic doctrine proposed by Simon Magus Sophia (Wisdom) is equated with Ennoia (the First Thought) of God. According to a Gnostic hymn:

She passed from body to body,
Always suffering disgrace from it;
Last of all
She was manifest as a prostitute;
This is the lost sheep.
For he sake He came,
To free her from her bonds,
And to offer men salvation
Through their recognition of him.

Simon appears to be stating that the wisdom is transmittable, 'it passed from body to body'. Even more intriguingly, he states that he found the 'lost sheep' in the prostitute in Tyre named Helen. G.R.S. Mead, writing in

Simon Magus: Gnostic Magician tells us this Helen was of unsurpassing beauty and the Trojan War came to pass on account of her. Sophia took up residence in this Helen, and thus when all the Powers laid claim to her, there arose faction and war among those nations to who she was manifested.

It is of immense value to us to ponder Schonfield's next remark. He states that the followers of Simon Magus worshipped Helen as the Goddess of Wisdom Athena (whose temple, the Parthenon, was rededicated to Mary)! This great goddess, in turn, was identified in Egypt as Isis. Plutarch states that Isis was sometimes called *Sophia*. She is also called As-Tarte or Is*, the goddess worshipped by Solomon and for whom his temple was built. Each of these goddesses, in turn is the Babylonian goddess *Inanna.

Schonfield concludes that there is no doubt that the beautiful woman's head of the Templars represents Sophia in her female and Isis aspect, *and she was linked with Mary Magdalene in the Christian interpretation.*

16.
MARY MAGDALENE AND THE SKULL OF GOD

Jesus' baptism, Mary Magdalene's illumination, the lost secret of the Templars: all revolved around a mysterious talking head or skull or the contents it protected.

This treasure skull, I propose, is a skill, a body of knowledge once shared by Jesus and MM (as well as Job's daughters).

A favorite painting of MM that combines many symbols of her secrets is Georges De La Tour's *The Penitent Magdalen.* The Illuminator poses before the lighted taper presented to the illuminati. She has a skull in her lap.

Probably painted between 1638 and 1643, it's one of four representations that La Tour did of the penitent Magdalene. Today it hangs in the Metropolitan Museum of Art in New York City. La Tour was known for his incredible use of realism as well as his preoccupation with the use of light. If we view this painting from outside the box we can certainly see that La Tour may even have seen the light, so to speak. It's loaded with symbols carrying mystical meaning that lead us deeper into the mysteries of Mary Magdalene.

The Penitent Magdalene. Georges La Tour.

Traditional readings of this painting, as for example the commentary provided in *The Guidebook to the Metropolitan Museum*, say La Tour's *The Penitent Magdalen* is unique in depicting MM at the dramatic moment of her conversion. Her jewels lay on the table beside her, having just cast them aside, though she still wears the luxurious clothes of her former life. In her lap, she holds a skull, a common feature of allegorical paintings of MM. It is usually interpreted as a symbol of mortality. In fact, the museum guidebook states as much saying, "The skull upon which her clasped hands rest may stand for peaceful acceptance of death."

MM is portrayed in front of an elaborate silver mirror that symbolizes luxury. The flame of the candle provides a soft and almost mysterious air to the work. To the writer of the *Guidebook* the self-consuming candle reflected in the mirror suggests the frailty of human life.

Interpreting the taper or candle as symbolic of the frailty of human life is certainly poetic enough for some. On the other hand, skeptics might argue that sometimes a candle is just a candle. But hang fire. This is a religious painting. It can only be fully understood when its components are interpreted in religious terms. Putting a religious scope on these symbols reveals that there's a lot more meaning intended here.

In religious symbolism, the candlestick is the symbol of spiritual illumination, of the Light, and of the seed of life and of salvation, says Cirlot in *The Dictionary of Symbols*. In Christian symbolism it is the divine light shining into the world and Christ as the light of the world. These suggest our Lord's words, "I am the light of the world." [John 8:12]

They also represent His two-fold nature - human and divine, when two candlesticks are used.

This interpretation changes things a bit, doesn't it? We now see Mary Magdalene holding a symbol for a body of wisdom (the *caput mortem* or dead head of God ) and posing beside a symbol for the divine light of Christ.

Another layer of meaning is revealed in this symbolism when viewed through a Hebrew lens where the candle is a reference to the *menorah*, the seven-branched 'candlestick of the Children of Israel', which represents the divine presence.

Following the trail of symbolism of the candlestick as the menorah leads to quite a surprising and astounding conjunction of facts.

According to Exodus (25:31-32), the menorah was made of pure gold. It had six branches, three on each side with three bowls made like almonds ... in one branch; and three bowls made like almonds in the other branch (25:33). The seven candles symbolize the sun, moon, and principal planets, also the seven days of the week *and the seven stars of **the Great Bear, Ursa Major***.

Once again, we find ourselves in the grip of a riddle or a pun. To release ourselves from this grip we need to recall that Mount *Moriah* is cognate with Mount *Meru*, the world axis. Meru is also another name for the Great Bear.

Hermes with the menorah.

With its almond-shaped bowls the menorah 'candlestick' thus represents an almond tree. Why almonds?

The almond tree bears its blossoms in the midst of winter, on a naked, leafless stem, and these blossoms seem at the time of their fall *exactly like white snow-flakes* or like manna?

This description may have been meant to remind us of Aaron's *rod that budded.* In the Bible, Aaron ('Ark', 'enlightened') is the brother of Moses and his spokesman in Egypt, and the first high priest of the Hebrews. He is presented as the instrument of God in performing many signs, such as the turning of his rod into a serpent and causing the rod to bud, blossom, and bear almonds. He may well have been the traditional 'head' of the priesthood. (It is also interesting to note that the Gospel of Luke tells us that John the Baptist was the son of Elizabeth, an elderly woman 'of the daughters of Aaron'.)

When the miracle occurred, the rod, having no root, bore leaves, flowers and almonds overnight (Numbers 17;8).

A similar blossoming rod is highlighted in a story recounted by Saint Jerome (*c.* 341-420). He wrote that all Mary's suitors brought a rod to the high priest of the temple, but Joseph's was the only one that blossomed. This was a sign from heaven that he was chosen to be her husband.

Aaron's rod is considered a branch that grew on the Tree of Life. Moreover, the menorah was placed in the Holy Place of the Temple on Mount *Moriah* in Jerusalem, where the original Tree of Life was said to have grown.

An essential clue relating to the (almond) Tree of Life and the menorah is found in the earliest known name for Mount Moriah (the site of Solomon's Temple), *Luz*.

It was at this mysterious place called *Luz* ('light', 'almond') that Jacob lay his head on a *stone* and saw a ladder with angels on either side. He ascended this ladder to a heavenly realm. Upon his return he declared the spot of real estate (the oracle) a "blessed gate to god."

And Jacob rose up early in the morning, and took the stone that he had put for his pillows, and set it up for a pillar, and *poured* ***oil*** *upon the top of it*." Gen. 28:13-15, 18

Why Jacob poured oil on top of this pillar/tower is a mystery, and one that made even more intriguing to us in light of MM's oil and tower connections. The fact that the Hebrew for oil is *shemen ha Mishcha* and is traditionally reckoned as the "anointing oil" of the messiahs should give us a clue. Near it in pronunciation is *shaman*. *Shem* is the Babylonian word for Name. *Shambhala* shares the shem root. From shem derives the *Semite*. By far the most interesting *shem* word is *shem-an-na*, which Gardner renders as "the highward fire-stone of the white powder gold." This, he says, is the Philosopher's Stone of the Messiah.

Nothing should grab us more than to learn that the base of the oiled almond tree of *Luz* is hollow. Through this 'hole' one enters an underground passage; this passage leads to the city itself, which remains completely hidden.

French mystic René Guénon saw Luz as another version of the archetypal mountain/tree/cave complex symbolizing Shambhala. *Luz* is called 'the blue city'. Writing in *History of the Cross*, he says that, in India, it is said that the blue color of the atmosphere is produced by reflection of light on the southern face of mystic Mount *Meru* -- the Cosmic Axis, the Tree of Life – which, it is thought, is a Tree of Sapphire. The stem of the menorah candlestick is thought to represent the *Babylonian Tree of Light*, the *Cosmic Tree*, the *Cosmic Axis*. Again, the menorah symbolizes Meru.

As a matter of fact, the place name (or description), Luz, is the exact clue that will lead us to an extraordinary discovery. It is one that answers one of the greatest mysteries of the Magdalene… the meaning of her name.

17.
THE LOST MEANING OF MAGDALENE

So, what does this incredibly provocative sounding place name *Luz* mean? The Hebrew word *luz*, translated "hazel" in the King James Bible (Gen. 30:37), is translated as "almond" in the Revised Version, New King James Version, New International Version and the New Revised Standard Version. It is probable that *luz* means the wild almond. In fact, it means "almond tree" in Aramaic, Arabic, Egyptian and Ethiopic.

According to *The Torah Anthology*, the city of Luz (Mount Moriah) was, indeed, associated with an immense 'almond tree'. This apparently harkens back to the Tree of Life – an almond tree – and the *water of life* that nourished it (more later), located in the center of the Garden of Eden. It is said that the 'Angel of Death' could not enter this city, and wielded no power over it.

This association Luz ('almond') = candlestick = menorah with the lit candle beside Mary Magdalene in LaTour's *Penitent Magdalene* could well be a lightly veiled reference to the almond Tree of Life planted at Luz.

This is highly important in and of itself. However, let's remove another layer of obscurity from this symbolism by noting that *luz* is the Portuguese and Spanish word for *light.*

I repeat for emphasis. *Luz* means *light.*

Think *illumination* with *ilu* as the root for a very good example of how this carried over into the English. In fact, a whole cluster of words beginning with *ilu* or *lu* -- *lux*, *luke, lucis* and *Lucifer* -- mean 'light' (and then, of course, there is *lust*).

Interestingly, the English word *almond* is composed of the two words *al* 'light' (the same as *il* and *el*, the Old Testament name for the *Shining Ones*), and *mond*, which is 'mound' or 'mount'. Hence, almond, , could be rendered as 'mountain of light'. That's Mount Moriah, the mount of Luz ('light'). This was the Bethel (House of God) (Genesis 28:19; Judges 1:23).

It only seems like we're going in circles here. In actuality we are tourists circling what may well be one of the deepest secrets of antiquity. The Bethel or House of God located atop the mound of Moriah was a house of light (Luz). Hence, it was the al-mond, the mound with the Tree of light.

These puns suggest that Solomon's Temple was a house of light ☉. Normally, when one thinks of a lighthouse the image of a tall, tower-like structure topped by a powerful light used as a beacon giving guidance through signals comes to mind. But Solomon's Temple is never described in these terms. Well, usually not anyway…

Before making the connection between the meaning of the word 'Magdalene' and the tower of Solomon's Temple I'd like to make one more highly important connection. The word *menorah* is strikingly similar to *menhir*, in archaeology, the name given to the single standing stones of Western Europe, and by extension to those of other lands. *Menorah*, *menhir*. In English the two words are almost interchangeable.

Traditionally, menhir applies to two to three hundred *ton* stones that pre-historic people moved to Brittany as stone markers. Often these phallic stone pillars were sited over or beside burial places. More often yet, these stones were placed at locations of pilgrimage. There are 'power places' where one breathes in spirit, where one can bathe in energies and feel a sense of the divine in their being. The ancients made treks to such geysers of cosmic energy to awaken their inner faculties. Jerusalem was certainly such a place in the ancient world.

Today we call the spiritual forces 'telluric'. They are often associated with subterranean water flows. The telluric forces 'snake' through the ground. The tall stones marked the location where these serpents rose to the surface and took flight. This may explain why the ancients represented them by winged serpents and sometimes birds: the 'sirens'. When the ancients transported enormous menhir stones and erected them at particular dots of real estate it was not for aesthetic reasons. It was for religious reasons.

Among the roles played by the menhir was that of tomb-guardian. In Celtic tradition, such pillars were raised in honor of important Druids and sited on the borders of the lands of the living looking out over the Happy Fields where the dead dwelt. Caesar regarded menhirs as images of Mercury or Hermes. In this context the stone is akin to the Tree of Life and the World Axis.

Thus, the words menorah and menhir share not only phonetic resonance, but share the exact same meanings.

MAGDALENE = LIGHT

This conjunction or cross of facts leads us to an astounding insight into the meaning of Mary Magdalene's name never before seen in print.

I am now going to relate another fact to you that left me awestruck and led to this insight.

Here it is. The Latins called the almond, , *amygdala*.

Amygdala. Magdala. Without vowels both words are identical: *mgdl*. An astounding angle on the meaning of Mary Magdalene comes when we replace the word Magdalene ('Tower') with Amygdala, almond or *Luz*, and relate to the references to Luz we have documented.

What this reveals to us is that Mary Magdalene can be thought of as Mary (of) Luz, the almond-gate or Light. In other words she is Mary Lucifer. She is the Illuminator.

The accumulation of these word meanings leads me to conclude that the Tower the place name Migdal refers to is the Tree of Light, as in the cabalistic tree climbed by the initiate.

I propose that the Beloved Tower (Mary Magdalene) is the Tree of Light that opens a gate, , in the brain to the Empire of Light.

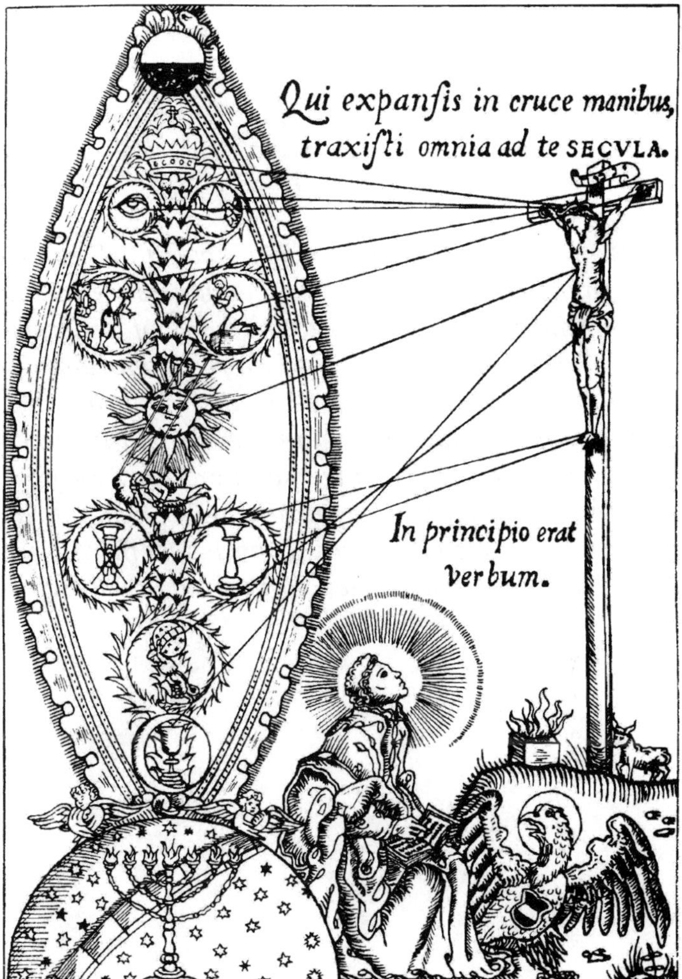
Qui expansis in cruce manibus,
traxisti omnia ad te SECVLA.
In principio erat
verbum.

The Tree of Life in an almond. The Cabalistic Tree of Life featured in the frontispiece of a sixteenth-century Gospel of John, with lines of attribution to the body of Jesus on the pillar of crucifixion. The Tree of Life rises above a sphere containing the Stairway to Heaven, the Menorah and the starry heavens. Contained within the almond is the Grail Cup, Atlas up-holding the universe, the Pillars Jachin and Boaz, Jacob's Ladder going through the Sun, Abraham prepared to sacrifice his innocent son Isaac, the All-seeing eye, the Horn of Plenty (the cornucopia) and Heavenly Crown.

The *amygdala* is the region of the human brain responsible for emotion. It is a primary arousal center, *originating in early fishes*, which is central to the expression of negative emotions in man. The amygdala coordinates the autonomic and endocrine systems. This gate is the point of exchange (another *Mercantile* term) between the worlds of matter and spirit.

To fully understand this gate we must note that the almond-shaped Egyptian glyph (*rus*) means *gate*. *Rus* is so close to *ros*, the French word for *rose*, and also *dew*. There is a definite connection to be made between the *dew* or *manna* and the gate to Heaven.

The link is provided by mystic painter William Blake, who believed the image of Jacob's Ladder as a gate to heaven was closely allied to the anatomy of the ear, whose passage he calls "the endlessly twisting spiral ascents to the Heaven of Heavens." The "opening of the ear" is the precondition for making contact with the higher worlds. Significantly, the Cathars believed the Holy Spirit of Christ entered Mary through her ear.

With this in mind let us study the alchemical image of Jacob's Ladder on the next page. Jacob dreams his dream of the ladder to heaven at Luz. An angel blows a horn – broadcasts a frequency – into Jacob's ear. Three sequences of numbers, read backwards, are Genesis 28:11-12, Genesis 27:28-36 and Deuteronomy 33:19-28. All three passages refer to the various passages in the bible dealing with the blessings of celestial dew. The roses also refer to it. Dew in French is *rosee*. In Latin *Ros*.

MUTUS LIBER IN QUO TAMEN
tota Philosophia her metica figuris hiero-
glyphicis depingitur, ter optimo maximo Deo mi-
sericordi consecratus solis que filiis artis
dedicatus authore cujus nomen
est Altus.
21. 11. 82. Neg
93. 82. 72. Neg
82. 91. 33. Tued.

From these connections it appears that there is a deep connection between almond (amydala, Magdala) and resurrection. Luz signifies a light house, a pillar of light, but also a gate of light or a stargate.

Through redefining "Magdalene" as "light house" or "tower of light" (ala the Tower of Siloam) we may be so far out the box that we're in: deep in between the temples that is.

The amygdala's resonance is amplified by a Jewish legend that tells of a special bone in the human spinal cord that never dies. And that God would use this bone in the act of resurrection, other bones coalescing with it to form the new body that, duly breathed upon by the divine spirit, would be raised from the dead. The name of the bone is *luz.*

One wonders what is the connection between the stone that Mary Magdalene moved away on Easter morning and the Luz bone.

18.
INCHRISTED LADDER = 153

There is much ambiguity in the Gospel accounts involving Mary Magdalene and these mysteries. For instance, the bible does not specifically describe the instrument of torture used to execute Jesus. It is assumed it was a cross she stood beside. However, as in the painting on the next page it is also thought of as a ladder.

The cross is an important symbol for Christians because it is on a cross that Jesus was hung, died for their sins and blazed a trail to a better world, the Otherworld. The book of Acts contradicts this saying Jesus was hung on a tree. Christian tradition reconciles the two. It maintains the True Cross was made of the same wood that grew as the Tree of Life in the Garden of Eden.

Early Christian images of Jesus didn't even represent him on a cross or a tree. Instead, he was a clean-shaven young man in the guise of Osiris or other "good shepherds" and civilization-bearers, carrying a pail, the symbol for wisdom and the inner realms or a magic wand.

Historically, the (C)*ross* did not become prominent in Christian imagery until after the 4th century. The first reference (there are few others) to the cross was established in Clement of Alexandria's unfinished *Stromateis* or 'Miscellanies' (book VI): he speaks of the Cross as "the symbol of the Lord." His contemporary Tertullian designated the body of Christian believers as *crucis religiosi*, *i.e.* "devotees of the Cross" (*Apol.*, chapter xvi). It is likely these were astronomical observations and referred to a cross in the heavens.

So, just what was it exactly that MM stood at the foot of? A closer look at the meaning of the word cross will serve us here.

Interestingly, the Greek word loosely translated cross in the original bible texts was *Stau-ros* (corresponding to the verb *stauroo*), which means 'stake' or 'pole', one without a cross beam. Some maintain that the exact translation of Stau ros is 'torture stake'.

Long before the time of Jesus pillars were featured instruments of messianic figures. The Egyptian god of Resurrection, Osiris, for example, was represented as a tall pillar placed atop a stable 'ark' or platform and flanked by two smaller pillars. The two 'Tat' or 'Tet' pillars have four arms, prefiguring the four arms of the cross. Osiris' pillar was connected with wisdom (hence the serpent, the symbol of wisdom) and was perceived as a stairway.

Historical findings, such as the relief portraying the complete Osiris pillar (or Tree) on the next page, sheds light on this subject.

Isis tending the Pillar or Tower of Osiris from Abydos, Egypt (c. 1400 BC). According to Egyptian myth, this tower held the soul of Osiris, the Egyptian savior. The hieroglyph of Osiris  *features this pillar.*

A rendition of the Tower by digital artist Dana Augustine. Beside the Ark platform are oxen. This is an interesting parallel with the biblical ark. While it was being transported on an oxcart, it teetered "because the oxen shook it". [2 Samuel 6:3]

Discovered in the Temple of Abydos at Egypt – the gate to the Underworld -- and now in the Egyptian hall at the New York Metropolitan Museum of Art this limestone fresco from the 3,300-year old chapel at Abydos that encapsulates Egyptian resurrection symbolism.

Significantly, *stau ros* is the mirror image of *ros stau*, the name of the secret sanctuary located in the Am-Tuat, the Underworld of Osiris described in the Egyptian *Book of the Dead. Ros* is a Hebrew word meaning 'dew' and 'wisdom', allowing 'pillar of wisdom' as one interpretation of *Stau ros*. In my opinion, this word play connects the myths, mysteries and metaphysics of the resurrection of Jesus with the resurrection science of Osiris.

In the relief we see Ramses I offering a platter (Grail) of food – a *cornucopia* -- including grapes, and a floral offering to the massive Osiris symbol. Isis stands beside the pillar. Its hieroglyph 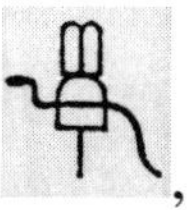, which features the levitating serpent is the symbol *ta-wer* and meant '"Eldest Land." In addition, the growth of the religion of Osiris, says Egyptologist Richard H. Wilkinson in *Reading Egyptian Art*, seems to have been responsible for the reinterpretation of the sign as a reliquary for the *head* of the god, which was supposed to reside at Abydos. In other instances, he says, the *ta-wer* is represented in scenes that allude to the concept of rebirth.

It is clear that this sign functioned as a symbol both for Osiris and his earthly domain, but also of the underworld Empire of the god accessed via Abydos and the hope of the afterlife.

Isis and the Tower of Osiris. From a bas-relief at Abydos. It may house the head of Hat.hor  *, known as the Syrian Ishtar Massey called Mufkt.*

The Ta-Wer of Osiris overlaid upon the human body reveals a powerful insight. This tower or pillar is our body.

The chakras, the body and the pillar.

I have presented the Ta-wer of Osiris for the reason that Jesus and Mary Magdalene are often compared to Isis and Osiris. The Ta-Wer of Osiris is also often called Jacob's Ladder or the Stairway to Heaven. On the previous page is another scene from the temple of Abydos, Egypt that connects to MM features Isis setting up the Pillar/Tower with what Egyptologist E.A. Wallis Budge says in *Osiris and the Egyptian Resurrection* is a *BOX* containing the *HEAD of Osiris* upon it. In Budge's illustration below, a priest anoints it with *holy oil* (or procures the oil from it).

THE CATHAR CROSS

In one incredibly provocative watermarks catalogued by Harold Bayley, an ox is seen with the serpent of Ascelpius, the symbol of healing, wound around a cross or a Tree of Life. Bayley does not offer an interpretation of this remarkable watermark. I propose the ox is the symbol for the Ark of the Covenant, which was carried on an ox cart. From the serpent's mouth emerges three circles bound together . This symbol is called the *trefoil*, the emblem of the Trinity. Notably, it is the symbol for the fifth element, *Wood*, also known as *quintessence*.

It is clear that this mark is describing the Ta-wer of Osiris.

The word Chirst, "anointed" comes from the Greek *krisma* (which rings of *charisma*), and *krio*, "to anoint." Thus we have a *krio*, a HORN, or vessel, in which the anointing oil poured upon Jesus' body is stored.

Cathar Pillar of 'Osiris' watermark.

There is an additional interesting function of Isis' Ta-wer that is worth noting. Literally translated, says Wilkinson in *Reading Egyptian Art*, the Egyptian word Ta-Wer means "the Bond between Heaven and Earth" – the same meaning as the Sumerian DUR.AN.KI., according to Sitchin in *The Stairway to Heaven.* The Sumerians described the Dur.An.Ki as a tall pillar reaching into the heavens. This pillar was secured to the platform atop Mount Moriah and was used by the Shining Ones to "pronounce the word" heavenward. In other words it was an antenna of some kind.

Phonetically, the letters 'd' and 't' are interchangeable. Thus, the 'Duranki' could be rendered as the 'Tur' or Tower (of) Anki. Anki is very close to wise Enki, the head of the Annunaki who as symbolized by a serpent ala the serpent and the Tree of Eden. The Plain of Dura is the location where Nebuchadnezzar erected the Golden Image.

Now, this is quite interesting as at Abydos we see the Head of Osiris 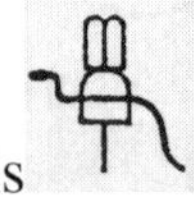 is placed upon a platform that resembles the Ark of the Covenant. Housed in Solomon's Temple, which was built on the same site as the Anuannki communications tower, the Ark was a device the Israelites used to communicate with Yahweh. In it were stored the Tablets or Commandments from Heaven.

Turning once more to Sitchin's *Stairway to Heaven* we find a line drawing of a Sumerian cylinder seal depicting the appearance of a deity to a shepherd. The deity, probably the sun god Shamash, appears through the double mountain. Significantly, additional names for Abydos are

Abju and *Abtu*, which was *Abz* or *Abyss*. Abz matches the Sumerian AB.ZU, 'Great Deep', the domain of Enki from whence came the gods of the Sumerians. We note that despite its simplicity the pillar beside the gate of the Sumerian god is a near perfect match for the pillar of Osiris.

A RELIC OF THE DESPOSYNI

In *The Magdalene Legacy* Laurence Gardner points out that the 3rd century Fisher King **Aminadab**, who was the grandson of Mary Magdalene's son Josephes, entered into an historically significantly marriage that cemented the Grail bloodlines of Jesus and his brother, James.

Pictured on the next page is "The Symbolic Quadriga of Aminadab", a 13th century medallion in a window at St. Denis, Paris. As we can see, it is a ringer for the Pillar/Tower of Osiris. Jesus is hanging from this Tree of Life, as prescribed in Acts 5:30, 10:39 and 13:29. One 13th century French commentator on the Song of Songs, Honorius of Autun, explains that Aminadab standing in the pillar is represents the Crucifixion. The Ark of the Covenant is seen to be the pedestal for the Cross, as in the example of the Abydos pillar. This Ark-Cross combination *is* the *Quadriga of Aminadab.*

The Symbolic Quadriga of Aminadab. *Note Jesus' head is pointed at approximately 25 Sagittarius as the Eagle is Scorpio and the angel is Aquarius... So did the wormhole take him to a Sagittarius star wormhole?*

Located a few miles north of the Ile de Citie, the Abbey of St. Denis, patron saint of Paris, Abbot Suger envisioned the church as the center of a new illuminated Christianity. In his three books on the building and consecration of the church, the brilliant Abbot penned thirteen separate inscriptions celebrating the Holy Light. In one of these illustrious inscriptions, a verse inscribed on the golden doors of west façade Suger tells us:

"Bright is the noble work, this work shining nobly/ Enlightens the mind so that it may travel through the true lights/To the True Light where Christ is the true door."

From such words Suger developed his theory of *lux continua*, or continuous light. His aim was to bring the True Light of God into the world.

Named after Denis the old abbey church of St. Denis had been completed in 775. The abbey had been founded in the seventh century by the Frankish king Dagobert in honor of Denis, and his legendary companions Rusticus and Eleutherius. King Dagobert II, and the Merovingian dynasty from which he came, have been romantically mythologized in the annals of both local legend and modern mystical pseudo-history, which upholds them as the supposed bloodline of Christ.

The Templar are often connected with the Merovingians. Their bloodline is called the 'Red Serpent'. The Merovingian sculpture shown here demonstrates their belief in Christ as the Serpent, and connects them with the Shining Ones.

Two crosses flank the serpent around the Tree of Life; symbol of the Shining Ones. Merovingian sculpture in the church at Pouille in Vendee.

According to legend, the Merovingian bloodline was founded by King Merovee, who is said to have been the spawn of a "Quinotaur", a giant fish or a sea monster, who raped his mother when she went out to swim in the ocean. He is called "Merovee', because in French, *Mer* means sea.

This half-human, half-fish is E.A. or one of his successors.

Dagobert's name reveals the divine origins of his bloodline. "Dagobert" comes, of course, from Dagon. 'Dag' means "fish". The word "Bert" has its roots in the word *Bahir*. So Dagobert's name literally means "Priest-King of the House of the Fish."

Significantly, Suger's medallion was placed in St. Denis shortly after the Templars returned to Paris from Jerusalem where they recovered the secrets of the Grail family. I have proposed elsewhere that this is the skull or 'head' called Baphomet, which the Catholic Church claimed the Templars used to perform miracles. Is the 'Quadiga' the property of Aminadab's royal family, i.e. of Jesus and Mary Magdalene? Is this evidence of Isis-Osiris (or Anunnaki) technology in the Grail family? What if the skill MM possessed was what modern science calls *hyperdimensional physics* and Jesus crossed the galaxy in a stargate or a wormhole?

Isis wearing the fish and bird headpiece.

In this detail we can see that Isis has a combined FISH and BIRD HEADPIECE. She tends Osiris's HEAD/BOX. To the right of his 'Head' are the hieroglyphs for 'bread' , 'water' (or 'vibration') and the Key of Life . Beside the Key of Life is the *Uas* scepter. In the next register to the right is the glyph shown in detail to the right (below). It is called the *Asgat-Nefer* glyph.

The top of Osiris's head (left). The Asgat-Nefer glyph (right). It means 'Harmony of Water'. Its presence suggests the Pillar of Osiris emitted water or even was a ***fountain of Living Waters****.*

Tu uab *"holy mountain". (This place name is followed by tubaat, a hill of metal, or a hill containing mines. It is very close to Tubal Cain, the smith).*

Ta aub-t, 'to purify'.

Egyptologists translate this glyph as "beautiful water" or "good water." However, according to Stephens S. Mehler, writing in *The Land of Osiris*, the indigenous Egyptian teacher Abd'El Hakim Awyan translates it as "Harmony of Water." Harmony in this sense, says Mehler, means *beyond polarity consciousness, beyond a concept of good and evil, the state of balance or bliss.* (In other words beyond the fear of death?)

In *The Making of the Egyptians*, Michael Rice notes that there is a special usage of this hieroglyph in the Pyramid Texts. The meaning here is 'Pure', 'Clean', as in Utterance **513** from the Pyramid Texts: 'Be pure: occupy your seat in the Bark of Re: row over the sky and mount up to the distant ones: row with the imperishable stars, navigate with the Unwearying Stars'.

The Bark of Re, I propose, is the Stargate of the Gods.

THE PULSER AND EMMITTER

Before her departure into the underworld Inanna had warned her chamberlain to send help if she did not return. He appealed to Inanna's Uncle, Enki, who crafted two beings and sent them on a rescue mission. To one of these beings he gave the Food of Life, to the other the Water of Life. Both were likely alchemical substances. According to Laurence Gardner the 'bread' of life is 'monatomic gold', an alchemical powder with many magical capabilities, including possibly the ability to open gateways to other realms. So prepared, these helpers descended into the underworld to rescue Inanna. Then,

> *Upon the corpse, hung from the stake,*
> *They directed the* **Pulser and the Emitter.**
> *Upon the flesh that had been smitten,*
> *Sixty times the Food of Life,*
> *Sixty times the Water of Life,*
> *They sprinkled upon it;*
> *And Inanna arose.*

The Pulser and the Emitter? Is this some form of a device that transmitted or spit the Water of Life capable of raising the dead to life? If MM personified this goddess is it possible she possessed such a device too? We shall return to this question momentarily.

Inanna's descent into this holy hole, ☉ (later known as Hell), lasted three days and culminated in the Day of Joy, when Tammuz was restored to life, wholeness. This sacred drama was re-enacted at the Temple of Solomon in Jerusalem (Ezekiel 8:14) during which the women "wailed" (crying 'hallileua') for Tammuz.

As I have proposed, this state of bliss was triggered by Mary Magdalene's oil. This substance was created by the Head of God, the Pillar of Osiris.

Turning to E.A. Wallis Budge's Egyptian Hieroglyphic Dictionary we find additional meanings of significance to the Divine Head:

'Mer – Head'
'Mer – Sacred Serpent'
'Mer – Likeness'
'Mer – To see'
'Merr – Beloved one' (the root of marry?)
'M'Her – Vessel or container'

This last definition – vessel or container – is most interesting in light of the Cathar symbol of the fleur-de-lis topped vase engraved MR.

The Cathars called a vase or container MR the 'Flower of Light'. It shows two serpents gathered at the head of the container topped by a fleur-de-lis.

MR (*mister* or provider of *mist*) is a key mystery term.

MR is a Sumerian term for *brightness*, *shining*, as in Mar-Duk, the Bright One. (MR is the root of the name Nimrod or Ni-Meru-od).

Speaking of towers and plates, let us return to the tower on a platter presented to King Tutankhamun. The two Nubians guard a pillar, which we can now appreciate, is the 'head' of Osiris.

In this context the two guardians fulfill a role strikingly similar to the two cherubim who guarded the Gate of Eden. Because Adam and Eve were disobedient to Yahweh, the god of Eden sent them out of the Garden (Genesis 3:23). He placed at the east of Eden Cherubims, and a flaming sword, which turned every way (it rotated gyroscopically), to keep the way of the way of the tree of life. Significantly, the Tree of Life is equated with the Cross.

Two Nubian figures stand beside the Osiris Ta-wer pillar in the middle of the Egyptian symbol for gate.

Now, let us examine a depiction of this tower from Denderah on the next page. Here we find that the lotus ship of the gods has been added. This ship clearly resembles the shape modern science uses to depict a wormhole:

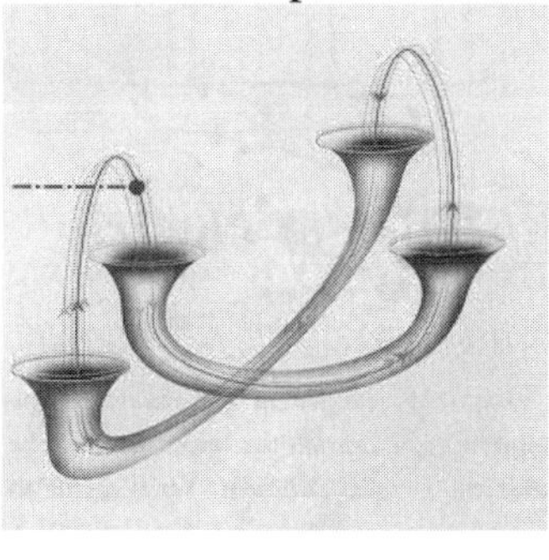

At Abydos we see this head is placed upon a platform that resembles the Ark of the Covenant, as well as the modern scientific symbol for a wormhole.

The striking similarity between the shape used by modern science to depict a wormhole and the Egyptian image of the (b)ark Osiris rode into the Nether World  raises astounding implications.

If we view Jesus and Mary Magdalene as exemplars of the archetypes once typified by Isis and Osiris, then this imagery suggests we must view them as advanced scientists, and dedicated esoteric researchers, who were more like quantum physicists than holier-than-thou religious figure-heads dressed in expensive clothing.

The work or reanalyzing Egyptian myth and Christian imagery through this lens needs to be performed by both spiritual theorists and physicists.

Ancient Egyptian hieroglyphs, in particular, are loaded with wormhole imagery and concepts about the fabric or cloth of the cosmos. For instance, take the Egyptian glyph for *Nether*, meaning 'cloth'.

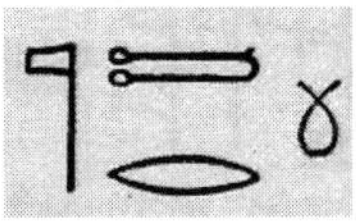

The Nether glyph contains an ax or flag, the open-mouth Ra symbol, the Egyptian *shen* glyph for the heron, the bird of light, and a fourth symbol, , which, amazingly, resembles not only a tuning fork, but also the symbol used by modern science to represent a wormhole.

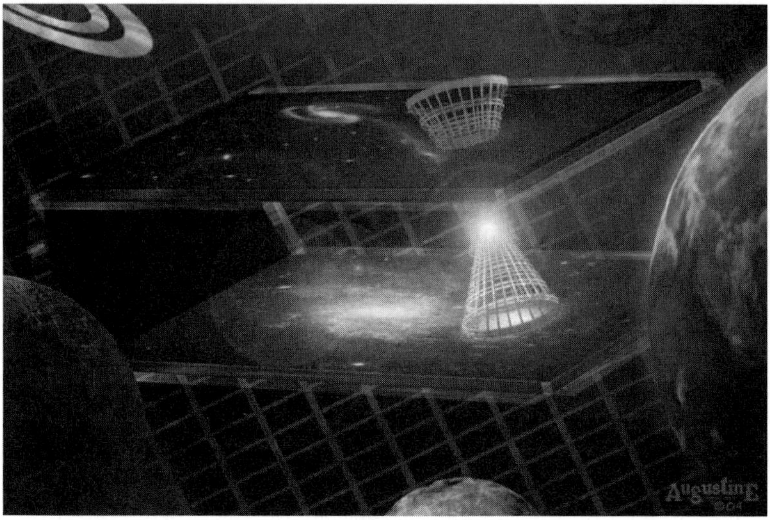

Representation of an Einstein-Rosen bridge.

In addition to a folded space, science imagines a wormhole as a serpent-rope or umbilical cord threading its way through the cosmos. Our entire conception of the Bible would be changed if it were revealed that this is the serpent of wisdom that is 'slayed' by all the heroes.

Who devised the Egyptian symbol system? The NTR, or *Neter*  (also rendered as *nuter* or *Nu*), meaning "one who watches." Neter is also the Egyptian name for "divine being" or "god".

This brings up the subject of 'celestial intermediaries' and the critical Gnostic word play between *Nazarene*, one title applied to Jesus, and *Neter*. Nazarene has been thought to refer to Nazareth, the town where Jesus is alleged to have lived. Bethlehem, Nazareth and Galilee all claim to be the home of Jesus. Scholars now claim, however, that the town of Nazareth did not exist at the time of Jesus.

Therefore, Nazarene must refer to something else. The words *Naaseni* and *Nazarene* are believed by some to have originated from *nazar*, meaning keep, guard, protect, and from *naas* or *nahash*, Hebrew for serpent.

Historian Michael Grant interprets *Nazoraios* as "guardian," and says it comes from the root *netser* (net-ser), meaning, "shoot" or "branch" (*klone* in Latin). Jesus was known as the *branch of David*, the long-awaited Messiah. (Isn't it interesting that the word "branch," earlier associated with 'mist', reappears in this context?)

Grant identifies Jesus as a member of an exclusive religious sect of priest-kings who guarded or "watched" the secrets of the ancient science of salvation and enlightenment. This group inherited this role from Egypt and the ancient *Neter* (also rendered as *nuter* or *Nu*), meaning "one who watches."

The word *neter* passed over directly into the Coptic (Egyptian Christian) language as *nouti* and *noute* (phonetically *note*), both terms meaning "God" and "Lord."

God, Lord, Watcher: all these terms were applied to Jesus. The secret knowledge I propose Jesus possessed and protected – and then passed to Mary Magdalene -- was the secrets of the transformation of humans into a neter (Shining One) preparatory to scaling the Stairway to Heaven and sailing to Neter-Neter land, the home of the gods.

19.
MISTRESS OF THE WATERS

We will now further explore the premise that Mary Magdalene's vigil at the foot of the cross[Mark 15:40] and Jesus' appearance to her after his Resurrection[Matthew 28:9], were part of an elaborate alchemical ceremony designed to help Jesus' body *resonate* with the *rays* or vibrations of the Empire of Light. Her liquid 'Christos potion (po-*shen*)' prepared Jesus, who called himself "the Door," to rise to the higher plane of the Empire of the Illumined and then fed "the dead" Jesus upon his *rai*-sing or return from that realm.

This places MM on the level of Isis who also raised Osiris and was impregnated by him after he had risen to a higher plane.

MM's oil was '*resin* for the *raisin* one', the bread/manna/Christ, symbolized in Cathar symbolism by a cluster of grapes (called *raisins* when dried in the sun). In fact, rai-sin comes from the Latine *racemus*, bunch of grapes. The (cosmic) rays that compose this resin trigger the Christos substance that *rises* within and *raises* us from sin.

A key reference to this fragrant 'raisin resin' is found in *Song of Songs*:

Until the king returns
I lie in fragrance,
Sweet anticipation
Of his entrance.

Between my breasts he'll lie –
Sachet of spices,
Spray of blossoms plucked
Form the oasis.

The term 'sachet' is important. A 'sachet' (s_-sh_') is a small packet or sack of perfumed powder. Sack carries with it a few thousand years of commercial or mercantile history and therefore cues us to evaluate its Mercurial meaning among the good people. It goes back to Middle Eastern antiquity and is easily recognizable in the Greek *sakkos*, the Hebrew *saq*, and the Akkadian *saqqu.*

Continuing, *sack* is the name of various light, dry, strong wines from Spain. The phonetically similar Japanese word *sake* is a liquor made from fermented rice. Of course, Christians believe Christ (the Grape) died for our *sake.*

"*A spray of blossoms plucked from the oasis.*" This line from the *Song of Songs* is more than poetry. I believe it is a major clue to identifying the nature of MM's mysterious balm that she rubbed or sprayed on Jesus (which, Tantrists believe, may have taken place while they were in the *sack*).

A spray is water or other liquid moving in a mass of dispersed droplets, as from a wave.

The noun spray is a dispenser that turns a liquid (such as perfume) into a fine spray.

The flower sacred to Astarte was the lily, the Easter flower. The alchemists portrayed Jesus as the spray of the blue lily.

Spray may be written (s)pray with the emphasis on *pray* (to ask) or (sp)ray, meaning essentially 'spread rays'.

A spray is also a flower arrangement consisting of a single branch or shoot bearing flowers and foliage.

Another word for a *fine spray* is *mist*. The connection between the word-concepts *messiah* and *mist*, I hypothesize, explains why the alche-mists portrayed 'Christos' as a blue lily spraying from Mary – the Oasis. In the illustration on the previous page, 'Mary' sits in a radiant orb. Mary and Jesus are one substance. In the five-part blue lily is Jesus.

'Mary' is symbolic of the mother of the sun, the Milky Way galaxy. What is located at the center of the Milky Way? Suns.

The fantastic collection of exotic objects found at the center of our Galaxy have been feeding the interests of astronomers for many decades. The Galactic Center harbors a variety of intriguing puzzles, including a strangely quiescent supermassive black hole, a collection of wispy magnetic filaments, a few dense stellar superclusters which host mysterious and massive stars, a star with a tail, and a family of gas streamers spiraling toward a central dark mass. Just to name a few.

The complex radio source Sagittarius A appears to be located almost exactly at the Galactic Center, and contains an intense compact radio source, Sagittarius A*, which many astronomers believe correspond with the supermassive black hole at the center of our Galaxy. They predict that in approximately 200 million years there will be an episode of starburst in the galactic center, with many stars forming rapidly and undergoing supernovas at a hundred times the current rate. The starburst may also be accompanied by the formation of galactic jets as matter falls into the central black hole.

David Aguilar, Harvard-Smithsonian Center for Astrophysics

A starburst galaxy. It is thought that the Milky Way undergoes a starburst of this sort every 500 million years.

Galactic jets are powerful jets of plasma which spray from the centers of active galaxies and quasars. A jet is created from subatomic particles and magnetic fields in the accretion disk of the supermassive black hole in the nucleus of an active galaxy. Similar jets, though on a much smaller scale, can develop around the accretion disks of neutron stars and stellar black holes.

Does the Cathar glyph on the left symbolize a galaxy spraying cosmic material represented by the figure 8 and the star?

One of the conclusions drawn in this work is that MM possessed a means to harvest a transformative substance spit from the center of our galaxy. This theory suggests that this material was originally ejected during a starburst event. One objection to this theory arises from the fact that the Milky Way has not gone starburst for over 200 million years.

This does not diminish my enthusiasm for this proposal. One well-known starburst galaxies is M82, located in ***Ursa Major***, the Great Bear. M82 is a tremendous star factory, observations show. Holy Grail legends are precise in locating Ursa Major as the source of high frequency cosmic rays that bathe Earth. This gusher of cosmic energy may be the source.

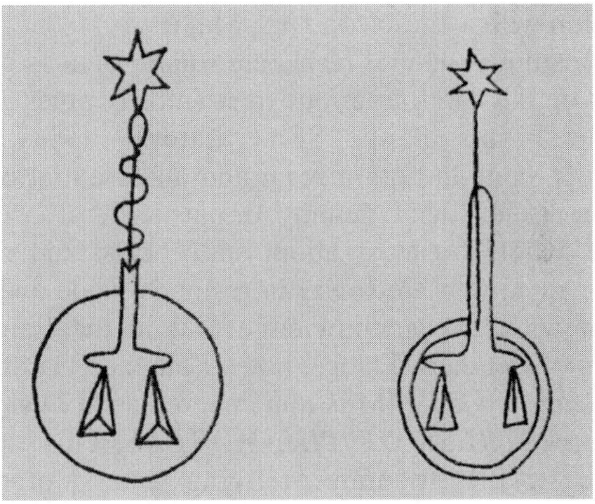

Two more Cathar glyphs that may show the galaxy spraying cosmic material.

The 'spray' that comes from this oasis, likely through the star nursery at the center of the Milky Way galaxy, is a mist of subatomic particles, and possibly even souls.

And so, we are confronted with an incredible story. When Mary washed Jesus' feet with her tears, I propose, it referred to this celestial substance. She knew how to draw from this medicinal fountain of the living water and the oil of joy. I find myself opining that this substance may have originated in Ursa Major, likely from the collision of two galaxies. While I cannot prove it at this time, new lines of research will soon offer such proof. After all, science now understands that tiny particles can communicate with each other over tremendous distances. It seems likely that the ancients also knew that a particle on earth is capable of interaction with a particle in Ursa Major.

Interestingly, natural resins are found often as globules or *tears* on the bark of various trees (mostly pines and firs) or other living plants. Some natural resins, called oleoresins, contain both a resin and an essential oil; they are often viscid, sticky, gummy, or plastic.

This whole business about spray, mist and celestial tears (or rays) that are found in resins is made even more relevant when we acknowledge that in the Languedoc tradition of Southern France, notes Laurence Gardner, *The Magdalene Legacy*, MM is remembered as *la Dompna del Aquae:* ***MISTRESS OF THE WATERS***. This title is a reference to the 'fountain of living waters' of the Old Testament's *Song of Solomon* (4:15), with which MM had become associated. It is thought that this title, Mistress of the Waters, is a reference to MM's sea voyage to France. However, it could equally refer to the 'heavenly waters' the Egyptians called the *Waters of Nun*.

Interestingly, according to the alchemist Fulcanelli, *alabastrum* refers to 'Pure Water' or 'Pure Matter'. Pure Water refers to the Heavenly Waters of Life.

The Greeks called the fundamental element *arche*, water.

Barbara Walker, in her *Woman's Encyclopedia of Myths and Secrets*, points out that the Vedic (early

Sanskrit) root word *puta*, "pure" or "holy," is also found in the Avestan *putika*, a mystical lake of the waters of birth.

Puta became the Spanish word for whore = *putti*. Puta, derives from the Latin term for a well, but the Latin term for grave, literally "a hole in the earth," is puticuli, meaning womb of rebirth. The Hebrew word hor means a cave, pit, or dark hole. These terms for whore were not derogatory.

As an *alche-mist* Joseph would have worked with the *arche*, the primary substance of creation, the primeval matter, the ultimate stuff of reality, which the alchemists symbolized with this symbol , the balance symbol.

MIST

The description of manna/Christ as rain is key. A synonym for rain is *mist*, defined as fine drops of a liquid, such as water, perfume, or medication, sprayed into the air. One of Mary Magdalene's specialties, according to Christian belief, is the manufacture of anointing oils and perfumes or *mists*.

Significantly, the Hebrew word *messeh* ('messiah'), which means 'anointed', is traced to the Egyptian word *messah* (' crocodile'). However, tracing this root *mes* into Egyptian hieroglyphs we find it derives from *mst* (mist). It means "*celestial tears*" or "*dew*," and portrays *three **drops*** or ***rays*** ,  of water (mist?) falling, radiating or misting from Heaven. The same hieroglyphic also means "instruction" or "teaching."

Mes or *ms* also means 'to bear', 'create', 'give birth' or 'birth'. This is an important pun on baru and the Great Bear, Ursa Major.

If one quietly contemplates these associations we see that right below the surface of the Egyptian and Christian teaching (or parallel to it), virtually intact, is an allusion to a galaxy-scale metaphysics and a spray of particles from another galaxy that instruct.

Clearly such a proposal, which unites spirit and the sciences of perfumery, astronomy, anatomy and alchemy, cannot be entirely proven through ordinary means.

Together, Isis, Osiris and Anubis are linked to the three stars of the blue-white Dog Star Sirius. Star light. Star bright. During the dog days of summer, Sirius disappears and the Nile floods. The Egyptians believed that Sirius was the *tear of Isis*, shed for the dead Osiris (who was *torn* to bits by Set), and that it would fall into the water, causing the yearly flood, a death and rebirth event. This lead to the Nile festival of the "Night of the Tear-Drop" (of Isis). Her name, Isis, means 'wisdom'. These drops of water/wisdom, the tears of Isis, were probably used to re-member or resurrect Osiris.

As Laird Scranton first pointed out in *Hidden Meanings*, the hieroglyph for '*tear*' 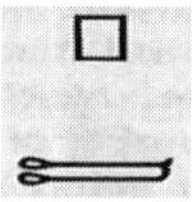 is remarkably similar in shape to the way modern science portrays the 'tearing' of space time and the birth of a wormhole.

This wormhole = tear symbolism, when applied to the *tear* of Isis raises a question. Beyond the dimensions of length, width, and breadth (one, two, and three) and beyond the dimension of space-time (four) into the fifth dimension and beyond is there a tear, a wormhole or portal, through which energy enter our region of the Milky Way? Were certain adepts able to capture this energy?

It would bring a radical new understanding if it turned out Mary Magdalene's 'tears' referred to the celestial tears, the rain (water), mist or dew of M82 (via Sirius or Venus). Particularly since shortly before the crucifixion MM also embalmed Jesus, just like Isis embalmed Osiris, preparing him for his journey to the Otherworld, when poetically speaking, he crossed the mist of the borderland between Earth and Heaven.

Interpreted in this light, Mary Magdalene's anointing of Jesus would bear a striking resemblance to the Archangel Michael's anointing of Enoch upon the prophet's arrival at the Seventh Heaven in *The Book of Enoch.* When the prophet arrived at a 'great house' of the Lord he was terrified. The Lord said to Michael: 'Go and strip Enoch of his own clothes; ***anoint him with fine oil***, and ***dress him like ourselves'***, and Michael did as he was told. He stripped me of my clothes, and *rubbed me over with* ***a wonderful oil like dew*** – with the scent of ***myrrh*** – *which* ***shone like a sunbeam***. And I looked at myself, *and I was like one of the others; there was no difference and all my fear and trembling let me.*" He had crossed the borderland into the world of the gods.

Strong religious connotations are associated with mist. Irish literary sources associate mist with the music of the

Otherworld or with the Otherworld itself. The Druids, for example, were imputed with the power to create a magical mist, the "Cleo Trom" in which to cloak themselves or make themselves invisible. In fact, according to one source, ability to raise the Druid Mist was a test of anyone claiming to be a Wizard.

Mist(s) are regarded as preludes to important revelations, prologues to manifestations. 'And the Lord said unto Moses, Lo, I come unto thee in a thick *cloud.*[Exodus 19:9] Clouds are formed when air containing water vapor or mist is cooled below a critical temperature called the *dew* point and the resulting moisture condenses into droplets on microscopic dust particles (condensation nuclei) in the atmosphere. The puns on mist and dew are evident and informative.

If this version of the anointing is the correct one, it confirms the use of perfume and reveals that Mary Magdalene was responsible for the transformation of Jesus from a man into *Christos*, the 'annointed', that would proclaim God's chosen Messiah. Henceforth, he would be portrayed in a cloud or a mist.

So let's follow the mist symbol  further.

As Egyptologist Stephen Mehler writes in *From Light Into Darkness*, according to indigenous Egyptian (or properly 'Khemetian') teaching this glyph, the *mes* or *mesu*, means *rebirth* and refers to a protective body that insures the deceased's body will not be consumed by negative entities (called jackals) nor reincarnate.

Mehler also notes that the Mesu (mist) glyph is the root of *Moses* or *Mosis*. This term should be correctly understood as that which insures rebirth, he says. Rebirth into the Otherworld, that is.

'Moses' is likely the title of the instructor who could produce this substance and the mystical awakening it caused. The Jews also call this instructor, the mist, 'the *Messiah*'. This makes clear that the terms 'Moses' and 'Mesu' or 'Messiah' are not names of people they are descriptions of a substance they can produce.

Like the Druid Mist it apparently makes one invisible to the jackals, in other words cloaked. The three rays are therefore not water, they're 'jackal skins' or 'jackal cloaks' (my term). Many described a tunnel of light that opens at the moment of death. Obviously, the jackal skin is a metaphor for a protective cloak that assists us when, at death, we tear open a hole in space and pass through the mist into the Other World, the shimmering sphere of space-time.

Following this trail, the jackal is usually associated with Anubis, the sun/son of Isis and Osiris, the Egyptian god of resurrection. This jackal-headed god was the conductor of souls to the underworld. This chain of Egyptian ideas suggests the mist glyph symbolizes the actual instructions or wisdom for making this journey.

All of these symbols represent this instruction: ,

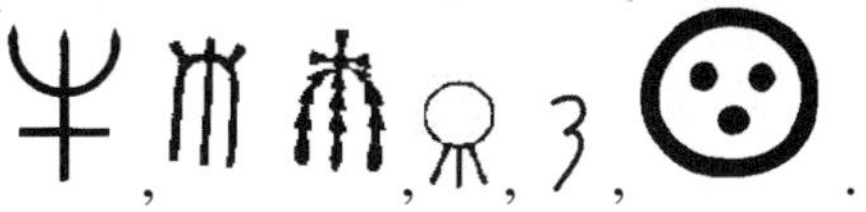

CONCLUSION
MARY, THE MAYA AND MANNA

In the wilderness of mystique that surrounds the manna/Christ substance and Mary Magdalene's important connection to it the Mayans, the indigenous people of Mexico and Central America, have vital knowledge to contribute. They describe a well of living water like Miriam's and Jacob's *and* a heavenly substance they too called *dew*. Before we explore the means by which MM might have made the Milky Way tear open and cry tears of golden rain we'll take a moment here to draw from the wisdom of the Maya concerning dew, which interestingly enough, they called *itz* (pronounced 'eats', as in the place name *Chichen Itza*).

What is *itz*? According to *Maya Cosmos* author Linda Schele, *itz* is a blessed, magical, liquid (watery) substance of heaven. As Martin Brennan notes in *The Hidden Maya* this precious substance was universally sought after by shamans through portals opened in the sky. They described it as 'cosmic sap'. Sound familiar?

It sounds exactly like manna to me, right down to the sap. Some modern critics of the Israelite story of manna believe this may simply have been an edible sap of a variety of cactus found in the Sinai Peninsula. However, the Mayans didn't find itz in the desert. They found it in the rainforest of Central America.

Adding to the Israelite-Maya connection is the Maya term *Itza*, which means both "saint and wise man" and "*water of the dew.*" This fact is one which I'd like to go into here as pertinent to the hypothesis that wise Mary Magdalene fulfilled the role of the Miriam, i.e. the prophetess who produced the water or mist of life.

In *The Mysteries of Chichen Itza*, Mayan religious interpreter Adalberto Rivera quotes Antonio Mendiz Bolio's translation of the Mayan book of prophecies, the *Chilam Balam de Chumayel*. He says the Itza were the race of mystical initiates that founded Mayan civilization. Their philosophy was embodied in a Solar Cult at Chichen Itza whose emblems were the Sun, a phallas, a serpent and the eagle. "Chitzen Itza's name means something like "*mouth of the well of the dew.*" It was ruled by high-ranking wise men who earned their posts and came to Chichen Itza from all over America. Those who emerged triumphant from the initiations of the Solar Cult became channels of divine energy. They were called "Quetzalcoatl," the feathered serpent (more momentarily).

An *Itzam* was an elite 'water wizard' who received *itz* from their encounters with the Otherworld. Notably, they accepted responsibility to wield this power wisely. Rivera reckons Chichen Itza means "*the sacred well of the Itza, the sorcerers of the water.*"

The definition of Itzam as 'water wizard' is most intriguing in light of the myth of Miriam's miraculous well and the possibility that MM took on the attributes of Miriam. Also, for the fact that Jesus appears to know the secret of a special living water that brings salvation (ala the Tower of Siloam story). As we have seen, Mary Magdalene was portrayed in the Gnostic gospels as thoroughly knowledgeable of the Otherworld. In France she was called *Mistress of the Waters*, supposedly because she traveled by water from Palestine to France. In addition, in Holy Grail myth, MM collected the transformed blood and *waters* that spurted from Jesus' body as he hung upon the cross, the mechanism that connected him with the Otherworld.

The definitions of itz and itza power my contention that the Mayans, Israelites and Jesus and Mary Magdalene experienced the same substance = manna = Christos. It was for information concerning this substance that the rabbis cornered Jesus in Capernaum. They expected Jesus to produce it. Based upon this I wonder. Is it a coincidence that it was at Capernaum that the 'Mistress of the Waters' entered Jesus' life? Based upon the Mayan model the sorcerers required super knowledge of dew (manna, bread) and water. Perhaps Jesus knew the secret of bread (manna) and MM knew the secrets of water or mist (oil, perfume). Put them together, and...

Let's resume our discussion on Itz. The scientifically minded Mayans said Itz ran from the Otherworld through the center of the Milky Way through a duct or canal they called a 'serpent rope'. *Itzamna*, the Lord of the Milky Way, controlled the portal from which it flowed at the other end. *Itzamna* (Itz-a-mna) coincidentally rings of '*Its manna*!' the exact declaration of excitement made by the

Israelites in Numbers 11 when they found this magical substance laying on the ground one morning.

Itzamna's spouse was Ix Chel. She was also known as the "Lady Rainbow" and was usually shown in Mayan art as an older woman dressed in a skirt with crossed bones on it. Ix Chel is frequently depicted with a great jug that is filled with water. As well, she was depicted with a serpent in her hand.

Somehow the Maya gleaned amazing knowledge of the Milky Way, which thcy accurately ascertained, was the giant celestial oasis in which we dwell. This knowledge is revealed by their symbolism. As noted, it is shared by the Good people of France.

How did two cultures separated by time and distance come to use the exact same obscure symbol? Did they draw from the same symbol bank? Or did some one give it to them?

In *Mayan Genesis* Maya scholar Graeme R. Kearsley connects the Maya iconography with that of India, as well as West Asia and China. Scholars have long connected the Israelites with India. Some even claim Jesus lived there. It is quite possible that India is the connecting link, although the myths of the respective peoples indicate they originated in the stars.

The connection between Mayan and Cathar symbolism returns us to Quetzalcoatl.

The Quetzalcoatl story hangs somewhat like an urban legend throughout American esoteric circles. Most people believe Quetzalcoatl was a white god figure who came mysteriously among the Aztecs, gave them direction for living, and then left them with a promise to someday return.

The belief among the Aztecs that their white god would someday return is told as the reason why the Aztecs submitted without a fight to a small band of Spanish conquerors, led by Hernando Cortez, in 1518.

Numerous traditions have made the connection between Jesus and Quetzalcoatl.

Quetzalcoatl 'earth dances' atop a Mayan pyramid with a staff in his hand. Note the crosses on his cloak. A Cathar glyph portrays a similar figure atop a Jacob's Ladder.

I am very curious about the connection between the Mayan stairway to the Milky Way glyph and its correspondence to the Cathar glyph from Southern France, very near where MM lived after the crucifixion, and these two glyphs of the figures atop Jacob's Ladders or stairways to heaven.

Is it possible the cross of Christ, called the ladder to god (Scala Dei in Latin), has been misinterpreted? Might it have been a device that certain initiates, namely Mary Magdalene, who stood at the foot of cross, and Jesus, used to connect with the galaxy in order to produce a cosmic substance? What, exactly, was this substance?

To repeat, the Mayans called it sap. Highly intrigued by this cosmic sap and wondering what it is, exactly, I consulted god or a form of god, Google.

Much to my amazement when I typed 'cosmic sap' into the search engine, and probed the consciousness of humanity, I found that sap is an acronym for 'sub atomic particle' (s.a.p.), i.e. photons, neutrinos, quarks, muons.

The incredible quantum world of subatomic particles isn't the realm of everyday human experience, what's called the 'real world', the realm in which we live, move, and have our being. It's the 'Other world'. Normally we think of subatomic particles as the stuff of particle physicists and not messiahs. However, as the master of the Word of God and Lord of the Otherworld it would seem logical that Jesus knew of this other world. Times have changed. We now know what the Word is composed of. In this way Jesus has everything to do with subatomic particles.

A question arises. Is manna/itz/Christ – or, shall we say, *Chr-itz* -- an oil imbued with a miraculous 'missing' or little known class of subatomic particle? Is it the same as *Christos* or *Chrestos*, the unidentified substance Christians were accused of being influenced by in Rome? Is this the same as the anointing oil of Mary Magdalene? If so, by what process might one distill this particle from the galaxy and manufacture this oil? Based upon the evidence I have presented in the pages I believe the answer is yes. Mary Magdalene's anointing oil was a cosmic substance. Rubbing it on one's body eliminated fear and brought about illumination, as in the example of Enoch's oil, and prepared us to climb the Stairway to Heaven. We may even be on the verge of rediscovering how to create it.

APPENDIX I

It was in the catacombs, the burial places outside the city walls of Rome that the first Christian images were made late in the second century AD (at the earliest). The Gospels, written in the first century after Jesus' crucifixion, give no description of what he looked like due to the prohibition against worshipping graven images or idols and because Jesus' appearance was unimportant. His teaching was the focus, rather than his personality, and Mary Magdalene was his chief apostle, his number one. Early Christians did not represent the person of Jesus, so much as the belief that he was the Lord (Adon), the Messiah, the Anointed One – 'Christ' in Greek -- who taught the Way. He was not the Way.

How beautiful are the feet of those who bring good news!
(Romans 10:15)

Jesus uses his rod or wand to raise Lazarus, from the catacombs of Rome.

Jesus rides a white horse and wields his rod or wand and holding a ring or chakra of power. This ring is likely taken from Babylonian ideas of the ring of cosmic sovereignty.

Beginning in the fourth century, when Christianity was proclaimed the Roman state religion by the emperor Constantine the Great (A.D. 323), these images of a magic wand (or is it a ray of light?) bearing Jesus disappear. So also does mention of Jesus and Mary Magdalene as a couple. Two centuries later Pope Gregory labeled her a prostitute. A program of disinformation by the Church began.

Constantine dammed up the stream of consciousness of mystical Christianity that had seeped into Rome from the east Mediterranean world. The connection with Oneness this stream led to offered Divinity to its aspirants. Soon, the idea that an individual could find this stream and drink from its waters on their own, with no help from a priest (or pimp) in a box became heresy. In fact, any document containing the original teachings of Jesus preserved by the Nazarenes, the Way to Divinity was suppressed, often violently.

During the first three centuries AD many of the Nazarene movement's *martyrs* ('witnesses') were *murdered*, crucified by Roman legions or fed to the lions of Rome for entertainment. They are recognized as martyrs because they have preferred to die rather than renounce their Christian faith.

According to legend, many disciples and saints, including Mary Magdalene, were sentenced to death by being thrown into a derelict hull, which had neither rudder nor gear, and cast adrift in the Mediterranean to drown. However, by God's grace (or by a ship similar to Solomon's, which moved by itself on the sea), they all arrived safely at the port of Marseilles.

Gardner tells us that after the crucifixion Mary Magdalene sought and was granted protection by young Herod –Agrippa II, who sent her to his family's estate near Lyon, France. When she fled to France some of history's greatest unsolved mysteries allegedly traveled with her. Chief among these is the Holy Grail, the awesome and terrible treasure of Jesus.

What became of Jesus' teachings? Did they go to France? If so, did they remain there?

Fascinatingly, in their book *In Search of the Holy Grail and the Precious Blood*, Ean and Deike Begg tell of the bizarre graffiti found in the chateau at Domme, France, where Knights Templar were imprisoned after the persecution by the Catholic Church in 1307. Here is found a depiction of the Crucifixion that is slightly twisted from the accepted Church version (or the Church version is twisted from the original event). Joseph of Arimathea (Jesus' brother James) is shown catching precious droplets of Jesus' blood (presumably with the Holy Grail).

On Jesus' left is a pregnant woman holding a wand or a rod. This woman, we presume, is Mary Magdalene. The wand is the tool of her husband, Jesus.

When I visited Domme in July, 2005 I was surprised to see several other astonishing details in the Templar graffiti including a fish with a Tree of Life coming out of its mouth and another larger 'fish' which will be discussed later.

As we can see the cross is portrayed atop a triangle or pyramid.

The Tree of Life is easily comparable to the Sepherotic Tree of Life. The Gnostics frequently called Jesus *the Tree of Life* and a *branch*. The Sephiroth are the ten qualities of the Mystical Tree, set forth as a major doctrine of the cabalistic *Book of Splendor* (*Sefer ha-Zohar*), which was first published about A.D. 1280 although its legend claimed a much earlier date.

The Mystical Tree stood for the "World of Union" showing the process of life flowing from divinity into the whole creation, and back again.

Cabalists call all ten Sephiroth collectively the *Merkabah* or "chariot" of God, whereby he could descend from heaven into men's souls.

This is an astonishing conglomeration of religious and philosophical symbolism, which taps into the root and runs into the branches of religious belief the world over. Like the Medieval Cabalists the Templars who engraved these drawings crammed a tremendous amount of information into a very small space.

There was a crudely drawn figure of a person (is it a he or she?) holding a rod that looked like a downward pointing arrow (or the Spear of Longinus?) to me.

Beside the figure is a spread eagle Jesus on a cross.

This surprised me in its similarity to early fifth century Christian depictions that show a muscular, almost superhuman, Jesus spread out against the cross; so different from the giant crosses with a small (or often no) Jesus Christians display in America today.

Why, I wondered, would Templars carve crucifixes on the wall of their prison at all? Denial of the crucifixion, or a Savior who hangs on a wooden cross, was *the* requirement of initiation into their order. To get in they spit on the cross. The reason for this remains a closely guarded secret.

Replica of the Templar grafitti engraved on a stone at Domme, France on display in the Templar Museum at Domme. Photo by the author.

A pregnant woman holds a rod or wand. The Crucifixion.

The Templar denial of the crucifixion is similar to that of the Cathars (who were first terrorized then systematically slaughtered by the Church only 60 years before) and their rejection of the cross as a symbol because it was an instrument of torture, a false idol of terrorists. The only source that *Christ* ('anointed') means "crucified", claimed the Templars, is the belief and the doctrine of the Church. The Templars rejected this belief.

Was this drawing some form of allusion to the secret Rule of the Order, a reminder of their oath? Did they ritualistically spit on it while imprisoned, perhaps to gain resolve? Remember, Jesus used spit on some healings. Did the Templars know his 'healing spit' secret?

Additional out of place details in the Templar graffiti included seven pierced pyramids topped by tall crosses.

Another non-Templar symbol is a fish and a Tree of Life and another larger creature or object topped by a cross, which we'll discuss momentarily.

When French king Philip the Fair ordered the arrest of the Knights Templar in 1307, the Order of the Templars was one of the most powerful forces in the world. Supposedly formed to protect pilgrims from the "infidels," most agree that during their travels throughout the Middle East during the early 12th century the Knights Templar were clandestinely in pursuit of ancient knowledge. It's claimed these militaristic monks reclaimed the secrets hidden beneath Solomon's Temple atop Jerusalem's Mount Moriah and subsequently acquired enormous wealth and knowledge… perhaps beyond earthly riches.

What could be more valuable than gold or other treasure? Whatever it was it posed a challenge to the temporal power of the king of France and to his supporter the Roman Catholic Church.

For a clue to this metaphysical treasure we return to the image of the fish and the tree beside the cross at Domme. They are easily comparable to the *Sephirotic Tree of Life* (see diagram). The Sephiroth are the ten qualities of the Mystical Tree, set forth as a major doctrine of the cabalistic *Book of Splendor* (*The Zohar*), which was first published about A.D. 1280 although its legend claimed a much earlier date.

Mastery of the principles of this enormously powerful spiritual tool allows the manifestation of the Divine into the world and the means by which Divine Union may be achieved. The *Zohar* compares itself to the Ark that gives shelter.

If we understand their graffiti correctly its symbolism suggests the Templars imprisoned at Domme had acquired esoteric knowledge. The only way to reconcile the appearance of the crucifix and the Kabbalistic Tree at Domme is to recognize that far from denying Jesus, like the Cathars, the Templars worshipped him as an angel of light who had entered human affairs to deliver a spiritual technology for escaping earth life and to cross into the Kingdom of Light via the Tree of Life.

The Gnostics frequently called Jesus *the Tree of Life* and a *branch*. At Domme, we have a figure holding what may be Jesus' wand. Is it a branch from the Tree of Life?

As noted, the Templars did not confuse Jesus, the man of light, with *Christ* = the timeless quantum cosmic essence that exists everywhere and nowhere. Instead, they accumulated technology (a cluster of principles including alchemy, sacred geometry and astronomy) that once belonged to this enlightened person and his apostles and enabled the manifestation of Christ. This 'Christ technology' could 'feed' us, transmute an individual into a higher being and even create an advanced social order, a new Kingdom of Heaven on Earth. Philip the Fair and the Church of Rome wanted this technology for their own purposes. Helter skelter. They planned to crush it out of the Templars like a bunch of grapes.

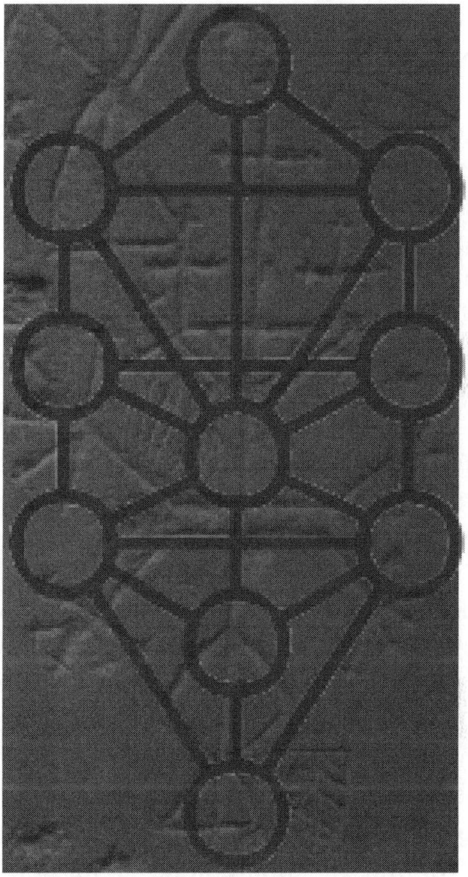

A fish with a Tree of Life (previous page) whose branches resemble grape stems (below). The Sephirothic tree overlaid on the Templar tree. A perfect match?

Cabalists call all ten Sephiroth collectively the *Merkabah* or "chariot" of God, whereby the Divine could descend from heaven into men's souls.

Lévi claims that Seth, Moses, David, Solomon and Jesus obtained from the same Kabalistc Tree of Life their royal wands. The saplings from this tree became the Burning Bush, in the midst of which God communicated to Moses his eternal name. When Moses asks His *Name what is it*, He replies I am That I Am. Moses plucked a triple branch of the sacred bush and used it as his miraculous wand. Although separated from its root, the branch continued to blossom, and it was subsequently preserved in the Ark. King David planted the branch on Mount Sion, and Solomon took wood from each section of the triple wand to make the two pillars *Jachin and Boaz*, which were placed at the entrance to his temple.

Returning to the 2nd century AD Coptic ("Egyptian") Christian portrayal of Jesus we notice he is wielding this triple branched rod and a ring... Solomon's Keys.

Beside the fish and Tree of Life at Domme is another larger 'fish creature'(?). Obviously any one can read anything they want into this symbolism. To me, this fish creature bears an amazing resemblance to a drawing presented by Robert Temple in *The Sirius Mystery* of the descent of Nommo, the amphibious savior being the Dogon tribe of Mali believed had been sent from Sirius to watch and educate humankind. Is Nommo's craft the Merkabah chariot?

Nommo divided his body to feed humankind. His name is thought to mean, "make one drink." Nommo was known as masters of waters.

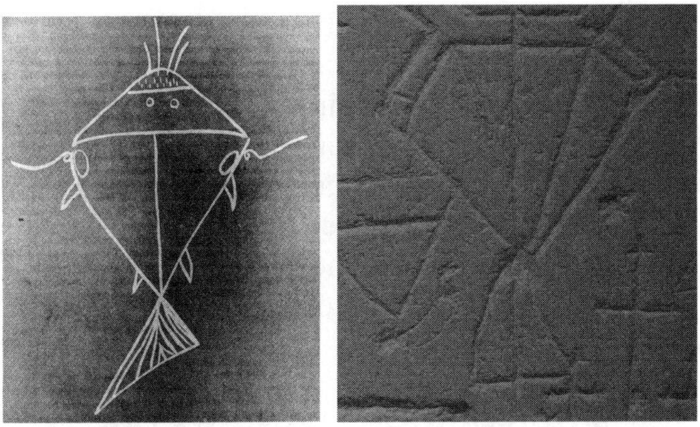

Dogon Nommo image.© Robert Temple. Righ. The Templar engraving cropped.

Interestingly, the Merovingians, the alleged 'offspring' of Jesus and Mary Magdalene who ruled this part of France, claimed descent from a fish creature that came out of the ocean. This fish-being is widely traced to Oannes in Babylonia and Enki in Sumeria. Both are equated with Nommo…and Jesus.

Enki is portrayed in the Babylonian seal shown earlier. He hovers in a winged ring or craft (an ark?) above a utensil operated by priests wearing fish suits. It appears to portray Enki descending in a Merkaba chariot. This is a purification ceremony.

In the catacombs of Rome we also find the identical theme is an astonishing Early Christian fish glyph.

The Early Christian symbol of the *anchor* with a cross with a pierced circle and a fish grasping a line of hope or salvation is plainly kin to, if not a copy of, the Sumerian seal portraying the fish priests beside a radiant tree or pillar above which hovers Enki.

Both are identical in meaning to fish grasping the Tree of Life in the Templar engraving.

The match between these emblems -- all three portray fish attached to a tree (or tower?) topped by a symbol for the Lord -- leads to a profound question. Were the Early Christians devotees of Enki/Nommo? Were the Templars, as well?

FOUNTAIN OF LIVING WATER

The fish at Domme may be the key that unlocks this engraving. In ancient Christian symbolism the fish stands for the concept of the *living water* referenced in so many traditions. This *living* water is different from ordinary water. It's cosmic. It has a *quickening* effect.

John's gospel provides insight into these mysterious waters. Jesus said "*the water that I give him shall become in him a fountain of water, springing up into life everlasting.*' [John 4: 10-14]

As Ezekiel 47:8-10 tells us its source is the Temple of Solomon in Jerusalem. The 'fountain of living waters' is mentioned in the Old Testament's *Song of Solomon* (4:15) The living waters flow *from the Temple.*

What is it about Solomon's Temple that produces the living water? And what does it have to do with the Templar excavations there and the graffiti portraying a Tree of Life/ *fount of living water*? I'm not certain, but this *living waters* connection is made even more relevant when we acknowledge that in French literary tradition introduced in the 12-13th century Mary Magdalene is remembered as *la Dompna del Aquae: Mistress of the Waters.* Is it she holding a branch of the Tree of Life at Domme? Or, could it be a beaker holding living water?

Like the Medieval Cabalists the Templars who engraved these drawings crammed a tremendous amount of information into a very small space. Whatever it means this astonishing conglomeration of religious and philosophical symbolism, which taps into the root and runs into the branches of religious beliefs of the ancient Middle East, certainly suggests the Templar prisoners at Domme utilized many mystic traditions.

BIBLIOGRAPHY

Michael Baigent, Richard Leigh, Henry Lincoln, *Holy Blood, Holy Grail* (Delacorte Press, New York, 19820.
Harold Bayley, *The Lost Language of Symbolism* (Citadel Press, New York, 1993).
Martin Brennan, *The Hidden Maya* (Bear & Co., Santa Fe, NM, 1998).
Rundle Clark, *Myth and Symbol in Ancient Egypt* (Thames & Hudson, London, 1959)
Mircea Eliade, *The Forge and the Crucible* (University of Chicago, Chicago, 1962).
Ralph Ellis, *Jesus: Last of the Pharaohs* (Edfu Books, Dorset, 1998).
Robert Feather, *The Secret Initiation of Jesus at Qumran* (Bear & Co., Rochester, VT, 2005).
David Fideler, *Jesus Christ, Sun of God* (Quest Books,

Chicago, 1996).
David Friedel, Linda Schele, Joy Parker, *Maya Cosmos* (New York, William Morrow, 1993).
Laurence Gardner, *The Magdalene Legacy* (Element, London, 2005).
Laurence Gardner, *Lost Secret of the Sacred Ark* (Element, London, 2003).
David Goddard, *The Tower of Alchemy* (Weiser Books, Boston, 1999).
Graeme R. Kearsley, *Mayan Genesis* (Yelsraek Publishing, London, 2001).
Robert Kraft, editor, *The Testament of Job* (Scholar's Press, Missoula, MT, 1974).
Paul LaViolette, *Earth Under Fire* (Starburst Publications, Schenectady, NY, 1997).
Jean Markale, *Montsegur and the Mystery of the Cathars* (Inner Traditions, Rochester, VT, 2003).
Gerald Massey, *Ancient Egypt: Light of the World* (Kessinger Publishing, Montana).
Stephen Mehler, *From Light Into Darkness* (Adventures Unlimited, Kempton, Ill., 2005).
Stephen Mehler, *Land of Osiris* (Adventures Unlimited, Kempton, Ill., 2001).
John Michell, *The Temple at Jerusalem: a Revelation* (Samuel Weiser, York Beach, Maine, 2000).
Greg Rigby, *On Earth As It Is In Heaven* (Rhaedus Publications, UK, 1996).
Michael Rice, *Egypt's Making* (Routledge, London, 1990).
Adalberto Rivera, *The Mysteries of Chichen Itza* (Univeral Image Enterprise, 1995).
Jane Schaberg, *The Resurrection of Mary Magdalene*

(Continuum, New York, 20030.
Hugh Schonfield, *The Essene Odyssey* (Element, Shaftesbury, Dorset, 1984).
Margaret Starbird, *The Woman with the Alabaster Jar* (Bear & Co., Santa Fe, NM, 1993).
Elizabeth VanBuren, *Refuge of the Apocalypse: Doorway Into Other Dimensions* (The C.W. Daniel Co., Saffron Waldon, 1986).
Jacobus de Voragine, *The Golden Legend* (Arno Press, New York, 1969).
Barbara G. Walker, *The Woman's Encyclopedia of Myths and Secrets* (HarperCollins, New York, 1996).

NASA, NAZIS & JFK:
The Torbitt Document & the JFK Assassination
introduction by Kenn Thomas

This book emphasizes the links between "Operation Paper Clip" Nazi scientists working for NASA, the assassination of JFK, and the secret Nevada air base Area 51. The Torbitt Document also talks about the roles played in the assassination by Division Five of the FBI, the Defense Industrial Security Command (DISC), the Las Vegas mob, and the shadow corporate entities Permindex and Centro-Mondiale Commerciale. The Torbitt Document claims that the same players planned the 1962 assassination attempt on Charles de Gaul, who ultimately pulled out of NATO because he traced the "Assassination Cabal" to Permindex in Switzerland and to NATO headquarters in Brussels. The Torbitt Document paints a dark picture of NASA, the military industrial complex, and the connections to Mercury, Nevada which headquarters the "secret space program."

258 PAGES. 5X8. PAPERBACK. ILLUSTRATED. $16.00. CODE: NNJ

INSIDE THE GEMSTONE FILE
Howard Hughes, Onassis & JFK
by Kenn Thomas & David Hatcher Childress

Steamshovel Press editor Thomas takes on the Gemstone File in this run-up and run-down of the most famous underground document ever circulated. Photocopied and distributed for over 20 years, the Gemstone File is the story of Bruce Roberts, the inventor of the synthetic ruby widely used in laser technology today, and his relationship with the Howard Hughes Company and ultimately with Aristotle Onassis, the Mafia, and the CIA. Hughes kidnapped and held a drugged-up prisoner for 10 years; Onassis and his role in the Kennedy Assassination; how the Mafia ran corporate America in the 1960s; the death of Onassis' son in the crash of a small private plane in Greece; Onassis as Ian Fleming's archvillain Ernst Stavro Blofeld; more.

320 PAGES. 6X9 PAPERBACK. ILLUSTRATED. $16.00. CODE: IGF

POPULAR PARANOIA
The Best of Steamshovel Press
edited by Kenn Thomas

The anthology exposes the biologocal warfare origins of AIDS; the Nazi/Nation of Islam link; the cult of Elizabeth Clare Prophet; the Oklahoma City bombing writings of the late Jim Keith, as well as an article on Keith's own strange death; the conspiratorial mind of John Judge; Marion Pettie and the shadowy Finders group in Washington, DC; demonic iconography; the death of Princess Diana, its connection to the Octopus and the Saudi aerospace contracts; spies among the Rajneeshis; scholarship on the historic Illuminati; and many other parapolitical topics. The book also includes the Steamshovel's last-ever interviews with the great Beat writers Allen Ginsberg and William S. Burroughs, and neuronaut Timothy Leary, and new views of the master Beat, Neal Cassady and Jack Kerouac's science fiction.

308 PAGES. 8X10 PAPERBACK. ILLUSTRATED. $19.95. CODE: POPA

MIND CONTROL, OSWALD & JFK:
Were We Controlled?
introduction by Kenn Thomas

Steamshovel Press editor Kenn Thomas examines the little-known book *Were We Controlled?*, first published in 1968. The book's author, the mysterious Lincoln Lawrence, maintained that Lee Harvey Oswald was a special agent who was a mind control subject, having received an implant in 1960 at a Russian hospital. Thomas examines the evidence for implant technology and the role it could have played in the Kennedy Assassination. Thomas also looks at the mind control aspects of the RFK assassination and details the history of implant technology. Looks at the case that the reporter Damon Runyon, Jr. was murdered because of this book.

256 PAGES. 6X9 PAPERBACK. ILLUSTRATED. NOTES. $16.00. CODE: MCOJ

THE SHADOW GOVERNMENT
9-11 and State Terror
by Len Bracken, introduction by Kenn Thomas

Bracken presents the alarming yet convincing theory that nation-states engage in or allow terror to be visited upon their citizens. It is not just liberation movements and radical groups that deploy terroristic tactics for offensive ends. States use terror defensively to directly intimidate their citizens and to indirectly attack themselves or harm their citizens under a false flag. Their motives? To provide pretexts for war or for increased police powers or both. This stratagem of indirectly using terrorism has been executed by statesmen in various ways but tends to involve the pretense of blind eyes, misdirection, and cover-ups that give statesmen plausible deniability. Lusitiania, Pearl Harbor, October Surprise, the first World Trade Center bombing, the Oklahoma City bombing and other well-known incidents suggest that terrorism is often and successfully used by states in an indirectly defensive way to take the offensive against enemies at home and abroad. Was 9-11 such an indirect defensive attack?

288 PAGES. 6X9 PAPERBACK. ILLUSTRATED. $16.00. CODE: SGOV

LIQUID CONSPIRACY
JFK, LSD, the CIA, Area 51 & UFOs
by George Piccard

Underground author George Piccard on the politics of LSD, mind control, and Kennedy's involvement with Area 51 and UFOs. Reveals JFK's LSD experiences with Mary Pinchot-Meyer. The plot thickens with an ever expanding web of CIA involvement, from underground bases with UFOs seen by JFK and Marilyn Monroe (among others) to a vaster conspiracy that affects every government agency from NASA to the Justice Department. This may have been the reason that Marilyn Monroe and actress-columnist Dorothy Kilgallen were both murdered. Focusing on the bizarre side of history, *Liquid Conspiracy* takes the reader on a psychedelic tour de force. This is your government on drugs!

264 PAGES. 6X9 PAPERBACK. ILLUSTRATED. $14.95. CODE: LIQC

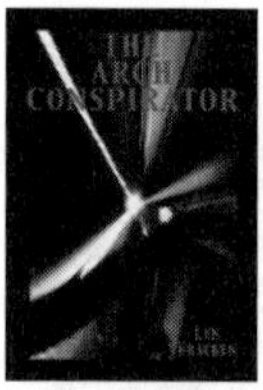

THE ARCH CONSPIRATOR
Essays and Actions
by Len Bracken

Veteran conspiracy author Len Bracken's witty essays and articles lead us down the dark corridors of conspiracy, politics, murder and mayhem. In 12 chapters Bracken takes us through a maze of interwoven tales from the Russian Conspiracy (and a few "extra notes" on conspiracies) to his interview with Costa Rican novelist Joaquin Gutierrez and his Psychogeographic Map into the Third Millennium. Other chapters in the book are A General Theory of Civil War; A False Report Exposes the Dirty Truth About South African Intelligence Services; The New-Catiline Conspiracy for the Cancellation of Debt; Anti-Labor Day; 1997 with selected Aphorisms Against Work; Solar Economics; and more. Bracken's work has appeared in such pop-conspiracy publications as *Paranoia*, *Steamshovel Press* and the *Village Voice*. Len Bracken lives in Arlington, Virginia and haunts the back alleys of Washington D.C., keeping an eye on the predators who run our country. With a gun to his head, he cranks out his rants for fringe publications and is the editor of *Extraphile*, described by *New Yorker Magazine* as "fusion conspiracy theory."

256 PAGES. 6X9 PAPERBACK. ILLUSTRATED. BIBLIOGRAPHY. $14.95. CODE: ACON.

PIRATES & THE LOST TEMPLAR FLEET
The Secret Naval War Between the Templars & the Vatican
by David Hatcher Childress

Childress takes us into the fascinating world of maverick sea captains who were Knights Templar (and later Scottish Rite Free Masons) who battled the Vatican, and the Spanish and Italian ships that sailed for the Pope. The lost Templar fleet was originally based at La Rochelle in southern France, but fled to the deep fiords of Scotland upon the dissolution of the Order by King Phillip. This banned fleet of ships was later commanded by the St. Clair family of Rosslyn Chapel (birthplace of Free Masonry). St. Clair and his Templars made a voyage to Canada in the year 1298 AD, nearly 100 years before Columbus! Later, this fleet of ships and new ones to come, flew the Skull and Crossbones, the symbol of the Knights Templar. They preyed on the ships of the Vatican coming from the rich ports of the Americas and were ultimately known as the Pirates of the Caribbean. Chapters include: 10,000 Years of Seafaring; The Knights Templar & the Crusades; The Templars and the Assassins; The Lost Templar Fleet and the Jolly Roger; Maps of the Ancient Sea Kings; Pirates, Templars and the New World; Christopher Columbus—Secret Templar Pirate?; Later Day Pirates and the War with the Vatican; Pirate Utopias and the New Jerusalem; more.

320 PAGES. 6X9 PAPERBACK. ILLUSTRATED. BIBLIOGRAPHY. $16.95. CODE: PLTF

THE HISTORY OF THE KNIGHTS TEMPLARS
by Charles G. Addison, introduction by David Hatcher Childress

Chapters on the origin of the Templars, their popularity in Europe and their rivalry with the Knights of St. John, later to be known as the Knights of Malta. Detailed information on the activities of the Templars in the Holy Land, and the 1312 AD suppression of the Templars in France and other countries, which culminated in the execution of Jacques de Molay and the continuation of the Knights Templars in England and Scotland; the formation of the society of Knights Templars in London; and the rebuilding of the Temple in 1816. Plus a lengthy intro about the lost Templar fleet and its connections to the ancient North American sea routes.

395 PAGES. 6X9 PAPERBACK. ILLUSTRATED. $16.95. CODE: HKT

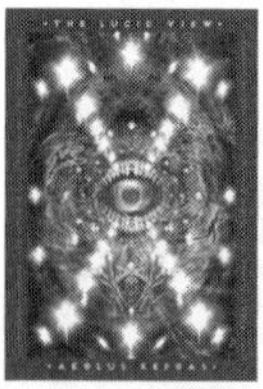

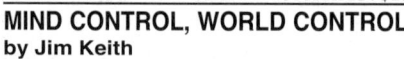

THE LUCID VIEW
Investigations in Occultism, Ufology & Paranoid Awareness
by Aeolus Kephas

An unorthodox analysis of conspiracy theory, ufology, extraterrestrialism and occultism. *The Lucid View* takes us on an impartial journey through secret history, including the Gnostics and Templars; Crowley and Hitler's occult alliance; the sorcery wars of Freemasonry and the Illuminati; "Alternative Three" covert space colonization; the JFK assassination; the Manson murders; Jonestown and 9/11. Also delves into UFOs and alien abductions, their relations to mind control technology and sorcery practices, with reference to inorganic beings and Kundalini energy. The book offers a balanced overview on religious, magical and paranoid beliefs pertaining to the 21st century, and their social, psychological, and spiritual implications for humanity, the leading game player in the grand mythic drama of Armageddon.

298 PAGES. 6X9 PAPERBACK. ILLUSTRATED. $16.95. CODE: LVEW

MIND CONTROL, WORLD CONTROL
by Jim Keith

Veteran author and investigator Jim Keith uncovers a surprising amount of information on the technology, experimentation and implementation of mind control. Various chapters in this shocking book are on early CIA experiments such as Project Artichoke and Project R.H.I.C.-EDOM, the methodology and technology of implants, mind control assassins and couriers, various famous Mind Control victims such as Sirhan Sirhan and Candy Jones. Also featured in this book are chapters on how mind control technology may be linked to some UFO activity and "UFO abductions."

256 PAGES. 6X9 PAPERBACK. ILLUSTRATED. FOOTNOTES. $14.95. CODE: MCWC

MASS CONTROL
Engineering Human Consciousness
by Jim Keith

Conspiracy expert Keith's final book on mind control, Project Monarch, and mass manipulation presents chilling evidence that we are indeed spinning a Matrix. Keith describes the New Man, where conception of reality is a dance of electronic images fired into his forebrain, a gossamer construction of his masters, designed so that he will not—under any circumstances—perceive the actual. His happiness is delivered to him through a tube or an electronic connection. His God lurks behind an electronic curtain; when the curtain is pulled away we find the CIA sorcerer, the media manipulatorÖ Chapters on the CIA, Tavistock, Jolly West and the Violence Center, Guerrilla Mindwar, Brice Taylor, other recent "victims," more.

256 PAGES. 6X9 PAPERBACK. ILLUSTRATED. INDEX. $16.95. CODE: MASC

PERPETUAL MOTION
The History of an Obsession
by Arthur W. J. G. Ord-Hume

Make a machine which gives out more work than the energy you put into it, and you have perpetual motion. The deceptively simple task of making a mechanism which would turn forever fascinated many an inventor, and a number of famous men and physicists applied themselves to the task. Despite the naivete and blatant trickery of many of the inventors, there are a handful of mechanisms which defy explanation. A vast canvas-covered wheel which turned by itself was erected in the Tower of London. Another wheel, equally surrounded by mystery and intrigue, turned endlessly in Germany. Chapters include: Elementary Physics and Perpetual Motion; Medieval Perpetual Motion; Self-moving Wheels and Overbalancing Weights; Lodestones, Electro-Magnetism and Steam; Capillary Attraction and Spongewheels; Cox's Perpetual Motion; Keely and his Amazing Motor; Odd Ideas about Vaporization and Liquefaction; The Astonishing Case of the Garabed Project; Ever-Ringing Bells and Radium Perpetual Motion; Perpetual Motion Inventors Barred from the US Patent Office; Rolling Ball Clocks; Perpetual Lamps; The Perpetuity of the Perpetual Motion Inventor; more.

260 PAGES. 6X9 PAPERBACK. ILLUSTRATED. BIBLIOGRAPHY. INDEX. $20.00. CODE: PPM

HIDDEN NATURE
The Startling Insights of Viktor Schauberger
by Alick Bartholomew, foreword by David Bellamy

Victor Schauberger (1885-1958) pioneered a new understanding of the Science of Nature, (re)discovering its primary laws and principles, unacknowledged by contemporary science. From studying the fast flowing streams of the unspoilt Alps, he gained insights into water as a living organism. He showed that water is like a magnetic tape; it can carry information that may either enhance or degrade the quality of organisms. Our failure to understand the need to protect the quality of water is the principle cause of environmental degradation on the planet. Schauberger warned of climatic chaos resulting from deforestation and called for work with free energy machines and energy generation. Chapters include: Schauberger's Vision; Different Kinds of Energy; Attraction & Repulsion of Opposites; Nature's Patterns & Shapes; Energy Production; Motion, Key to Balance; Atmosphere/Electricity; The Nature of Water; Hydrological Cycle; Formation of Springs; How Rivers Flow; Supplying Water; The Role of the Forests; Tree Metabolism; Soil Fertility and Cultivation; Organic Cultivation; The Energy Revolution; Harnessing Implosion Power; Viktor Schauberger & Society; more.

288 PAGES. 7X10 PAPERBACK. ILLUSTRATED. REFERENCES. INDEX. $22.95. CODE: HNAT

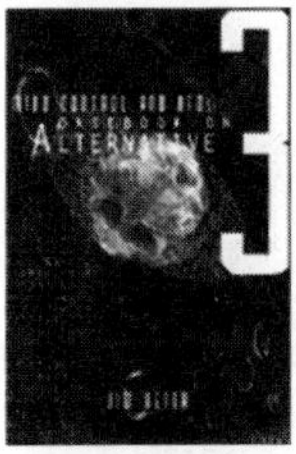

MIND CONTROL AND UFOS
Casebook on Alternative 3
by Jim Keith

Drawing on his diverse research and a wide variety of sources, Jim Keith delves into the bizarre story behind *Alternative 3*, including mind control programs, underground bases not only on the Earth but also on the Moon and Mars, the real origin of the UFO problem, the mysterious deaths of Marconi Electronics employees in Britain during the 1980s, top scientists around the world kidnapped to work at the secret government space bases, the Russian-American superpower arms race of the 50s, 60s and 70s as a massive hoax, and other startling arenas. Chapters include: Secret Societies and *Die Neuordning*; The Fourth Reich; UFOs and the Space Program; Government UFOs; Hot Jobs and Crop Circles; Missing Scientists and LGIBs; Ice Picks, Electrodes and LSD; Electronic Wars; Batch Consignments; The Depopulation Bomb; Veins and Tributaries; Lunar Base Alpha One; Disinfo; Other Alternatives; Noah's Ark II; *Das Marsprojekt*; more.

248 PAGES. 6X9 PAPERBACK. ILLUSTRATED. BIBLIOGRAPHY. $14.95. CODE: MCUF

UFOS, PSI AND SPIRITUAL EVOLUTION
A Journey through the Evolution of Interstellar Travel
by Christopher Humphries, Ph.D.

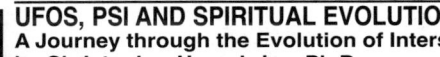

The modern era of UFOs began in May, 1947, one year and eight months after Hiroshima. This is no coincidence, and suggests there are beings in the universe with the ability to jump hundreds of light years in an instant. That is teleportation, a power of the mind. If it weren't for levitation and teleportation, star travel would not be possible at all, since physics rules out star travel by technology. So if we want to go to the stars, it is the mind and spirit we must study, not technology. The mind must be a dark matter object, since it is invisible and intangible and can freely pass through solid objects. A disembodied mind can see the de Broglie vibrations (the basis of quantum mechanics) radiated by both dark and ordinary matter during near-death or out-of-body experiences. Levitation requires warping the geodesics of space-time. The latest theory in physics is String Theory, which requires six extra spatial dimensions. The mind warps those higher geodesics to produce teleportation. We are a primitive and violent species. Our universities lack any sciences of mind, spirit or civilization. If we want to go to the stars, the first thing we must do is "grow up." That is the real Journey.

274 PAGES. 6X9 PAPERBACK. ILLUSTRATED. REFERENCES. $16.95. CODE: UPSE

INVISIBLE RESIDENTS
The Reality of Underwater UFOS
by Ivan T. Sanderson, Foreword by David Hatcher Childress

This book is a groundbreaking contribution to the study of the UFO enigma, originally published over 30 years ago. In this book, Sanderson, a renowned zoologist with a keen interest in the paranormal, puts forward the curious theory that "OINTS"—Other Intelligences—live under the Earth's oceans. This underwater, parallel, civilization may be twice as old as Homo sapiens, he proposes, and may have "developed what we call space flight." Sanderson postulates that the OINTS are behind many UFO sightings as well as the mysterious disappearances of aircraft and ships in the Bermuda Triangle. What better place to have an impenetrable base than deep within the oceans of the planet? Yet, if UFOs, or at least some of them, are coming from beneath our oceans or lakes, does it necessarily mean that there is another civilization besides our own that is responsible? In fact, could it be that since WWII a number of underwater UFO bases have been constructed by the very human governments of our planet? Whatever their source, Sanderson offers here an exhaustive study of USOs (Unidentified Submarine Objects) observed in nearly every part of the world. He presents many well-documented and exciting case studies of these unusual sightings.; more.

298 PAGES. 6X9 PAPERBACK. ILLUSTRATED. BIBLIOGRAPHY. INDEX. $16.95. CODE: INVS

THE WORLD CATACLYSM IN 2012
Maya Calendar Countdown
by Patrick Geryl

In his previous book, *The Orion Prophecy*, author Geryl theorized that the lost civilization of Atlantis was destroyed by a huge cataclysm engendered by changes in sunspot activity affecting Earth's magnetic poles and atmosphere. Having experienced earlier catastrophes, the Atlanteans had developed amazing astronomical and mathematical knowledge that enabled them to predict the date of their continent's demise. They devised a survival plan, and were able to pass along their knowledge to civilizations we know as the Maya and Old Egyptians. Here, Geryl shows that the mathematics and astronomy of the ancient Egyptians and Maya are related, and have similar predictive power which should be taken very seriously. He cracks their hidden codes that show definitively that the next earth-consuming cataclysm will occur in 2012, and calls urgently for the excavation of the Labyrinth of ancient Egypt, a storehouse of Atlantean knowledge which is linked in prophecy to the May predictions.

256 PAGES. 6X9 PAPERBACK. ILLUSTRATED. REFERENCES. $16.95. CODE: WC20

HAARP
The Ultimate Weapon of the Conspiracy
by Jerry Smith

The HAARP project in Alaska is one of the most controversial projects ever undertaken by the U.S. Government. Jerry Smith gives us the history of the HAARP project and explains how it works, in technically correct yet easy to understand language. At best, HAARP is science out-of-control; at worst, HAARP could be the most dangerous device ever created, a futuristic technology that is everything from super-beam weapon to world-wide mind control device. Topics include Over-the-Horizon Radar and HAARP; Mind Control, ELF and HAARP; The Telsa Connection; The Russian Woodpecker; GWEN & HAARP; Earth Penetrating Tomography; Weather Modification; Secret Science of the Conspiracy; more. Includes the complete 1987 Eastlund patent for his pulsed super-weapon that he claims was stolen by the HAARP Project.

256 PAGES. 6X9 PAPERBACK. ILLUSTRATED. $14.95. CODE: HARP

SECRETS OF THE HOLY LANCE
The Spear of Destiny in History & Legend
by Jerry E. Smith and George Piccard

As Jesus Christ hung on the cross a Roman centurion pieced the Savior's side with his spear. A legend has arisen that "whosoever possesses this Holy Lance and understands the powers it serves, holds in his hand the destiny of the world for good or evil." *Secrets of the Holy Lance* traces the Spear from its possession by Constantine, Rome's first Christian Caesar, to Charlemagne's claim that with it he ruled the Holy Roman Empire by Divine Right, and on through two thousand years of kings and emperors, until it came within Hitler's grasp—and beyond! Did it rest for a while in Antarctic ice? Is it now hidden in Europe, awaiting the next person to claim its awesome power? Neither debunking nor worshiping, *Secrets of the Holy Lance* seeks to pierce the veil of myth and mystery around the Spear. Mere belief that it was infused with magic by virtue of its shedding the Savior's blood has made men kings. But what if it's more? What are "the powers it serves"?

312 PAGES. 6X9 PAPERBACK. ILLUSTRATED. BIBLIOGRAPHY. $16.95. CODE: SOHL

FROM LIGHT INTO DARKNESS
The Evolution of Religion in Ancient Egypt
by Stephen S. Mehler

Building on the esoteric information first revealed in Land of Osiris, this exciting book presents more of Abd'El Hakim's oral traditions, with radical new interpretations of how religion evolved in prehistoric and dynastic Khemit, or Egypt. * Have popular modern religions developed out of practices in ancient Egypt? * Did religion in Egypt represent only a shadow of the spiritual practices of prehistoric people? * Have the Western Mystery Schools such as the Rosicrucian Order evolved from these ancient systems? * Author Mehler explores the teachings of the King Akhenaten and the real Moses, the true identity of the Hyksos, and Akhenaten's connections to The Exodus, Judaism and the Rosicrucian Order. Here for the first time in the West, are the spiritual teachings of the ancient Khemitians, the foundation for the coming new cycle of consciousness—The Awakening; more.

240 PAGES. 6X9 PAPERBACK. ILLUSTRATED. REFERENCES. $16.95. CODE: FLID

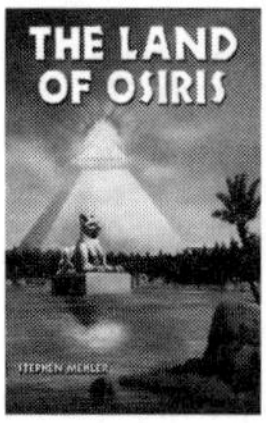

THE LAND OF OSIRIS
An Introduction to Khemitology
by Stephen S. Mehler

Was there an advanced prehistoric civilization in ancient Egypt who built the great pyramids and carved the Great Sphinx? Did the pyramids serve as energy devices and not as tombs for kings? Mehler has uncovered an indigenous oral tradition that still exists in Egypt, and has been fortunate to have studied with a living master of this tradition, Abd'El Hakim Awyan. Mehler has also been given permission to present these teachings to the Western world, teachings that unfold a whole new understanding of ancient Egypt . Chapters include: Egyptology and Its Paradigms; Asgat Nefer—The Harmony of Water; Khemit and the Myth of Atlantis; The Extraterrestrial Question; more.

272 PAGES. 6X9 PAPERBACK. ILLUSTRATED. COLOR SECTION. BIBLIOGRAPHY. $18.95. CODE: LOOS

ORACLE OF THE ILLUMINATI
Coincidence, Cocreation, Contact
By William Henry

Investigative mythologist William Henry follows up his best-selling Cloak of the Illuminati with this illustration-packed treatise on the secret codes, oracles and technology of ancient Illuminati. His primary expertise and mission is finding and interpreting ancient gateway stories which feature advanced technology for raising of spiritual vibration and increasing our body's innate healing ability. Chapters include: From Cloak to Oracle; The Return of Sophia; The Cosmic G-Spot Stimulator; The Reality of the Rulers; The Hymn of the Pearl; The Realm of the Illuminati; Francis Bacon: Oracle; Abydos and the Head of Sophia; Enki and the Flower of Light; The God Head and the Dodecahedron; The Star Walker; The Big Secret; more.

243 PAGES. 6X9 PAPERBACK. ILLUSTRATED. NOTES & REFERENCES. $16.95. CODE: ORIL

CLOAK OF THE ILLUMINATI
Secrets, Transformations, Crossing the Star Gate
by William Henry

Thousands of years ago the stargate technology of the gods was lost. Mayan Prophecy says it will return by 2012, along with our alignment with the center of our galaxy. In this book: Find examples of stargates and wormholes in the ancient world; Examine myths and scripture with hidden references to a stargate cloak worn by the Illuminati, including Mari, Nimrod, Elijah, and Jesus; See rare images of gods and goddesses wearing the Cloak of the illuminati; Learn about Saddam Hussein and the secret missing library of Jesus; Uncover the secret Roman-era eugenics experiments at the Temple of Hathor in Denderah, Egypt; Explore the duplicate of the Stargate Pillar of the Gods in the Illuminists' secret garden in Nashville, TN; Discover the secrets of manna, the food of the angels; Share the lost Peace Prayer posture of Osiris, Jesus and the Illuminati; more. Chapters include: Seven Stars Under Three Stars; The Long Walk; Squaring the Circle; The Mill of the Host; The Miracle Garment; The Fig; Nimrod: The Mighty Man; Nebuchadnezzar's Gate; The New Mighty Man; more.

238 PAGES. 6X9 PAPERBACK. ILLUSTRATED. BIBLIOGRAPHY. INDEX. $16.95. CODE: COIL

THE GIZA DEATH STAR
The Paleophysics of the Great Pyramid & the Military Complex at Giza
by Joseph P. Farrell

Was the Giza complex part of a military installation over 10,000 years ago? Chapters include: An Archaeology of Mass Destruction; Thoth and Theories; The Machine Hypothesis; Pythagoras, Plato, Planck, and the Pyramid; The Weapon Hypothesis; Encoded Harmonics of the Planck Units in the Great Pyramid; High Frequency Direct Current "Impulse" Technology; The Grand Gallery and its Crystals: Gravito-acoustic Resonators; The Other Two Large Pyramids, "Causeways," and the "Temples"; A Phase Conjugate Howitzer; Evidence of the Use of Weapons of Mass Destruction in Ancient Times; more.

290 PAGES. 6X9 PAPERBACK. ILLUSTRATED. $16.95. CODE: GDS

THE GIZA DEATH STAR DEPLOYED
The Physics & Engineering of the Great Pyramid
by Joseph P. Farrell

Farrell expands on his thesis that the Great Pyramid was a chemical maser, designed as a weapon and eventually deployed—with disastrous results to the solar system. Includes: Exploding Planets: The Movie, the Mirror, and the Model; Dating the Catastrophe and the Compound; A Brief History of the Exoteric and Esoteric Investigations of the Great Pyramid; No Machines, Please!; The Stargate Conspiracy; The Scalar Weapons; Message or Machine?; A Tesla Analysis of the Putative Physics and Engineering of the Giza Death Star; Cohering the Zero Point, Vacuum Energy, Flux: Synopsis of Scalar Physics and Paleophysics; Configuring the Scalar Pulse Wave; Inferred Applications in the Great Pyramid; Quantum Numerology, Feedback Loops and Tetrahedral Physics; and more.

290 PAGES. 6X9 PAPERBACK. ILLUSTRATED. BIBLIOGRAPHY. INDEX. $16.95. CODE: GDSD

THE GIZA DEATH STAR DESTROYED
The Ancient War For Future Science
by Joseph P. Farrell

This is the third and final volume in the popular *Giza Death Star* series, physicist Farrell looks at what eventually happened to the 10,000-year-old Giza Death Star after it was deployed—it was destroyed by an internal explosion. Recapping his earlier books, Farrell moves on to events of the final days of the Giza Death Star and its awesome power. These final events, eventually leading up to the destruction of this giant machine, are dissected one by one, leading us to the eventual abandonment of the Giza Military Complex—an event that hurled civilization back into the Stone Age. Chapters include: The Mars-Earth Connection; The Lost "Root Races" and the Moral Reasons for the Flood; The Destruction of Krypton: The Electrodynamic Solar System, Exploding Planets and Ancient Wars; Turning the Stream of the Flood: the Origin of Secret Societies and Esoteric Traditions; The Quest to Recover Ancient Mega-Technology; Non-Equilibrium Paleophysics; Monatomic Paleophysics; Frequencies, Vortices and Mass Particles: the Pyramid Power of Dr. Pat Flanagan and Joe Parr; The Topology of the Aether; A Final Physical Effect: "Acoustic" Intensity of Fields; The Pyramid of Crystals; tons more.

292 PAGES. 6X9 PAPERBACK. ILLUSTRATED. BIBLIOGRAPHY. $16.95. CODE: GDES

QUEST FOR ZERO-POINT ENERGY
Engineering Principles for "Free Energy"
by Moray B. King

King expands, with diagrams, on how free energy and anti-gravity are possible. The theories of zero point energy maintain there are tremendous fluctuations of electrical field energy embedded within the fabric of space. King explains the following topics: Tapping the Zero-Point Energy as an Energy Source; Fundamentals of a Zero-Point Energy Technology; Vacuum Energy Vortices; The Super Tube; Charge Clusters: The Basis of Zero-Point Energy Inventions; Vortex Filaments, Torsion Fields and the Zero-Point Energy; Transforming the Planet with a Zero-Point Energy Experiment; Dual Vortex Forms: The Key to a Large Zero-Point Energy Coherence. Packed with diagrams, patents and photos. With power shortages now a daily reality in many parts of the world, this book offers a fresh approach very rarely mentioned in the mainstream media.

224 PAGES. 6X9 PAPERBACK. ILLUSTRATED. $14.95. CODE: QZPE

TAPPING THE ZERO POINT ENERGY
Free Energy & Anti-Gravity in Today's Physics
by Moray B. King

King explains how free energy and anti-gravity are possible. The theories of the zero point energy maintain there are tremendous fluctuations of electrical field energy imbedded within the fabric of space. This book tells how, in the 1930s, inventor T. Henry Moray could produce a fifty kilowatt "free energy" machine; how an electrified plasma vortex creates anti-gravity; how the Pons/Fleischmann "cold fusion" experiment could produce tremendous heat without fusion; and how certain experiments might produce a gravitational anomaly.

180 PAGES. 5X8 PAPERBACK. ILLUSTRATED. $12.95. CODE: TAP

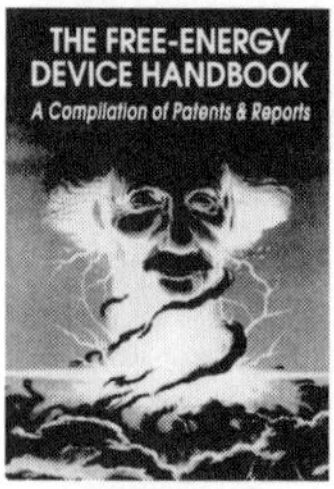

THE FREE-ENERGY DEVICE HANDBOOK
A Compilation of Patents and Reports
by David Hatcher Childress

A large-format compilation of various patents, papers, descriptions and diagrams concerning free-energy devices and systems. *The Free-Energy Device Handbook* is a visual tool for experimenters and researchers into magnetic motors and other "over-unity" devices. With chapters on the Adams Motor, the Hans Coler Generator, cold fusion, superconductors, "N" machines, space-energy generators, Nikola Tesla, T. Townsend Brown, and the latest in free-energy devices. Packed with photos, technical diagrams, patents and fascinating information, this book belongs on every science shelf. With energy and profit being a major political reason for fighting various wars, free-energy devices, if ever allowed to be mass distributed to consumers, could change the world! Get your copy now before the Department of Energy bans this book!

292 PAGES. 8X10 PAPERBACK. ILLUSTRATED. BIBLIOGRAPHY. $16.95. CODE: FEH

ETHER TECHNOLOGY
A Rational Approach to Gravity Control
by Rho Sigma

This classic book on anti-gravity and free energy is back in print and back in stock. Written by a well-known American scientist under the pseudonym of "Rho Sigma," this book delves into international efforts at gravity control and discoid craft propulsion. Before the Quantum Field, there was "Ether." This small, but informative book has chapters on John Searle and "Searle discs;" T. Townsend Brown and his work on anti-gravity and ether-vortex turbines. Includes a forward by former NASA astronaut Edgar Mitchell.

108 PAGES. 6X9 PAPERBACK. ILLUSTRATED. $12.95. CODE: ETT

THE TIME TRAVEL HANDBOOK
A Manual of Practical Teleportation & Time Travel
edited by David Hatcher Childress

In the tradition of *The Anti-Gravity Handbook* and *The Free-Energy Device Handbook,* science and UFO author David Hatcher Childress takes us into the weird world of time travel and teleportation. Not just a whacked-out look at science fiction, this book is an authoritative chronicling of real-life time travel experiments, teleportation devices and more. *The Time Travel Handbook* takes the reader beyond the government experiments and deep into the uncharted territory of early time travellers such as Nikola Tesla and Guglielmo Marconi and their alleged time travel experiments, as well as the Wilson Brothers of EMI and their connection to the Philadelphia Experiment—the U.S. Navy's forays into invisibility, time travel, and teleportation. Childress looks into the claims of time travelling individuals, and investigates the unusual claim that the pyramids on Mars were built in the future and sent back in time. A highly visual, large format book, with patents, photos and schematics. Be the first on your block to build your own time travel device!

316 PAGES. 7X10 PAPERBACK. ILLUSTRATED. $16.95. CODE: TTH

MAN-MADE UFOS 1944—1994
Fifty Years of Suppression
by Renato Vesco & David Hatcher Childress

A comprehensive look at the early "flying saucer" technology of Nazi Germany and the genesis of man-made UFOs. This book takes us from the work of captured German scientists to escaped battalions of Germans, secret communities in South America and Antarctica to todays state-of-the-art "Dreamland" flying machines. Heavily illustrated, this astonishing book blows the lid off the "government UFO conspiracy" and explains with technical diagrams the technology involved. Examined in detail are secret underground airfields and factories; German secret weapons; "suction" aircraft; the origin of NASA; gyroscopic stabilizers and engines; the secret Marconi aircraft factory in South America; and more. Introduction by W.A. Harbinson, author of the Dell novels *GENESIS* and *REVELATION*.

318 PAGES. 6X9 PAPERBACK. ILLUSTRATED. INDEX & FOOTNOTES. $18.95. CODE: MMU

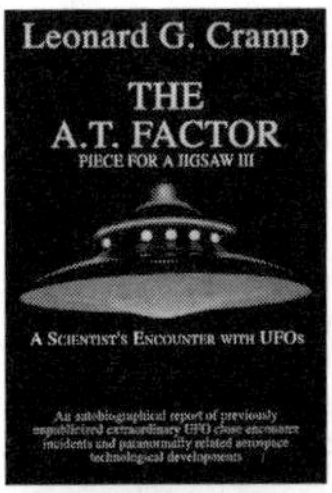

THE A.T. FACTOR

A Scientists Encounter with UFOs: Piece For A Jigsaw Part 3

by Leonard Cramp

British aerospace engineer Cramp began much of the scientific anti-gravity and UFO propulsion analysis back in 1955 with his landmark book *Space, Gravity & the Flying Saucer* (out-of-print and rare). His next books (available from Adventures Unlimited) *UFOs & Anti-Gravity: Piece for a Jig-Saw* and *The Cosmic Matrix: Piece for a Jig-Saw Part 2* began Cramp's in depth look into gravity control, free-energy, and the interlocking web of energy that pervades the universe. In this final book, Cramp brings to a close his detailed and controversial study of UFOs and Anti-Gravity.

324 PAGES. 6X9 PAPERBACK. ILLUSTRATED. BIBLIOGRAPHY. INDEX. $16.95. CODE: ATF

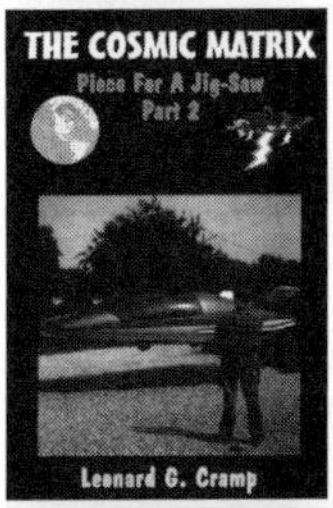

COSMIC MATRIX

Piece for a Jig-Saw, Part Two

by Leonard G. Cramp

Leonard G. Cramp, a British aerospace engineer, wrote his first book *Space Gravity and the Flying Saucer* in 1954. Cosmic Matrix is the long-awaited sequel to his 1966 book *UFOs & Anti-Gravity: Piece for a Jig-Saw.* Cramp has had a long history of examining UFO phenomena and has concluded that UFOs use the highest possible aeronautic science to move in the way they do. Cramp examines anti-gravity effects and theorizes that this super-science used by the craft—described in detail in the book—can lift mankind into a new level of technology, transportation and understanding of the universe. The book takes a close look at gravity control, time travel, and the interlocking web of energy between all planets in our solar system with Leonard's unique technical diagrams. A fantastic voyage into the present and future!

364 PAGES. 6X9 PAPERBACK. ILLUSTRATED. BIBLIOGRAPHY. $16.00. CODE: CMX

UFOS AND ANTI-GRAVITY

Piece For A Jig-Saw

by Leonard G. Cramp

Leonard G. Cramp's 1966 classic book on flying saucer propulsion and suppressed technology is a highly technical look at the UFO phenomena by a trained scientist. Cramp first introduces the idea of 'anti-gravity' and introduces us to the various theories of gravitation. He then examines the technology necessary to build a flying saucer and examines in great detail the technical aspects of such a craft. Cramp's book is a wealth of material and diagrams on flying saucers, anti-gravity, suppressed technology, G-fields and UFOs. Chapters include Crossroads of Aerodymanics, Aerodynamic Saucers, Limitations of Rocketry, Gravitation and the Ether, Gravitational Spaceships, G-Field Lift Effects, The Bi-Field Theory, VTOL and Hovercraft, Analysis of UFO photos, more.

388 PAGES. 6X9 PAPERBACK. ILLUSTRATED. $16.95. CODE: UAG

THE TESLA PAPERS

Nikola Tesla on Free Energy & Wireless Transmission of Power

by Nikola Tesla, edited by David Hatcher Childress

David Hatcher Childress takes us into the incredible world of Nikola Tesla and his amazing inventions. Tesla's rare article "The Problem of Increasing Human Energy with Special Reference to the Harnessing of the Sun's Energy" is included. This lengthy article was originally published in the June 1900 issue of *The Century Illustrated Monthly Magazine* and it was the outline for Tesla's master blueprint for the world. Tesla's fantastic vision of the future, including wireless power, anti-gravity, free energy and highly advanced solar power. Also included are some of the papers, patents and material collected on Tesla at the Colorado Springs Tesla Symposiums, including papers on: •The Secret History of Wireless Transmission •Tesla and the Magnifying Transmitter •Design and Construction of a Half-Wave Tesla Coil •Electrostatics: A Key to Free Energy •Progress in Zero-Point Energy Research •Electromagnetic Energy from Antennas to Atoms •Tesla's Particle Beam Technology •Fundamental Excitatory Modes of the Earth-Ionosphere Cavity

325 PAGES. 8X10 PAPERBACK. ILLUSTRATED. $16.95. CODE: TTP

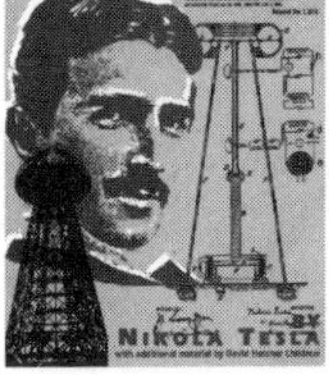

THE FANTASTIC INVENTIONS OF NIKOLA TESLA

by Nikola Tesla with additional material by David Hatcher Childress

This book is a readable compendium of patents, diagrams, photos and explanations of the many incredible inventions of the originator of the modern era of electrification. In Tesla's own words are such topics as wireless transmission of power, death rays, and radio-controlled airships. In addition, rare material on German bases in Antarctica and South America, and a secret city built at a remote jungle site in South America by one of Tesla's students, Guglielmo Marconi. Marconi's secret group claims to have built flying saucers in the 1940s and to have gone to Mars in the early 1950s! Incredible photos of these Tesla craft are included. The Ancient Atlantean system of broadcasting energy through a grid system of obelisks and pyramids is discussed, and a fascinating concept comes out of one chapter: that Egyptian engineers had to wear protective metal head-shields while in these power plants, hence the Egyptian Pharoah's head covering as well as the Face on Mars! •His plan to transmit free electricity into the atmosphere. •How electrical devices would work using only small antennas. •Why unlimited power could be utilized anywhere on earth. •How radio and radar technology can be used as death-ray weapons in Star Wars.

342 PAGES. 6X9 PAPERBACK. ILLUSTRATED. $16.95. CODE: FINT

REICH OF THE BLACK SUN

Nazi Secret Weapons and the Cold War Allied Legend

by Joseph P. Farrell

Why were the Allies worried about an atom bomb attack by the Germans in 1944? Why did the Soviets threaten to use poison gas against the Germans? Why did Hitler in 1945 insist that holding Prague could win the war for the Third Reich? Why did US General George Patton's Third Army race for the Skoda works at Pilsen in Czechoslovakia instead of Berlin? Why did the US Army not test the uranium atom bomb it dropped on Hiroshima? Why did the Luftwaffe fly a non-stop round trip mission to within twenty miles of New York City in 1944? *Reich of the Black Sun* takes the reader on a scientific-historical journey in order to answer these questions. Arguing that Nazi Germany actually won the race for the atom bomb in late 1944, and then goes on to explore the even more secretive research the Nazis were conducting into the occult, alternative physics and new energy sources.

352 PAGES. 6X9 PAPERBACK. ILLUSTRATED. BIBLIOGRAPHY. $16.95. CODE: ROBS

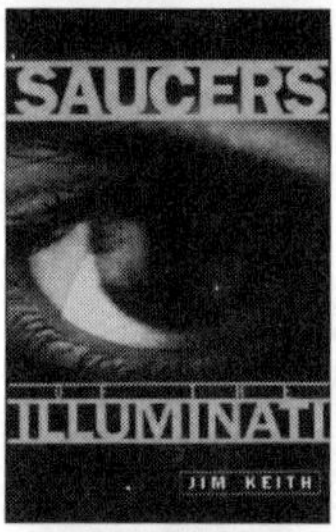

SAUCERS OF THE ILLUMINATI

by Jim Keith, Foreword by Kenn Thomas

Seeking the truth behind stories of alien invasion, secret underground bases, and the secret plans of the New World Order, *Saucers of the Illuminati* offers ground breaking research, uncovering clues to the nature of UFOs and to forces even more sinister: the secret cabal behind planetary control! Includes mind control, saucer abductions, the MJ-12 documents, cattle mutilations, government anti-gravity testing, the Sirius Connection, science fiction author Philip K. Dick and his efforts to expose the Illuminati, plus more from veteran conspiracy and UFO author Keith. Conspiracy expert Keith's final book on UFOs and the highly secret group that manufactures them and uses them for their own purposes: the control and manipulation of the population of planet Earth.

148 PAGES. 6X9 PAPERBACK. ILLUSTRATED. $12.95. CODE: SOIL

THE ENERGY MACHINE OF T. HENRY MORAY

by Moray B. King

In the 1920s T. Henry Moray invented a "free energy" device that reportedly output 50 kilowatts of electricity. It could not be explained by standard science at that time. The electricity exhibited a strange "cold current" characteristic where thin wires could conduct appreciable power without heating. Moray suffered ruthless suppression, and in 1939 the device was destroyed. Frontier science lecturer and author Moray B. King explains the invention with today's science. Modern physics recognizes that the vacuum contains tremendous energy called the zero-point energy. A way to coherently activate it appears surprisingly simple: first create a glow plasma or corona, then abruptly pulse it. Other inventors have discovered this approach (sometimes unwittingly) to create novel energy devices, and they too were suppressed. The common pattern of their technologies clarified the fundamental operating principle. King hopes to inspire engineers and inventors so that a new energy source can become available to mankind.

192 PAGES. 6X8 PAPERBACK. ILLUSTRATED. $14.95. CODE: EMHM

THE ENERGY GRID

Harmonic 695, The Pulse of the Universe

by Captain Bruce Cathie.

This is the breakthrough book that explores the incredible potential of the Energy Grid and the Earth's Unified Field all around us. Cathie's first book, *Harmonic 33*, was published in 1968 when he was a commercial pilot in New Zealand. Since then, Captain Bruce Cathie has been the premier investigator into the amazing potential of the infinite energy that surrounds our planet every microsecond. Cathie investigates the Harmonics of Light and how the Energy Grid is created. In this amazing book are chapters on UFO Propulsion, Nikola Tesla, Unified Equations, the Mysterious Aerials, Pythagoras & the Grid, Nuclear Detonation and the Grid, Maps of the Ancients, an Australian Stonehenge examined, more.

255 PAGES. 6X9 TRADEPAPER. ILLUSTRATED. $15.95. CODE: TEG

THE BRIDGE TO INFINITY

Harmonic 371244

by Captain Bruce Cathie

Cathie has popularized the concept that the earth is crisscrossed by an electromagnetic grid system that can be used for anti-gravity, free energy, levitation and more. The book includes a new analysis of the harmonic nature of reality, acoustic levitation, pyramid power, harmonic receiver towers and UFO propulsion. It concludes that today's scientists have at their command a fantastic store of knowledge with which to advance the welfare of the human race.

204 PAGES. 6X9 TRADEPAPER. ILLUSTRATED. $14.95. CODE: BTF

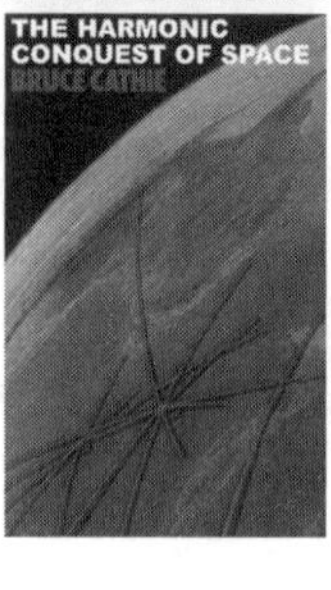

THE HARMONIC CONQUEST OF SPACE

by Captain Bruce Cathie

Chapters include: Mathematics of the World Grid; the Harmonics of Hiroshima and Nagasaki; Harmonic Transmission and Receiving; the Link Between Human Brain Waves; the Cavity Resonance between the Earth; the Ionosphere and Gravity; Edgar Cayce—the Harmonics of the Subconscious; Stonehenge; the Harmonics of the Moon; the Pyramids of Mars; Nikola Tesla's Electric Car; the Robert Adams Pulsed Electric Motor Generator; Harmonic Clues to the Unified Field; and more. Also included are tables showing the harmonic relations between the earth's magnetic field, the speed of light, and anti-gravity/gravity acceleration at different points on the earth's surface. New chapters in this edition on the giant stone spheres of Costa Rica, Atomic Tests and Volcanic Activity, and a chapter on Ayers Rock analysed with Stone Mountain, Georgia.

248 PAGES. 6X9. PAPERBACK. ILLUSTRATED. BIBLIOGRAPHY. $16.95. CODE: HCS

THE ANTI-GRAVITY HANDBOOK

edited by David Hatcher Childress, with Nikola Tesla, T.B. Paulicki, Bruce Cathie, Albert Einstein and others

The new expanded compilation of material on Anti-Gravity, Free Energy, Flying Saucer Propulsion, UFOs, Suppressed Technology, NASA Cover-ups and more. Highly illustrated with patents, technical illustrations and photos. This revised and expanded edition has more material, including photos of Area 51, Nevada, the government's secret testing facility. This classic on weird science is back in a 90s format!

- **How to build a flying saucer.**
- **Arthur C. Clarke on Anti-Gravity.**
- **Crystals and their role in levitation.**
- **Secret government research and development.**
- **Nikola Tesla on how anti-gravity airships could draw power from the atmosphere.**
- **Bruce Cathie's Anti-Gravity Equation.**
- **NASA, the Moon and Anti-Gravity.**

230 PAGES. 7X10 PAPERBACK. ILLUSTRATED. $14.95. CODE: AGH

ANTI–GRAVITY & THE WORLD GRID

Is the earth surrounded by an intricate electromagnetic grid network offering free energy? This compilation of material on ley lines and world power points contains chapters on the geography, mathematics, and light harmonics of the earth grid. Learn the purpose of ley lines and ancient megalithic structures located on the grid. Discover how the grid made the Philadelphia Experiment possible. Explore the Coral Castle and many other mysteries, including acoustic levitation, Tesla Shields and scalar wave weaponry. Browse through the section on anti-gravity patents, and research resources.

274 PAGES. 7X10 PAPERBACK. ILLUSTRATED. $14.95. CODE: AGW

ANTI–GRAVITY & THE UNIFIED FIELD

edited by David Hatcher Childress

Is Einstein's Unified Field Theory the answer to all of our energy problems? Explored in this compilation of material is how gravity, electricity and magnetism manifest from a unified field around us. Why artificial gravity is possible; secrets of UFO propulsion; free energy; Nikola Tesla and anti-gravity airships of the 20s and 30s; flying saucers as superconducting whirls of plasma; anti-mass generators; vortex propulsion; suppressed technology; government cover-ups; gravitational pulse drive; spacecraft & more.

240 PAGES. 7X10 PAPERBACK. ILLUSTRATED. $14.95. CODE: AGU

THE GIZA DEATH STAR

The Paleophysics of the Great Pyramid & the Military Complex at Giza

by Joseph P. Farrell

Physicist Joseph Farrell's amazing book on the secrets of Great Pyramid of Giza. *The Giza Death Star* starts where British engineer Christopher Dunn leaves off in his 1998 book, *The Giza Power Plant*. Was the Giza complex part of a military installation over 10,000 years ago? Chapters include: An Archaeology of Mass Destruction, Thoth and Theories; The Machine Hypothesis; Pythagoras, Plato, Planck, and the Pyramid; The Weapon Hypothesis; Encoded Harmonics of the Planck Units in the Great Pyramid; High Fregquency Direct Current "Impulse" Technology; The Grand Gallery and its Crystals: Gravito-acoustic Resonators; The Other Two Large Pyramids; the "Causeways," and the "Temples"; A Phase Conjugate Howitzer; Evidence of the Use of Weapons of Mass Destruction in Ancient Times; more.

290 PAGES. 6X9 PAPERBACK. ILLUSTRATED. $16.95. CODE: GDS

DARK MOON

Apollo and the Whistleblowers

by Mary Bennett and David Percy

- Was Neil Armstrong really the first man on the Moon?
- Did you know a second craft was going to the Moon at the same time as Apollo 11?
- Do you know that potentially lethal radiation is prevalent throughout deep space?
- Do you know there are serious discrepancies in the account of the Apollo 13 'accident'?
- Did you know that 'live' color TV from the Moon was not actually live at all?
- Did you know that the Lunar Surface Camera had no viewfinder?
- Do you know that lighting was used in the Apollo photographs—yet no lighting equipment was taken to the Moon?

All these questions, and more, are discussed in great detail by British researchers Bennett and Percy in *Dark Moon*, the definitive book (nearly 600 pages) on the possible faking of the Apollo Moon missions. Bennett and Percy delve into every possible aspect of this beguiling theory, one that rocks the very foundation of our beliefs concerning NASA and the space program. Tons of NASA photos analyzed for possible deceptions.

568 PAGES. 6X9 PAPERBACK. ILLUSTRATED. BIBLIOGRAPHY. INDEX. $25.00. CODE: DMO

TECHNOLOGY OF THE GODS

The Incredible Sciences of the Ancients

by David Hatcher Childress

Popular *Lost Cities* author David Hatcher Childress takes us into the amazing world of ancient technology, from computers in antiquity to the "flying machines of the gods." Childress looks at the technology that was allegedly used in Atlantis and the theory that the Great Pyramid of Egypt was originally a gigantic power station. He examines tales of ancient flight and the technology that it involved; how the ancients used electricity; megalithic building techniques; the use of crystal lenses and the fire from the gods; evidence of various high tech weapons in the past, including atomic weapons; ancient metallurgy and heavy machinery; the role of modern inventors such as Nikola Tesla in bringing ancient technology back into modern use; impossible artifacts; and more.

356 PAGES. 6X9 PAPERBACK. ILLUSTRATED. BIBLIOGRAPHY. $16.95. CODE: TGOD

VIMANA AIRCRAFT OF ANCIENT INDIA & ATLANTIS

by David Hatcher Childress, introduction by Ivan T. Sanderson

Did the ancients have the technology of flight? In this incredible volume on ancient India, authentic Indian texts such as the *Ramayana* and the *Mahabharata* are used to prove that ancient aircraft were in use more than four thousand years ago. Included in this book is the entire Fourth Century BC manuscript *Vimaanika Shastra* by the ancient author Maharishi Bharadwaaja, translated into English by the Mysore Sanskrit professor G.R. Josyer. Also included are chapters on Atlantean technology, the incredible Rama Empire of India and the devastating wars that destroyed it. Also an entire chapter on mercury vortex propulsion and mercury gyros, the power source described in the ancient Indian texts. Not to be missed by those interested in ancient civilizations or the UFO enigma.

334 PAGES. 6X9 PAPERBACK. ILLUSTRATED. $15.95. CODE: VAA

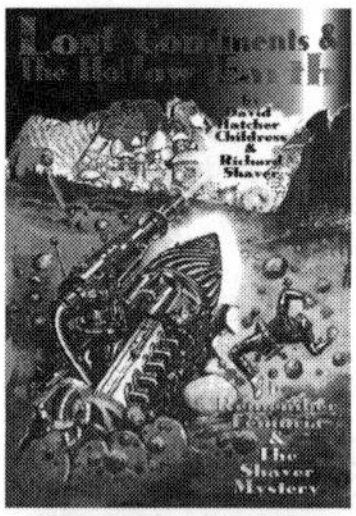

LOST CONTINENTS & THE HOLLOW EARTH

I Remember Lemuria and the Shaver Mystery

by David Hatcher Childress & Richard Shaver

Lost Continents & the Hollow Earth is Childress' thorough examination of the early hollow earth stories of Richard Shaver and the fascination that fringe fantasy subjects such as lost continents and the hollow earth have had for the American public. Shaver's rare 1948 book *I Remember Lemuria* is reprinted in its entirety, and the book is packed with illustrations from Ray Palmer's *Amazing Stories* magazine of the 1940s. Palmer and Shaver told of tunnels running through the earth—tunnels inhabited by the Deros and Teros, humanoids from an ancient spacefaring race that had inhabited the earth, eventually going underground, hundreds of thousands of years ago. Childress discusses the famous hollow earth books and delves deep into whatever reality may be behind the stories of tunnels in the earth. Operation High Jump to Antarctica in 1947 and Admiral Byrd's bizarre statements, tunnel systems in South America and Tibet, the underground world of Agartha, the belief of UFOs coming from the South Pole, more.

344 PAGES. 6X9 PAPERBACK. ILLUSTRATED. $16.95. CODE: LCHE

ATLANTIS & THE POWER SYSTEM OF THE GODS

Mercury Vortex Generators & the Power System of Atlantis

by David Hatcher Childress and Bill Clendenon

Atlantis and the Power System of the Gods starts with a reprinting of the rare 1990 book *Mercury: UFO Messenger of the Gods* by Bill Clendenon. Clendenon takes on an unusual voyage into the world of ancient flying vehicles, strange personal UFO sightings, a meeting with a "Man In Black" and then to a centuries-old library in India where he got his ideas for the diagrams of mercury vortex engines. The second part of the book is Childress' fascinating analysis of Nikola Tesla's broadcast system in light of Edgar Cayce's "Terrible Crystal" and the obelisks of ancient Egypt and Ethiopia. Includes: Atlantis and its crystal power towers that broadcast energy; how these incredible power stations may still exist today; inventor Nikola Tesla's nearly identical system of power transmission; Mercury Proton Gyros and mercury vortex propulsion; more. Richly illustrated, and packed with evidence that Atlantis not only existed—it had a world-wide energy system more sophisticated than ours today.

246 PAGES. 6X9 PAPERBACK. ILLUSTRATED. $15.95. CODE: APSG

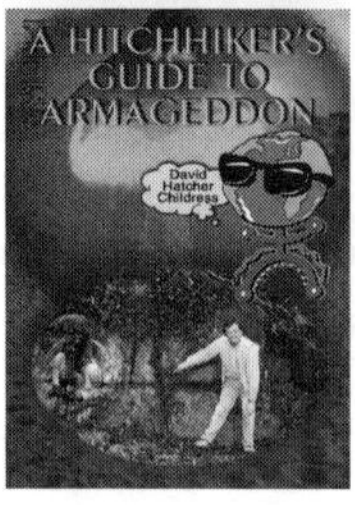

A HITCHHIKER'S GUIDE TO ARMAGEDDON

by David Hatcher Childress

With wit and humor, popular Lost Cities author David Hatcher Childress takes us around the world and back in his trippy finalé to the Lost Cities series. He's off on an adventure in search of the apocalypse and end times. Childress hits the road from the fortress of Megiddo, the legendary citadel in northern Israel where Armageddon is prophesied to start. Hitchhiking around the world, Childress takes us from one adventure to another, to ancient cities in the deserts and the legends of worlds before our own. Childress muses on the rise and fall of civilizations, and the forces that have shaped mankind over the millennia, including wars, invasions and cataclysms. He discusses the ancient Armageddons of the past, and chronicles recent Middle East developments and their ominous undertones. In the meantime, he becomes a cargo cult god on a remote island off New Guinea, gets dragged into the Kennedy Assassination by one of the "conspirators," investigates a strange power operating out of the Altai Mountains of Mongolia, and discovers how the Knights Templar and their off-shoots have driven the world toward an epic battle centered around Jerusalem and the Middle East.

320 PAGES. 6X9 PAPERBACK. ILLUSTRATED. BIBLIOGRAPHY. INDEX. $16.95. CODE: HGA

ADVENTURES UNLIMITED

One Adventure Place
P.O. Box 74
Kempton, Illinois 60946
United States of America
Tel.: 815-253-6390 • Fax: 815-253-6300
Email: auphq@frontiernet.net
http://www.adventuresunlimitedpress.com
or www.adventuresunlimited.nl

ORDERING INSTRUCTIONS

- Remit by USD$ Check, Money Order or Credit Card
- Visa, Master Card, Discover & AmEx Accepted
- Prices May Change Without Notice
- 10% Discount for 3 or more Items

SHIPPING CHARGES

United States

- Postal Book Rate { $3.00 First Item; 50¢ Each Additional Item }
- Priority Mail { $4.50 First Item; $2.00 Each Additional Item }
- UPS { $5.00 First Item; $1.50 Each Additional Item }

NOTE: UPS Delivery Available to Mainland USA Only

Canada

- Postal Book Rate { $6.00 First Item; $2.00 Each Additional Item }
- Postal Air Mail { $8.00 First Item; $2.50 Each Additional Item }
- Personal Checks or Bank Drafts MUST BE USD$ and Drawn on a US Bank
- Canadian Postal Money Orders OK
- Payment MUST BE USD$

All Other Countries

- Surface Delivery { $10.00 First Item; $4.00 Each Additional Item }
- Postal Air Mail { $14.00 First Item; $5.00 Each Additional Item }
- Payment MUST BE USD$
- Checks and Money Orders MUST BE USD$ and Drawn on a US Bank or branch.
- Add $5.00 for Air Mail Subscription to Future *Adventures Unlimited* Catalogs

SPECIAL NOTES

- RETAILERS: Standard Discounts Available
- BACKORDERS: We Backorder all Out-of-Stock Items Unless Otherwise Requested
- PRO FORMA INVOICES: Available on Request
- VIDEOS: NTSC Mode Only. Replacement only.
- For PAL mode videos contact our other offices:

Please check: ☑

☐ This is my first order ☐ I have ordered before

Name

Address

City

State/Province | Postal Code

Country

Phone day | Evening

Fax

Item Code	Item Description	Qty	Total

Please check: ☑

☐ Postal-Surface

☐ Postal-Air Mail (Priority in USA)

☐ UPS (Mainland USA only)

Subtotal ➠

Less Discount-10% for 3 or more items ➠

Balance ➠

Illinois Residents 6.25% Sales Tax ➠

Previous Credit ➠

Shipping ➠

Total (check/MO in USD$ only) ➠

☐ Visa/MasterCard/Discover/Amex

Card Number

Expiration Date

10% Discount When You Order 3 or More Items!

William Henry is an investigative mythologist. His primary expertise and mission is finding and interpreting ancient gateway stories which feature advanced technology for raising of spiritual vibration and increasing our body's innate healing ability.

He regularly appears on radio programs and lectures internationally. He has inspired a new generation of seekers with his interpretations of ancient mysteries, edgy science and the promise of the new millennium. He lives in Nashville, Tennessee.

He is the author of many books, including:
Cloak of the Illuminati
Oracle of the Illuminati
Mary Magdalene: The Illuminator
The Peacemaker
Blue Apples
The Language of Birds
God Making
The Crystal Halls of Christ's Court

Visit his website:
www.Williamhenry.net